EXILES

A journey through Ireland from Beara to Ballycastle

(Book Three in the Pilgrim Trilogy)

DERMOT BREEN

Cover photo by Dermot Breen:
Children of Lir sculpture, Ballycastle

ISBN: 978-1-095768-97-6

*Dedicated to all who have lost
and are still searching*

*"But though life's valley be a vale of tears,
A brighter scene beyond that vale appears"*

from the poem Conversation
by William Cowper

About the Author

Dermot Breen was born in Northern Ireland in 1960. He took early retirement from a senior management post in the NI Civil Service in 2016 following the death of his beloved wife Jacqui from ovarian cancer. He has since devoted his time to raising funds for cancer research and has undertaken several long-distance walks in Ireland, Spain and China as part of his fundraising efforts. This book is the third and final book in the author's Pilgrim Trilogy. He has also written *The Edge: Walking the Ulster Way with my Angels & Demons* and *The Man with the Camino Tattoo*, Books One and Two in the Pilgrim Trilogy respectively. All author profits from the sales of his Pilgrim Trilogy books are donated to Cancer Research UK to fund its important work in the fight against cancer.

Foreword

I am delighted to have been given the opportunity to write the foreword to this wonderful book. For those of you who don't know me, my name is Donal Cam O'Sullivan Beare and I was born in Ireland in 1561 and I died in exile in Spain in 1618. Yes, you read that correctly. I realise that it's highly unusual to have a foreword written by a deceased person, but please bear with me. Just think of me as a sort of 'ghost-writer'.

Dermot's book makes many references to me and my epic march out of Munster in 1603. I feel that it may be helpful, before you begin reading his story, for me to provide a little historical background - to set the scene, as it were. During the early seventeenth century, I was Prince of Beare and First Count of Berehaven. I was the last independent ruler of the O'Sullivan Beare sept (clan), and thus the last O'Sullivan Beare (a Gaelic princely title) on the Beara Peninsula in the southwest of Ireland.

Unfortunately, I lived during a time when the English Crown was attempting to secure its rule over the whole island of Ireland. Queen Elizabeth feared that the Spanish would use Ireland as a 'backdoor' to attack England. She therefore believed that England needed to take direct control of Ireland. One tactic they used was the system of 'surrender and regrant', where they 'persuaded' many Irish chieftains to relinquish their Gaelic titles and lands and then granted them, or part of them, back again, but under royal assent. In this way the retitled lords became subject to the dictates of government policy and English law. Under Elizabeth's rule, many Irish chieftains had succumbed to 'surrender and regrant' and acknowledged the English crown.

My father, Lord of Beara and Bantry, was chieftain before me. But when he was slain in 1563, the succession passed, not to me, but to my uncle, Owen O'Sullivan, under tanistry, the traditional Gaelic system of inheritance. Although I was my father's first born, I was only a child of two at the time and under Gaelic law was considered unsuitable to inherit the title of Chieftain. Not long after becoming chieftain, Owen decided to accept the terms of 'surrender and regrant' and pledged his allegiance to the Queen. He subsequently became Sir Owen O'Sullivan and was confirmed as Lord of Beara.

Like the sons of many other Irish chieftains, I received an

5

Anglicized education. I went to school in Waterford and there learnt both Latin and English. In 1587, educated and older, I took advantage of the general trend towards the adoption of English laws in Ireland and challenged my uncle's right to the chieftaincy of Beara. After two years of legal argument and family quarrel, the case was decided in my favour. This fitted well with England's desire to eradicate the tradition of Gaelic tanistry in Ireland. The title of Chieftain was subsequently awarded to me under English law and I was granted the greater part of my father's territory including the harbour of Berehaven and Dunboy Castle. The English may very well have assumed that deciding in my favour would have also encouraged me to pledge allegiance to the Crown, but this was not to be the case - quite the opposite in fact.

Sir Owen died around 1593 and was succeeded by his son, a second Sir Owen, who, perhaps understandably, didn't have much love for me, his cousin. He would later join forces with the English against me in order to win favour with the Crown and reclaim the inheritance that he felt was rightfully his. Many of the most important Irish families of the time were divided in this way – some siding with the Crown while others rebelled.

In addition to the 'surrender and regrant' tactic, the English also followed a strategic campaign of settlement in Ireland and more than half a million acres of land in Munster had already been confiscated for the settlers. It seemed to me only a matter of time before my newly acquired inheritance and livelihood was claimed by force. However, even when Munster reached breaking point in 1600 and the province erupted in rebellion, I continued to 'keep my powder dry'. The rebels were quickly defeated by Sir George Carew, the Lord President of Munster. However, things changed dramatically when the Spanish finally came to the aid of their Catholic allies.

In 1601, twelve years after the Spanish Armada, King Philip of Spain sent another fleet to land on Ireland's south coast and Spanish forces subsequently took over the town of Kinsale. The Nine Years' War, or Tyrone's Rebellion, was also taking place at this time, with Hugh O'Neill and Hugh Roe O'Donnell leading highly successful rebellions in Ulster. When they marched with their armies to join the Spanish forces at Kinsale, I was finally persuaded to join the rebellion. I delivered up my castle in Dunboy to the Spanish, assembled an army of one thousand men and set about marching to Kinsale to support O'Neill and O'Donnell.

And so it came about that I was present at the Battle of Kinsale, the final disastrous battle, which is said to have marked the death knell of Gaelic Ireland. It should have been a great victory for us, but, due to a lack of communication between the Irish and Spanish forces, it was a humiliating defeat. At dawn on Christmas Eve 1601, it took only a few hours for Lord Deputy Mountjoy's English army to win an overwhelming victory. We suffered dreadful losses - up to twelve hundred dead and eight hundred wounded. The Spanish surrendered and O'Neill and his army retreated back to Ulster, while O'Donnell went to Spain to seek further help from King Philip. Under the terms of their surrender, the Spanish were shipped back to Spain and the castles that had been given over to the Spanish by the Irish, including Dunboy Castle, were to be handed over to the English.

I returned to the Beara Peninsula and persuaded the Spaniards to surrender Dunboy castle back to me. Dunboy was now the main rebel fortress in Munster holding out against the English and it became a supremely important objective for Sir George Carew. In March 1602, he set out from Cork to take Dunboy and over the next couple of months he assembled an army of over four thousand in Beara. Meanwhile, I had left Dunboy and gone across the Caha Mountains to the other side of the peninsula to meet further Spanish ships I had been assured would be arriving imminently. However, I waited in vain. The promised Spanish reinforcements never arrived. After Kinsale, it seems that King Philip's interests in Irish affairs had steadily dwindled.

On 16th June, Carew launched his attack on Dunboy. The defenders, under Captain MacGeoghegan, put up a brave fight, but the superior forces under Carew eventually overwhelmed them. The siege of Dunboy ended on 22nd June 1602, when the castle was blown to pieces. Out of the one hundred and forty men defending it, seventy-seven were killed in the fighting and the remaining sixty-three finally surrendered and were subsequently hanged.

While the siege of Dunboy was underway, the Dursey Massacre also took place. On 20th June, an expedition under the command of John Bostock, accompanied by my cousin Owen, set off for Dursey Island. Dursey was where I had planned to make a last stand in the event of Dunboy's surrender. I had stationed a small garrison of forty men there to defend both the island and the three hundred refugees who had flocked over from the mainland. The attackers *hanged the defenders and then brutally slaughtered all of the refugees.*

The loss of Dunboy and Dursey was a serious personal blow to me and marked a significant reduction in the rebel stronghold in Munster. But I still commanded a force of over one thousand men and had Spanish gold with which to pay my soldiers. In addition, my creaght, or livestock, had not yet been captured. I knew the country well and it was terrain perfectly suited to guerrilla warfare. For a short time my forces had some success, retaking a number of the more important castles. However, I began to lose allies as it became clear to other rebels that the Spanish were never going to come to our aid again.

In late 1602, Sir Charles Wilmot, Governor of Beare, was detailed to attack my bases on the peninsula. Wilmot concentrated his force of five thousand near Glengarriff. At that time we were camped in a forested area known as Derrynafulla, which was only two or three miles away from the English camp. However, the forests were so thick then that for some time we were unaware of each other's location. But our camp was eventually spotted and, in late December, Wilmot attacked it and managed to capture my creaght of two thousand cows and four thousand sheep. It spelt disaster for us and, on top of this, two of my best commanders left our ranks and returned to Connacht with their men.

Now without enough soldiers remaining and our position known by Wilmot's troops, I made the decision to leave the Beara Peninsula. We left Glengarriff on New Year's Eve 1602, before Wilmot's army launched a further attack. Our initial destination was Brian Og O'Rourke's castle in Leitrim and my route cut across the western half of Ireland for three hundred miles. I took with me one thousand people; about four hundred soldiers and six hundred civilians. We had only one day's rations with us and we set off in bitterly cold weather in the middle of winter to cross the high mountain passes behind Glengarriff. What followed was an epic two-week march that saw us face the most difficult of challenges that the winter weather, the rough terrain and our persistent enemies could throw at us. Only a small number of us who left the camp near Glengarriff actually made it to O'Rourke's castle.

Our journey has been held up as a historic tale of unbelievable endurance, courage and survival against the odds. Today, the Beara-Breifne Way closely follows the route of our epic march from the Beara Peninsula to Leitrim Village in what was then the Kingdom of Breifne. The Ireland Way links the Beara-Breifne Way in the Republic of Ireland to the Ulster Way in Northern Ireland and continues the journey onwards to Ballycastle on the north coast of Ireland.

As I said at the outset, I died in exile in Spain in the year 1618. Exactly four hundred years later, in 2018, Dermot arrived in Castletownbere on the Beara Peninsula to follow in my footsteps and what follows is his truly incredible story. Although he walked in much more peaceful times, his journey was nevertheless full of risk and adventure and, in many ways, was just as remarkable as my own. I am certain that you will enjoy it.

Donal Cam O'Sullivan Beare

PS. I am delighted to say that I am finally to be released from my longest exile. This won't make any sense to you now, but don't worry, it will all become clear in time!

Portrait of Donal Cam O'Sullivan Beare,
painted in 1613 when exiled in Spain

The Ireland Way Route

Contents

Prologue
(Knocklayde Mountain, Ballycastle)

I deliberately suppressed a rising feeling of panic. "Time for a cool head," I muttered to myself - immediately laughing at the irony of my words. For at that moment, I stood trapped waist deep in pristine white snow, with an icy wind whipping past my ears. My laugh was short lived. The seriousness of my situation quickly came back into focus. I was three quarters of the way up Knocklayde Mountain in the middle of a snow storm and I had just dropped into a deep hollow that had been completely hidden by the deep layer of snow blanketing the upper regions of the mountain. While unsuspectingly approaching the concealed hollow, the snow had only been knee deep at most. Then, without warning, I had suddenly found my feet dropping away from beneath me and now the lower half of my body was imprisoned in a very close fitting cocoon of ice crystals. But it was only snow - soft and yielding snowflakes - easy to extricate myself from, surely? But, try as I might, I couldn't move my legs; either upwards, forwards or sideways. I was well and truly stuck. And now that I was rendered immobile, I began to feel the cold much more acutely. Was this it? Was this how it was going to end? Frozen to death on the mountain I was climbing to mark the third anniversary of my wife's death?

I have to admit that, even then, my possible fate struck me as having a certain tragicomic quality to it. It might even end up being reported in the tabloid press; no doubt in suitably ghoulish fashion, under an appropriately melodramatic and pun laden headline such as, *"Widower's devotion to late wife snows no limits"* or *"Frozen!*

He wouldn't let it go!" I might even achieve some sort of posthumous fame as a result. Who knows, it might even generate a spike in book sales. The public always seem to renew their interest in singers and actors when they die. Perhaps that same phenomenon might apply to writers; even obscure ones!

So, that was me keeping a cool head. I have to admit that it wasn't getting me anywhere. Okay, time to panic instead then! I tried even harder to wriggle my legs free, but without success and I cried out in frustration; the sound immediately snatched away hopelessly in the wind, as if it had never existed. A different strategy was required. I leaned forward, hinging my upper body at the waist, until my arms and chest were laying on the surface of the snow. I then roared with effort and used my elbows to drag myself forward, commando fashion, over the snow. With great relief I found that my legs and feet followed behind as they reluctantly slid out of their icy moulds. I maintained a spread-eagled crawling position for a time in the belief that a prone body would be less likely to sink into the snow again than an upright one. I then used one of my walking poles to test the depth of the snow ahead (something I probably should have been doing earlier!) and once I reckoned I had passed over the hollow, I climbed slowly to my feet again; slightly exhausted by my endeavours, but mightily relieved at the same time.

Not for the first time, a very familiar and totally irrational question popped unwelcome into my mind. Why did she have to die in the middle of winter? Of course, Jacqui had no say over the timing of her death. That had been determined by the evil cancer that had cruelly and indiscriminately decided to cut her beautiful life short. "Careful now," I cautioned myself, "Don't let the bugger get to you." I knew from experience that such thoughts could quickly drag me down a slippery slope – which certainly wasn't a good idea given my present location and the current weather conditions! A distraction was needed. Some humour. My default position of black humour would have to do. "You picked a fine time to leave me, Jacqui", I sang at the top of my voice to the tune of the old Kenny Rodgers song. "With the wind blowing hard and snow on the ground", I continued as I resumed my climb up the side of Knocklayde, through the near blizzard conditions that had descended on the mountain.

Treading more carefully now, testing ahead with my poles, peering through the horizontal snow flurry, immensely thankful for the fence line that would eventually guide me to the summit. More than once I paused to admire the incredible ice sculptures that had formed on the wires and posts of the fence – elongated, wind-blown shapes that stretched out perpendicularly from the southern edge of every solid object caught in the path of the biting northerly airstream. The wire squares of the fence had formed into multiple deep ice 'window frames' and the posts had formed otherworldly shapes that the sculptor Henry Moore would no doubt have found pleasing.

Onwards I pushed through the almost total whiteout; the angle of the fence line providing the only visual clue as to the fact that I was indeed climbing higher. Thankfully, the sky cleared a little as I reached the summit, or what I assumed to be the summit, of Knocklayde. The diffuse light of a pale, watery sun barely penetrated the gloom of my surroundings, but I felt that it was sufficient for me to risk leaving the security of the fence line in order to traverse the summit to reach the central mound that I knew to rest on top of this mountain. This was *Carn an Truagh*, the Cairn of Sorrows, a megalithic cairn that is believed to contain a passage tomb. I set off across the mountain top in the direction I believed the cairn to be, looking back frequently to see that the fence was still visible should I need to turn back. Just as I was seriously considering doing just that, the wind whipped the curtain of snow away for a brief moment and revealed the mound shape of the cairn ahead of me.

I trudged on through the thick snow; the only sound in the icy stillness, apart from the wind, being the soft 'crump' of my boots repeatedly sinking into and compacting the snow with each step. I reached the cairn, climbed the short distance to the top and stuck one of my walking poles into the snow beside the stone triangulation pillar, as if planting a flag and declaring the mountain well and truly conquered. "Made it", I muttered quietly to myself, enjoying a brief moment of satisfaction at having achieved my objective. Four hours after leaving Jacqui's grave at Ramoan Parish Church on the edge of Ballycastle town, I had reached my goal – from one place of sorrows to another. I searched around the southern slopes of the cairn to see if I could find the little stash of Jacqui's shells and pebbles that I had carefully hidden in a small hollow two years previously. However, even though this sheltered side of the cairn was relatively clear of snow, I was unable to find any sign of them. Either I had hidden them too well or someone else had come across them and taken them - like modern day tomb raiders. I gave up searching and chose to believe that I had hidden them too well. The thought of some stranger taking them was just a little too much for me to bear.

It was now time to get off the mountain before the weather turned even worse. The fence had disappeared from view, but I was able to retrace my steps fairly easily – there was only one set of footprints on this mountain today. The descent was much easier and quicker and two hours later I was once again standing by Jacqui's graveside in the graveyard of Ramoan Parish Church. "You picked a fine time to leave me, Jacqui", I repeated, speaking the words this time; not feeling like singing. Then after a moment's reflection, I added, "I don't think I can do this anymore. Climbing that mountain can be dangerous at this time of year. The weather is just too unpredictable. I need to think of something else. Perhaps a walk to coincide with our wedding anniversary on 1st August? Yes, that sounds like a much more hospitable time of year. What do you think?" I didn't get a response, so I took that as a tacit agreement.

Chapter One: Beara Peninsula
(Days one and two - Castletownbere to Glengarriff)

Five months after my graveside monologue, I was up against the window of the Cork to Castletownbere bus, as it rounded a long sweeping bend a few miles out from its destination. I was mesmerized by what was my first clear view of the Beara Peninsula and the Caha Mountains rising majestically behind. Good God! I thought to myself anxiously, I'm not expected to go over those on my first day, am I? I quickly referred to my guidebook and, regrettably, it confirmed that the first day of my walk would indeed take me up into the Caha Mountains. Thankfully not over the highest peaks, but still at an elevation that added to my growing concern that I might not make my first planned stop before nightfall. My bus was heading to the Beara Peninsula where I would begin walking a route known as the Ireland Way. It stretched from Castletownbere in the extreme south-west of Ireland to Ballycastle in the extreme north-east and covered a distance of over 1,000 kilometres. It was my third 1,000 kilometre walk in memory of Jacqui; known as '1000K4J' for short. I was also walking to help raise further funds for Cancer Research UK and hoped to raise my total, since I had begun my fundraising 'obsession' three years earlier, by another few thousand pounds.

I had left my home in Belfast the previous day and stayed in Cork City overnight, before catching the express to Castletownbere at 8:30am that morning. It would get me in at just after 11:30am and I estimated that, after grabbing a bite of lunch and finding my bearings, it would probably be close to 12:30pm before I actually started my first day's walk to Hungry Hill Lodge in Adrigole, about thirty kilometres away. However, while on the bus to Castletownbere I had been reading a blog posted by a previous Ireland Way walker, who claimed that it had taken her and her colleagues twelve hours to cover the section to Adrigole! This had concerned me so much that I had phoned the owner of the Hungry Hill Lodge to seek his advice. But Owen at the Lodge assured me in an English accent that I should be able to cover the distance in about half the time quoted in the blog. "They must have been numpties and carrying ridiculously heavy rucksacks", he said, confidently dismissing my recently acquired intelligence. "If you're experienced and carrying a reasonable load, you should make it in five to six hours easy!"

I declined to make any comment on either my experience or my load, but simply thanked him for his reassurance and informed him that I would stick to my plan and would hopefully see him later that day. My rucksack wasn't too heavy at 13kg and I suppose I could call myself experienced. After all, I had already completed two long distance hikes. However, the last one had been two years ago and I hadn't done a lot of what you might call 'serious walking' since. I felt out of condition and my preparation and training for this walk had been rather limited, to say the least. Although I had felt that another walk was in the air five months previously, I had only seriously committed myself to this challenge about three weeks before setting off! So the sight of the Caha Mountains, looming ominously before me, did reawaken those familiar fears that, on this occasion, I had perhaps bitten off more than I could chew.

The bus pulled into a rather inauspicious stop, just short of the crammed harbour of the busy little fishing port of Castletownbere. I stepped down onto the dry and dusty ground along with a handful of fellow passengers and collected my rucksack from the hold. I slung it casually over one shoulder and, as the bus set off on its return journey in a cloud of exhaust fumes and dust, I headed to a café a short distance away. I had brought some food supplies with me, but I decided to save these for during my walk and instead ordered a nice bowl of seafood chowder and wheaten bread, which I had sitting at a table outside, under the shade of a large parasol. The sun was beating down from between the gaps in the light, patchy cloud cover and the temperature was rising. The forecast for the next few days ahead looked really good –

perhaps too good! I didn't realise it then, but I had arrived at the start of the Ireland Way at the same time as a heat wave was about to begin its relentless assault on the island of Ireland. Over the coming weeks, the exceptional weather conditions would see hose pipe bans introduced nationwide and would temporarily rob Ireland of any claim to being the 'Emerald Isle', as fields and hillsides alike were scorched dry and, in some places, even ignited under an unforgiving sun.

As I enjoyed my lunch, I reflected on the marvellous mystical connection that existed between Beara and Ballycastle at either end of the Ireland Way route. This related to the legendary story of the Children of Lir. Although the Ireland Way was a relatively new route, a particular sculpture in Ballycastle had already become an iconic 'touchstone' for walkers reaching the end point. This was a beautiful metal sculpture, depicting the Children of Lir as swans flying over the Sea of Moyle, which lies between Scotland and the north coast of Ireland. Indeed, there had already been a small number of photographs posted on social media of various tired, relieved and joyous pilgrims standing under the sculpture in celebration at reaching the end of their epic journeys. And the connection to Beara on the south coast of the Ireland? Well, on the Beara Peninsula, less than ten kilometres from where I was sitting, is a little seaside village called Allihies. And just outside that village is a small, sacred site dedicated to the Children of Lir.

The Children of Lir is a well-known legend in Ireland and also one I was very familiar with given its connection to Jacqui's home town of Ballycastle. The story goes that in ancient Ireland, Lir was blissfully married to Aobh, the first daughter of King Bov, and they had four children called Aodh, Fionnghuala, Fiachra and Conn. Unfortunately, Aobh died and Lir, not wanting his children growing up without the love of a mother, married Aoife, King Bov's second daughter. This was a happy marriage until Aoife became jealous of Lir's devotion to his children. Overcome with hatred she brought the children to Lough Derravaragh in County Westmeath, in the centre of Ireland, and transformed them into swans. Realising what she had done and overcome with remorse, she attempted to release the spell but could only ease their distress by enabling them to speak and sing and to remain as swans for nine hundred years. The swans spent the first three hundred years on Lough Derravaragh, the next three hundred years on the Sea of Moyle and the last three hundred years on the Atlantic sea to the west of Ireland. When their time in exile was over, the swans, attracted by the ringing of a bell by a monk living in Allihies village, came ashore and immediately were changed back into their human form. The children, who were now very old men and women, were baptised by the monk. A short time later they died and were buried at a site marked with a number of large white boulders, which can still be found outside Allihies on the Beara Peninsula. It was certainly a sad story, known as one of the 'three sorrows' of Irish storytelling, but it was, I felt, important to acknowledge this mystical link between the start and end points of my journey. It also reminded me of my own feelings of being exiled since Jacqui had died. I had felt abandoned; left exiled on this Earth to live out the rest of my days without her.

Lunch finished, I shrugged off my melancholy and pulled on my rucksack. I automatically patted my pocket to check that the folded sheets of paper I carried with me were still there. It was time to set off and begin my long journey home. But it would be a stuttering start. I walked through the centre of the colourful little town of Castletownbere and almost immediately spotted MacCarthy's Bar across the street. This was the very bar that featured on the front cover of the popular book 'McCarthy's Bar', written by Pete McCarthy in 2000. In his book, Pete sets off on a trip around Ireland, obeying the rule 'never pass a pub with your name on it'. I waved to a woman who had just come out of the bar and was about to sit outside at one of the wooden picnic tables. "Do you mind me taking a photo?" I called over to her, adding, "this bar is quite famous, you know." "Oh, I do know", she said, laughing and waving a paperback over her head triumphantly, "I'm just about to sit down here and read Pete McCarthy's book!" I took my shot and headed over to say hello. "I've just noticed that the name above the pub door says 'MacCarthy's', while the photo on the cover of the book clearly shows it as 'McCarthy's'," she pointed out to me, obviously puzzled by the minor discrepancy. Whether this was a case of a name change in the intervening years or a judicious use of 'Photoshop' I'm not sure, but I simply said, "A little artistic license, no doubt. And, if you're after a pint in a bar with your name on it, you're not likely to let a minor spelling variation stand in your way!" She seemed satisfied with this and laughed, "I suppose you're right."

Pete McCarthy unfortunately died of cancer in 2004, just a few weeks before turning 54 – my Jacqui had only just turned 54 by less than a week when she was taken by the same cruel and indiscriminate disease. A reminder, as if I needed any, of the purpose behind my walk. On impulse, I decided to step into the bar for a few minutes, at the same time thinking that this is hardly the proper way to begin my Ireland Way walk; by visiting the first pub I encountered! But drink wasn't on my mind on this occasion. I simply didn't want to pass this legendary establishment by without at least being able to say that I had gone inside. The pub was full of all the old world charm that you might expect and was fairly busy with tourists and locals alike enjoying the food and drink on offer. My rucksack was adorned with a banner reading *'Walking the Ireland Way for Cancer Research UK*' and the bar lady, Adrianne, was very interested in my challenge, as were a few of her customers. Adrianne was a MacCarthy herself and she give me a donation and proudly presented me with one of the Bar's personalised tee shirts, both of which I gratefully accepted; although, in all honesty, I didn't particularly want to add any more clothing to my already straining rucksack. Adrianne then turned towards one of the crowded shelves behind the counter, displaying everything from 'Weetabix' to 'Walnut Whips', and lifted down an 'antique' hand press, which she described as a family heirloom. She used this to produce the very first stamp in my Ireland Way passport. A member of staff then took a photo of me and Adrianne behind the bar and with that I departed MacCarthy's Bar, my load ever so slightly heavier, but my mood considerably lighter.

A few hundred metres up the street and I came to a busy road junction with an even busier signpost. I counted at least fifteen separate directional signs, all competing for attention on the single metal pole bearing both the weight and the responsibility of sending people off in a multitude of different directions. As well as the signs pointing to the various surrounding towns and villages, there were also signs directing folk to the Wild Atlantic Way, the Beara Way and the Beara-Breifne Way. It was this latter sign that I was particularly interested in and there on the sign, next to the lettering, was the small image of what looked like a Spanish nobleman, dressed in armour and wearing an 'Elizabethan' style ruff around his neck. This was actually an image of Donal Cam O'Sullivan Beare (1561–1618), one of the last Gaelic Chieftains in

Ireland when Queen Elizabeth I was attempting to secure English rule over the whole island. In the early 1600's this region was ravaged by war. The forces of Elizabeth I had defeated the Irish and Spanish at the Battle of Kinsale and advanced west to capture O'Sullivan Beare's lands on the Beara Peninsula, including his main stronghold at Dunboy Castle just a few kilometres from where I was standing. Nothing much remains of the original castle; just part of a tower and a fragment of staircase. On New Year's Eve 1602, O'Sullivan Beare led one thousand men and women, including four hundred soldiers, on an epic march north, hoping to join forces with rebel leaders in Ulster. It was O'Sullivan Beare's march from the Beara Peninsula to the kingdom of Breifne in Leitrim that gave rise to the Beara-Breifne Way that I was now following. The Ireland Way joins the Beara-Breifne Way in the Republic of Ireland with the Ulster Way in Northern Ireland, creating a continuous route that runs the entire length of Ireland. I recorded a 'video blog' under O'Sullivan Beare's image and, once I was satisfied that my post had successfully left my phone to travel the super-fast highways of the World Wide Web, I finally took my first steps on the super-slow byways of the Ireland Way Walk. There was no fanfare or waving or cheering crowds to see me off, but I did allow myself a little celebratory "Whey-hey" as I ventured forth to begin my epic journey north.

With the towering mountains of Caha to my left and the islands of Dinish and the much larger Bere languishing in the serene waters of Bantry Bay to my right, I followed the main road for about half a kilometre to Brandy Hall Bridge, before turning inland up a quiet country road. The country road soon turned to country lanes, often corralled between hedges of blackthorn intermingled with sweet smelling honeysuckle, which provided a heady perfume in the summer heat. After about half an hour of walking, I came across a sign announcing the start of the 'off-road' section that would take me up into the mountains and eventually down into Adrigole, my destination for the day. I was horrified to note that the sign advised that walkers should allow seven to eight hours to complete this section! I checked my wristwatch. It would be 8:30pm before I had a chance to tell Owen to his face that his estimated walking time was totally up the left! Thankfully, the sign also pointed out that there was an 'escape route' should I need to get off the hills sooner. Unfortunately, I didn't pay attention to the section of the sign that mentioned a 'detour' to Princess Beara's grave. I left the sign behind and followed the long winding hard track that took me higher up into the hills, meandering for miles under the peaks of Maulin and Knocknagree. The higher I got, the more frequently I paused, not only to catch my breath, but also to take in the spectacular views back down into Bantry Bay, which looked absolutely splendid in the fine afternoon sunshine. The hustle and bustle of the towns and villages were long forgotten as I moved further into the peace and solitude of the mountains. Only the occasional bleating of the hill sheep and the song of the skylarks risked interrupting, but never disturbing, the tranquillity. It was wonderful to watch the skylarks, as they suddenly rose up from the long grass singing as they went higher and higher and then, just as suddenly, dropped back down to disappear into the long grass again, as if they had never existed.

The route through the Cork mountains was rather circuitous and I was so grateful to meet my Ireland Way walking companion, Pacman, who appeared along the way to reassure me that I was still on the correct path. Pacman was the name I had given to the little yellow figure carrying a backpack that adorned the top of the way-marker posts often accompanied by a yellow arrow to point you in the right direction. However, I was to subsequently discover that Pacman wasn't always as reliable as he was on my first day. He could disappear without warning for days on end and then reappear without so much as a 'how do you do'! Nevertheless, he was invaluable in terms of helping me find my way through the hills and valleys of the Caha Mountains. So, I can't blame him for my missing a crucial turn off the dirt track I was blindly following at one point. Instead of turning right and descending into a valley to cross the Owgarriff River, I headed straight on along the track that took me higher into the hills towards Tooreenbeg. It wasn't until I arrived at Princess Beara's grave that I realised my mistake.

Beara was a Spanish princess, the daughter of the King of Castille, who married a local Irish chieftain called Owen Mór when he was in Spain. On return to Ireland, Owen took his wife to the highest hill on Greenane Island and, looking across the harbour, he named the island and the whole peninsula Beara in her honour. According to local tradition, when Princess Beara died, Owen had her remains buried in this remote and peaceful valley between Maulin and Knocknagree Mountains. To be honest, I didn't immediately realise that I was at the princess' grave until a young woman suddenly appeared out of nowhere. I hadn't met a single soul since I had left Castletownbere a few hours before and I certainly hadn't expected to meet anyone else in this isolated spot. She appeared just as startled as me to find her sense of isolation suddenly no more than an illusion. "Sorry," I blurted out, as if I was somehow in the wrong for being on the same mountain, "I didn't mean to startle you. I think I may have taken a wrong turn or missed a turn or something. Anyway, I think I'm lost." She seemed to relax a little, now that she realised that I wasn't a threat. "Oh, hi," she replied, "Let's see. I have some maps here. Let's have a look." It turned out that Isabel was hiking in the mountains with her two young boys and was in the process of setting up camp behind a wall in a small stone compound that was perhaps once, and possibly still was, used by sheep farmers. I explained that I was on the first day of walking the length of Ireland. I may have detected a look in her eye that suggested a slight questioning of my ability to achieve my goal given that I was already lost after just a few hours. However, she disguised it well and called to her boys and proceeded to enthusiastically tell them about my challenge. They did appear to be suitably impressed, despite the fact that I was clearly heading in the wrong direction. Isabel found the appropriate map, which was much more detailed than mine, and we were soon able to see where I had gone wrong about half a kilometre back. Before I set off again, Isabel, who was in her early forties, confided in me that she was a cancer survivor, having been diagnosed with breast cancer seven years before, and that she now managed a blog under the name of 'The Cancer Queen Bee' to give other people hope that there can be life after cancer. "Not for my Jacqui, unfortunately," the words came into my head but remained unspoken. She was really delighted that I was walking for cancer research and we hugged before I turned and headed downhill again to re-join the correct route, reflecting as I did so that not every wrong turn was waste of time. It's not every day that you visit the grave of a princess and meet a queen! As I proceeded back down the valley, it was easy to appreciate why Owen Mór had chosen this beautiful and peaceful location for his beloved's final resting place. My thought's immediately turned to another resting place located between the majesty of Fair Head and Knocklayde Mountain in Ballycastle, where my own princess lay.

It wasn't too long before I got back on the right track and dropped down into the valley to cross the narrow but fast flowing Owgarriff River. I met a small group of German walkers coming up out of the valley as I was going down and discovered that they had set off from Adrigole that morning - six hours earlier! This of course meant I had at least another six hours of walking to go before I reached my destination for the day. The scenery remained spectacular and the weather remained beautiful, but the heat and the terrain were starting to take their toll. My legs still felt strong, but my feet were beginning to suffer a bit – I felt the familiar telltale 'hotspot' signs of blisters beginning to form on my right heel and left sole. I sat against a boulder and removed my boots and socks and applied a few 'Compeed' plasters as necessary. I also pulled the orthopaedic insoles out of my boots. I normally wore these to deal with a mild case of plantar fasciitis in both heels, but I felt that they were now causing my boots to rub in places they hadn't rubbed before. Adjustments made, socks and boots on again, snack consumed (as I had stopped anyway) and I was good to go. My feet were still sore though. As usual, I had endured the warning signs for too long before stopping to take corrective action.

I passed the rotting carcass of a fox on the track. It looked like it had been run over by something. A group of German hikers perhaps? There certainly weren't many vehicles that could handle the terrain even if one felt the need to drive over the mountains. There were a couple of crows perched on a rocky outcrop above, probably waiting for me to move on so they could resume their meal of sun-ripened fox. They cawed eerily as I passed by their rocky enclave. The grassy hills of the lower slopes, often softened by white puffs of bog cotton, had now given way to the harder, rugged terrain of the higher reaches of the mountains. Here the ground was littered with random boulders, glacial erratics, together with some quite extensive layers of exposed rock. It was unyielding ground that was certainly much rougher on my poor feet. It was also quite slippery underfoot in places where water had seeped onto the rocks from the hills above. I gradually made my way round the slopes beneath the imposing peak of Hungry Hill, the highest peak in the Caha Mountains at 685 metres. It was aptly named, as I was now beginning to feel the pangs of hunger and had long ago exhausted my meagre travel rations. Hungry Hill is also the title and setting of a famous novel by Daphne du

Maurier about local copper-mining barons of the nineteenth century. In the novel, the name of the mountain is metaphoric, as during the course of the story the mountain seems to 'swallow' successive generations of the Broderick family, who own and mine the mountain. Incidentally, Daphne du Maurier also penned a short story called "The Birds", which was the inspiration for the movie horror masterpiece of the same name directed by Alfred Hitchcock. The crows on the rock above continued to caw menacingly, as if telling me to hurry on and I was only too happy to oblige, before they, or the mountain, could consume me.

It was around 7pm and I estimated that I was still a couple of hours away from Adrigole. It was then that I came across a sign that threw me a possible life line. It was my friend Pacman indicating that I could either continue walking the route to Adrigole, a distance of about six kilometres, or leave the route and walk less than two kilometres to the main road. This second option was tantalisingly labelled the "Escape Route". It was at this very point that I was beset with the worst case of indecision that I had ever experienced. I subsequently walked repeatedly one way and then the other and must have added another half a kilometre to my journey in the process! I was torn between the attraction of cutting my journey short and saving my feet any more discomfort and sticking to the route and not bottling it on the very first day of my challenge. I felt ridiculous going one way and then the other only to turn back once again. I think the sun had gone to my head! More in exasperation than in actually making a conscious decision, I finally settled on continuing to walk the route to Adrigole.

Eight hours and twenty-seven kilometres after leaving Castletownbere, I finally came down off the mountains and trudged up the long driveway to the Hungry Hill Lodge and Campsite on tired legs and aching feet. Here I was welcomed by Owen, a very friendly middle-aged Englishman, who had found the attraction of life on the Beara Peninsula so tempting that he and his wife Barbara had moved from Yorkshire and settled here many years ago. Together they had established the extensive holiday accommodation that, in addition to the lodge and campsite, also boasted a cottage and log cabin, all against the magnificent backdrop of Hungry Hill itself. Not wishing to get off on the wrong foot with my host, I decided to hold my tongue regarding his very optimistic estimation of the time it would take me to walk from Castletownbere to Adrigole. Owen equally chose not to make any comment on my late arrival, perhaps now simply marking me down as another one of those inexperienced numpties. Anyway, collective avoidance of the time issue ensured a trouble free and genial welcome and Owen quickly registered me and showed me to my comfortable room in the lodge and then to the large kitchen/dining room. After showering and applying a little first aid to my long suffering feet, I headed back to the kitchen where Owen very kindly rustled up a tasty chicken curry for me. The kitchen also had a large drinks cooler in the corner with a great selection of alcoholic and non-alcoholic beverages, with an honesty box for payment. I chose a wonderfully cold can of draught Guinness and, while my meal was heating, asked another resident, Dom from Australia, to take a photo of me with my pint of Guinness and my Cancer Research flag. It was a spur of the moment thing on that first evening, but would go on to become my trademark finishing ritual after each day's walk. I don't necessarily recommend going to such lengths, but I can tell you now, hand on heart, that a pint of Guinness tastes so much more refreshing, more smooth, more sublime, more 'good for you', after walking twenty-seven kilometres in twenty-five degrees centigrade heat to reach it!

****

I had the most sublime sleep at the Hungry Hill Lodge, undoubtedly aided to a large extent by my tiring trek over the mountains the day before. Owen provided me with a super breakfast and we had a chat about a number of things of local interest, including the previously avoided subject of the time it takes to walk from Castletownbere to Adrigole! I'm not sure I entirely convinced him that I wasn't a numpty though. To be fair though, he was very impressed with the challenge I had embarked upon and as I was checking out he very kindly slipped me a donation. Before I left the lodge, Owen also took some time out to show me to an old laneway that passed behind the hostel. Owen believed that this was the actual route taken by Donal Cam O'Sullivan Beare and his followers prior to their flight from the Beara Peninsula in the early 1600's. From here, they had made their way to camp in a forest in the Coomerkane Valley, which was just to the west of Glengarriff, my destination for today. The laneway was very heavily overgrown, but Owen had started the process of clearing it and had plans to turn it into a bit of a tourist attraction. It was fair to say that he still had a lot of work ahead of him and that, for now anyway, I would be best sticking to the route set out in my guidebook.

My brief history lesson over, it was now time for me to resume my own long trek. I bade farewell to Owen and made my way down the long drive again to join the main road, which was fairly quiet. It was only a short distance into what might be regarded as the centre of Adrigole, where 'Peg's Shop', which doubles as the local post office, was located. I called in to Peg's to pick up some supplies for the day ahead and bumped into Australian couple Dom and Heidi, who I had met a few times at the Hungry Hill Lodge the previous evening. They were in Ireland touring and, being keen hikers, were preparing to head into the mountains for the day, starting with Hungry Hill. Exchanging information, as hikers tend to do, about the condition of our feet, Heidi enthusiastically extolled the virtues of New Zealand wool as an excellent treatment for blisters. I'd never known an Australian to give credit to anything from New Zealand before, so I reckoned the stuff must be good. Filled with zeal, Heidi dug into her rucksack and pulled out a small box of the wool and handed it to me to keep. "We're near the end of our trip," she said, adding, "You'll perhaps need it more than us given the distance you still have to go." I was extremely grateful, but I have to admit that an ungenerous thought also flitted through my mind. If people keep giving me stuff – a tee shirt yesterday, a box of wool today – I was going to need a bigger rucksack to carry it all. I thanked her and after grabbing a selfie with both her and Dom, we went our separate ways and I finally left Adrigole at just after 10am.

It was only a couple of hundred metres past Peg's before I climbed over a stile to leave the road and pass through a few fields and woods, before heading up into the hills once again. And once again it was a case of fabulous weather and fabulous views. The music app on my phone played 'The Boys of Summer' by Don Henley as I climbed higher. "Don't look back. You can never look back," he sang, but I begged to differ. When you are climbing up hills and mountains, you must always look back. And indeed, every time I took the time to stop and turn around, I was rewarded with the most wonderful views back towards the picturesque landscape of Bantry Bay and the surrounding hills. The pale blue waters of the ocean almost seemed to have been decanted gently over the green headlands and islands to fill all the depressions and inlets along the undulating coastline, creating a smooth and even surface that beautifully reflected the blue sky and white clouds above. It was truly glorious. However, the route gradually became steeper and more taxing and it consequently became harder to always fully appreciate the stunning beauty of the landscape around me. I tried not to be overly concerned when I came across a defibrillator station located at a road junction, with a 'break glass in case of emergency' sign. It wouldn't have been much use to me in an emergency anyway, as self-application might have proved problematic. Pacman, my little yellow hiker friend, wouldn't have been much help on that score either. But, regardless, he appeared quite frequently today to at least provide the necessary reassurance that I was on the right path. Not even I could have taken a wrong turn today!

A stony dirt track carried me higher before petering out to leave me to cross open hillsides for a time. I came to a fence line and followed it for about one and a half kilometres, climbing so steeply at times that I had to use the fence wire to help haul myself and my rucksack upwards. I could now understand why the wire was bent the way it was – misshapen by countless previous hikers doing the same thing, no doubt. At an elevation close to five hundred metres, I came over a rise to be met with a wonderful view down into a small but beautiful lake nestled amongst the peaks of Sugarloaf Mountain. This was Lough Toberavanaha, which is from the Irish meaning 'well of the blessing', and it was here that I met three German lads, who were probably only in their late teens. They were in Ireland for a week and in the process of walking to Killarney. I proudly told them that I was walking the whole length of Ireland and that it would take me about six weeks. However, the smug smile that I felt creeping its way across my lips, kind of stuck mid-smirk when they announced that they were intending to climb Carrauntoohil, Beenkeragh and Caher Mountains on the way to Killarney, which just happened to be the three highest peaks in Ireland – all over one thousand metres high and twice the height of where we were standing at that moment! Only slightly envious of their youth and energy, I wished them good luck as they set off on their way again, while I looked about for somewhere to rest my old bones and have my lunch.

I found a boulder on a nice elevated position overlooking the lake and sat there to have my break, while being entertained by a pair of rams about a hundred metres away continually head butting each other. It was quite a spectacle to watch and the sound of their heads cracking together carried quite clearly to where I was sitting and seemed to echo around the hills. There was nothing gentile about it as they faced each other and rose up on their hind legs before launching themselves forward at each other. The ewes in the small flock appeared to be totally disinterested in proceedings and just kept grazing nonchalantly. They'd seen it all before no doubt. I could imagine them chatting among themselves, "Stupid males; always trying to prove a point. Let them finish their ridiculous shenanigans and then we'll take the one with the least brain damage."

After my lunch break, I headed on up the hill beyond the lake and between the peaks of Sugar Loaf Mountain. As I came over the top of the rise, the view that opened up before me looking towards Glengarriff was truly breath-taking. The multiple rolling peaks of the Cork and Kerry mountains stretched into the distance to meet an impossibly blue sky, a colour that was reflected in the waters of Glengarriff Bay below. My subsequent traversing of the slopes of the long valley, cut through by the Coomerkane River, down towards Glengarriff was truly beautiful. However, it included a very steep descent on a loose rocky path that was quite challenging. I wasn't surprised to learn that Glengarriff comes from the Irish *An Gleann Garbh*, meaning 'the rugged glen'. It certainly lived up to its name, although I had a very friendly sheep to welcome me near the bottom. We spotted each other when still about a hundred metres apart and, rather than it turning on its heels as I would have expected, it wandered up the track towards me. I naturally assumed that it wanted to go on up the track and would probably dash past me when I came too close. But no - it came straight up to me and rubbed its head against my legs and was very happy to be petted. It was obviously well used to humans and I'm guessing that it must have been hand reared. It proceeded to accompany me for the next few hundred metres down the track, only stopping when we came to a stile, which I could climb over and it obviously couldn't.

The route then passed through a forested area known as *Derrynafulla*, meaning 'Oakwood of the blood'. This was where, in the winter of 1602, Donal Cam O'Sullivan Beare and his followers had camped, hiding from the newly appointed Governor of Beare, Sir Charles Wilmot, and his English forces. Wilmot and his troops were camped less than two miles away and eventually discovered where the rebels were hiding out. Sometime late in December, Wilmot's army raided the Irish camp and, after fierce fighting and heavy casualties on both sides, they captured O'Sullivan Beare's herds of two thousand cows and four thousand sheep. The loss of his livestock spelt disaster for O'Sullivan Beare. The means of his people's survival had been taken and he was left with little option but to flee from the Beara Peninsula before they either starved or were attacked once again by Wilmot and his men. In an audacious 'flight' for survival, he decided to take one thousand of his people, four hundred troops and six hundred civilians, on a five hundred kilometre march to Leitrim, where he knew they would be safe. They departed on 31st December 1602, on a bitterly cold New Year's Eve night. Not everyone who had been camped in the wood was fit to set out on such a long, arduous march and O'Sullivan Beare must have realised that the old, weak, injured and ill left behind would face certain death at the hands of the crown forces. Nevertheless, he asked these abandoned souls to help with their escape by keeping the camp fires burning in the woods to fool Wilmot's men into believing that the entire camp was still intact and settled in for the night. The ruse worked and allowed O'Sullivan Beare and his thousand followers to escape unhindered, but once Wilmot's army discovered that the majority of the rebels had scarpered from under their noses, those who had remained behind were slaughtered. Although it was known as 'Oakwood of the blood' well before O'Sullivan Beare's time, there is little doubt that this slaughter only further ingrained the wood's eternally haunting name. As I listened to the birds twittering in the trees and the buzz of insects hovering over the brambles, it was hard to imagine that such a bloody massacre could have taken place in such peaceful surroundings all those years ago.

I finally got into Glengarriff at just after 5:30pm, which was a lot later than expected. My feet were sore and my shoulders were aching from the weight of my rucksack, both of which had contributed to my slow pace. I made my way up the main street to the Blue Pool Hostel, where I had reserved a room for the night, and was signed in by Siobhan, one half of the couple who ran this great little hostel in the centre of town. The window of my upstairs room looked out onto the main street and there, right across the road from the hostel was MacCarthy's Bar! What were the chances? This was obviously a sign. My name wasn't 'MacCarthy', or 'McCarthy' for that matter, but I nevertheless felt that I was being summoned. Fifteen minutes later I was sitting outside the bar with a pint of Guinness and my flag, wearing my recently acquired MacCarthy's Bar tee shirt and getting my photo taken by an unsuspecting stranger that I had just commandeered from inside the pub.

Chapter Two: Wild Camping
(Days three and four - Glengarriff to Gougane Barra)

The following morning, I decided to lighten my rucksack a little to help my aching shoulders and feet. I stripped out everything that I felt I could manage without, including a belt, my orthopaedic insoles, high-viz jacket, spare trousers and the MacCarthy's Bar tee shirt. After a self-service breakfast at the Blue Moon Hostel and a chat with some of the guests and the owners, Mike and Siobhan, I headed down the street to the local post office with my surplus goods to post them back to Belfast. Having lightened my load, I then called into a pharmacy and added to it by purchasing a pair of the gaudiest flip-flops I had ever seen. I had foolishly neglected to pack a pair of sandals and was finding it difficult to manage with hiking boots as my only form of footwear. The flip-flops were very lightweight, didn't take up much room in my rucksack and were only four Euros, all of which was great. However, they were a ladies size five, bright orange and green with pink flamingos and the only pair left in town, all of which was not great! But, they would have to do until I found something better.

Having finally sorted my rucksack out, I hoisted it onto my tired shoulders once again and set off on day three, enjoying a pleasant walk out of town, past the pretty harbour lined with lobster pots. The sky was a pale, morning blue, with only the merest wisps of white cloud lingering wistfully in the air. The darker blue waters of Glengarriff Bay were dotted with small fishing boats and lush green islands that drew the eye out towards the deeper waters of Bantry Bay. It took me a lot longer than I expected to find the turn off I was seeking in order to head inland for the hills once again. I was over three kilometres out of town before I left the road and climbed over a stile to pass through a delightful, leaf-shaded path. I then followed a rugged track that gradually climbed into the hills, providing superb uninterrupted views over Bantry Bay, Whiddy Island, Sheep's Head Peninsula and even Mizen Peninsula beyond. The route continued to skirt round the upper and mainly grassy slopes of Derroograne Hill and Coomhola Mountain and once again I kept stopping and turning to drink in the wonderful vistas on display, everything looking resplendent in the glorious sunshine. I wondered if O'Sullivan Beare had done the same as he led his people over the mountains and away from Beara and Bantry. If he had, the views might not have been as glorious beneath the grey winter skies they were escaping under, but I'm sure he would have nevertheless looked at them longingly, perhaps wondering if he would ever see them again. As I continued on, I was pleased to find that some of the boggier stretches on the hills had been 'planted' with flat stepping stones that provided easy passage through the waterlogged meadows, each step bringing with it a satisfying squelch as the stone settled into its soggy bed.

When I reached the highest point of today's Ireland Way route, which a sign indicated was also part of the 'Corrycommane Loop Walk', I came across a small rocky hill with a single standing stone resting on top. The hill was fenced off right around its perimeter and at this point I had to decide on whether to skirt round it to the right or to the left. Pacman was nowhere to be seen. I chose to go left. I chose wrong. Unfortunately, it wasn't until I had spent twenty minutes negotiating my way down a steep and very rough slope that I realised that the way ahead was pretty much impassable. I then had to turn and retrace my steps back up the slope. I showed remarkable restraint and only cursed for the first half of the way. When I got back to where I had made the wrong choice, I started off around the hill with the standing stone once again, but going to the right this time. I had only gone a few metres when Pacman suddenly appeared from behind a rock! The sneaky wee sod had been hiding on me! More cursing ensued before the beauty and tranquillity of my surroundings worked their magic and calmed me down once again. I headed on down the right slope, following the fence line with its posts conspicuously dubbed with bright yellow paint, so that no one, except an idiot like me, could possibly take the wrong side of the hill! At the bottom, I climbed over a couple of stiles to enter into a wood, the floor of which was carpeted with soft moss. It was such a lovely peaceful place that I decided to stop here for a little while and have a bite of lunch. My unfortunate wrong turn at the standing stone aside, it had been a beautiful journey so far, with superb views and glorious weather once again. My trek through the hills had also been punctuated with lovely glimpses of the sights and sounds of nature - butterflies, dragonflies and damselflies flitting over pools of water dotted with soft white flags of bog cotton, a lonely cuckoo calling, skylarks singing, hawthorn, foxglove and honeysuckle - all of which added to the beauty of the morning. It had been truly sublime. Unfortunately it didn't last!

I left the wood and almost immediately ran into Mr. McAdam. I'd met him many times before and I didn't really care for him that much. You probably know him well. He gets around a lot. Goes by the first name of Tar. Tar McAdam - that's the very one! He's a hard, unforgiving fecker. And he can go on relentlessly for miles and miles. On this occasion, he stayed with me for the entire second half of my journey. All the way to my final destination in Kealkill, in fact. And to make matters worse, he's a devious fecker! He bores you so much that you lose your concentration and then stop paying attention to where you're going. And the next thing you know, you're way off route and having to circle back, adding miles onto your already tedious journey. And he slowly and methodically wears you down. You feel like he's beating the soles of your feet with a rod of iron, so that each step is so painful that you seek out the grass verge whenever you can. And then he toys with you, like a cat cruelly playing with a mouse. He grows a green Mohawk and offers your feet a soft cushion to walk upon. But it's only temporary. Just as you begin to feel the benefit, he shaves it off again and it's back to his bald blacktop!

Yes, after I had left the woods I joined a quiet country road that brought me to Coomhola Bridge. The heat of the day had increased significantly and I reckon it was now close to thirty degrees. I was sweaty, tired and distracted and, as a consequence, I took the second wrong turn of the day and ended up on a road running parallel to, but perhaps a kilometre away from, the road I should have been on. In my defence, I would also maintain that the signage at Coomhola Bridge was not particularly helpful and the map in my guidebook not sufficiently detailed. Anyway, I set off on the wrong road and blindly followed it in the blistering heat for over an hour before I began to realise that something was wrong. I was looking out for a right turn that showed clearly on my map, which I should have come across by this stage, but it never appeared. I kept on going, hoping that I would encounter it soon. The heat was relentless, both from the sun above and from the hot road beneath my feet. It eventually occurred to me that I was perhaps on the wrong road. Further scrutiny of the guidebook map, in conjunction with Google maps on my phone, confirmed that I was indeed off course. It seems that I may have been on the cycle route rather than the walking route. And, unfortunately, I was so far off course that it was pointless turning back. No, I was best to keep going until I came to a turn in the road that would enable me to take a long loop back round towards Kealkill. I must have added a good six kilometres and two hours or more onto my journey. And it was absolutely torturous in the unremitting heat. The only relief for my feet came when a strip of weeds or grass appeared along the centre of the road – the 'green Mohawk'. But this reprieve from the hot, black tarmacadam was sporadic and often very short lived. By the time I got to Kealkill, the soles of my feet were burning! So no, I don't like Mr. McAdam at all.

However, the village of Kealkill, pronounced "Key-kill", provided some much needed relief (initially anyway) for a weary traveller. First, there were the picturesque ruins of Carriganass Castle sitting prominently on the north bank of the Ouvane River. Carriganass is from the Irish *Carraig an Easa*, meaning 'the rock of the waterfall'. I stopped briefly at a small picnic area beside the castle and stripped off my boots and socks as fast as I could to plunge my hot feet into the cold, shallow waters of the river. I almost expected clouds of steam to hiss up as I submerged my feet, but the only sound was a long sigh of satisfaction from my lips at the immediate relief imparted by the clear, cold water. After my feet had cooled sufficiently, I wandered up to the castle and from the information sign outside I discovered that it had at one time been occupied by Donal Cam O'Sullivan Beare and his cousin Owen O'Sullivan. I strongly suspected that it was never occupied by both cousins at the same time though. They were bitter enemies due to arguments over family inheritance and they were very much on opposing sides when it came to their allegiance to Queen Elizabeth I. Owen's father was knighted by Elizabeth and, after his death, Owen subsequently retained his title and became a Sir, while Donal Cam was to be hunted by forces loyal to the Queen and effectively became an outlaw.

Another notice recounted the legend of 'The Revenge of Donal Cam', a rather fanciful tale in the form of a rather gruesome poem. It told how Donal Cam had sought vengeance for the murder of his wife by St. Ledger, the leader of a band of English soldiers who, at one time, had occupied Carriganass Castle. Apparently Donal Cam made a rather blood curdling vow over the body of his dead wife, described in the poem as follows:

> *No food, no rest shall Donal know*
> *Until he lays thy murderer low*
> *Until each severed quivering limb*
> *In its own lustful blood shall swim*

The legend goes on to describe how Donal Cam, disguised as a monk, gained access to Carriganass Castle and hurled St. Ledger from the upper tower onto the rocks below in the Ouvane River.

> *Saxon, 'tis Aoife gives this grave*
> *And saying plunged him in the wave*
> *One piercing shriek was heard, no more*
> *Up flashed the billows dyed with gore*

Donal Cam then made a miraculous escape by jumping from the tower across the river. All very melodramatic indeed; never mind rather gory. The notice finished by pointing out that there is no historical basis for the events described in the poem, but cheekily added, *"why should history get in the way of a good story?"* Despite this story that obviously hailed deep from the realms of fantasy, I was further intrigued by this character Donal Cam O'Sullivan Beare, who had obviously gained legendary status in Ireland as a result of his epic march north in the early 1600's. There was a picture of Donal Cam above the poem and I recognised it as the same image used on the Beara-Breifne Way road signs, showing him as a Spanish nobleman in armour and ruff. I could now see more clearly the carefully teased moustache and the neatly groomed Van Dyke beard. A medallion hung from a ribbon around his neck and, although the picture wasn't the clearest, it looked very much like the medallion displayed the red

Cross of St James that I had encountered on my Spanish Camino de Santiago. I wanted to find out more about this Irish Chieftain and rebel who dressed in Spanish garb and took so much care over his appearance. I was also intrigued as to why an Irishman was wearing what appeared to be the Cross of St James, a symbol of the Order of Santiago, a religious and military order founded in twelfth century Spain. One of the primary objectives of the order, also known as the Order of St James of the Sword, was to protect pilgrims walking the Camino de Santiago – the Way of St James.

I continued on into the heart of Kealkill, passing Kealkill Parkland on the way and idly wondering if it was the woods of this parkland that gave the village its name. Kealkill is from the Irish *An Chaolchoill,* meaning 'the narrow wood'. I soon came to my intended destination, which was Collins Bar, and my reward, which was of a pint of Guinness. After hours of tramping along the hot black top, it was so nice to sit down and enjoy the cold black stuff. I enquired about food, but the barman looked at his watch, as if to check the time, and then said, "I'm afraid you're too late. We stopped serving food....oh....about two years ago!" He laughed at his own little joke and then, seeing my crestfallen face, he advised me that I would be able to pick up something to eat at Burke's Foodstore, which was about half a kilometre away. Brilliant! Just what I needed. Another bloody walk! Thankfully the barman said he would look after my rucksack while I headed to Burke's to stock up on sufficient supplies. I followed the busy road to the store, picked up a selection of unhealthy snacks to see me through to lunchtime the next day and then headed back to Collins to linger over another pint.

I was sitting alone, sipping my drink and composing my daily blog, when a young couple at the table next to me noticed my rucksack and banner. My not so subtle advertising had worked again. They were very interested in the Ireland Way and we subsequently chatted at length about my walks for Jacqui, writing and fundraising. Andy Hall was a professional singer/songwriter, originally from Stoke-on-Trent, who had settled in Ireland about a year ago with his partner Louise McCarthy from Wexford - it seemed that I couldn't escape the McCarthy's! They were touring around the Beara Peninsula for a few days catching up with some of Louise's family. Despite my feeble protests, they insisted on buying me another pint and we ended up sitting on enjoying the craic for much longer than I had ever intended. I was very conscious of the fact that it was getting late and that I still hadn't sorted out somewhere to stay for the night, but I was enjoying the company so much that I hadn't really given my sleeping arrangements much thought. There was no accommodation nearby and so I knew that I would be resorting to 'wild camping' somewhere tonight, perhaps back near the castle at the picnic spot. But I would worry about that later. What is it that they say? When the drink is in, the wit is out! Sometime before closing time, our collective remaining wit decided that it would probably be a good idea to call it a night. However, before we parted company, Louise insisted that Andy play me a song. Andy was very willing and headed out to his car to fetch his guitar. He was reluctant to play in the bar and so we headed outside instead. We stood on the street outside Collins Bar and Andy launched into one of his own rousing compositions called "Atlas". It was quite a surreal experience listening to Andy perform in the dark of the night with the only light coming from the street lamps and the headlights of the occasional car going past. But it was quite a performance and he gave it his all; even if he did only have an audience of two on this occasion.

Promising to keep in touch, Andy and Louise then headed back to Glengarriff, where they were staying for the night, and I collected my rucksack from inside the bar and went to find a place to pitch my tent. Only then did it fully dawn on me just how foolish it had been to leave it so late. It was not only dark, but it was also very, very cold. So cold in fact that I was shivering and my breath was misting before me as I went. Despite the searing heat I had experienced during the day, the lack of cloud cover meant that when the sun had disappeared all the heat had gone with it and as a result the temperatures had plummeted. Rather than head all the way back to the castle, I decided to set up camp in the parkland, which had a large grassy area near the entrance. There was a little light coming from an almost full moon overhead, but it was insufficient to see what I was doing in relation to pitching the tent. Thankfully, I had invested in a small head torch, which proved invaluable. Regardless, it was still quite a challenge to erect the small one-man tent that I had no previous experience of erecting. My friend, Brendan McManus SJ, who I had borrowed the tent from, had given me a quick demonstration of how to put it up a few weeks earlier and I had always intended to practice, but had never gotten round to it. Oh no, I thought that I would leave it until a bitterly cold and dark night in a strange environment and after I had downed a few pints of Guinness before giving it a go - like any idiot would! Anyway, thankfully the tent was pretty much idiot proof and I eventually got it up and, after blowing up my inflatable mattress with a few alcoholic puffs, I wriggled into my sleeping bag inside and closed all the zips. The tent was of a low profile compact design, apparently known in the trade as a 'coffin tent' due to the fact that there is just room for one body inside, and only if it was lying down! However, I was under cover and, for that, I was at least thankful. It had been so cold whilst putting the tent up that I had decided to keep all my clothes on; the only things I had removed before bedding down were my boots. So, I had fully expected to be nice and cosy inside my sleeping bag. But, try as I might, I simply could not get warm and consequently could not get over to sleep. The whole night was spent twisting and turning and trying to get warm and comfortable, but it was simply impossible Perhaps I should have gone for a couple of laps round the green before getting into the tent. I have since heard it said that you should never get into a sleeping bag cold. I can now personally vouch for that. Despite being in a 'coffin tent', I did not 'rest in peace'!

****

As dawn was breaking, I gave up on the possibility of getting any sleep and I finally decided to throw in the towel. Or at least I would have if there had been enough room inside my 'coffin' to throw a towel! I struggled to extricate myself from my twisted sleeping bag inside the narrow confines of the tent and pull on my boots before emerging like a drunken moth from my canvas cocoon onto the damp grass outside. I slowly unfolded and stretched my tired aching body into the cold pre-light of the new day as my muttered cursing simultaneously turned the air both white and blue. I began the process of dismantling the tent and packing everything back into my rucksack again. I fumbled a fresh pair of contact lenses into my eyes before hauling on my pack and getting on the road for 5am. It was still so cold that I needed my fleece, jacket, hat and even gloves on, as I began my dawn dander towards the wonderfully named Gougane Barra. Surprisingly though, it was actually quite pleasant walking in the cool of the early morning and

I was able to get some nice photographs as the sun was coming up. Photographers often wax lyrical about 'the golden hour' after sunrise, when the daylight has a much redder and softer quality than when the sun is higher in the sky. Being a 'night owl', I rarely got to experience the beauty of a summer sunrise, but now I was reminded of just how special this time of the day could be. It almost made up for my lack of sleep; almost! It was quite ethereal at times walking along some of the minor roads that were lined with tall trees, their leaf canopies creating a tunnel like effect ahead of me, leading towards this beautiful, warm, glowing light created by a sun still low in the sky. You can perhaps imagine my surprise when I came across a large angel standing by the roadside. Someone had very skilfully carved its figure from the trunk of a tree, which was still rooted in the ground. Previously, in more vulnerable times following my loss of Jacqui, I would have seen this as some sort of divine sign from my loved one. Now, I supposed that I was less prone to such fantasies. Or so I thought!

Things started to gradually warm up around 8am and then proceeded to get very hot once again after 10am. A mixture of country roads were followed by boggy tracks around and through forests, before I was deposited once again on long, winding, torturous minor roads and lanes that gradually climbed towards the Shehy Mountains. I had long since stripped off and packed away my warm clothing and was now down to shorts and a tee shirt, but I was slowly roasting as the sun climbed higher in the sky. The 'golden hour' had been replaced by the 'crisping hour' and I was glad of my factor 30 sun lotion, but once again my poor feet were overheating. It was therefore an absolute delight to come across a small bridge over a stream flowing down off the rocky hillside. I fought the natural urge to keep going and forced myself to take a break here and removed my footwear once again to enjoy the instant relief of the icy cold waters cascading down between the rocks. It was a moment of shear bliss as I sat on a boulder with my feet dangling into a small pool and closed my eyes to listen to the soothing water music. It was hard to drag myself away from this Nirvana, but I knew that I still had the hardest part of the day's journey ahead of me. So I dried off my feet and reluctantly pulled on my socks and boots once again and set off for the mountains.

The sun-bleached skull of some sort of long-horned steer, fixed to a telegraph pole at the roadside, didn't exactly fill me with confidence as I proceeded upwards under the hot sun – quite a contrast to the ethereal effect of the carved angel I had encountered earlier in the cool of the morning. Perhaps the skull was just a reminder that the name Shehy Mountains is from the Irish *Cnoic na Síofra*, meaning 'hills of the animal hides' – this particular animal had certainly given up its hide long ago. A small group of peacocks on the lower slopes of the mountains provided some amusement as they hurried ahead of me and eventually scattered into the undergrowth. There are several collective nouns to choose from when referring to a group of peacocks. You can use muster, pride, bevy or party, but my personal favourite is ostentation. It just seems to fit the strutting, flamboyant nature of the birds perfectly. The ascent and eventual descent from the Shehy Mountains was as spectacular as it was exhausting. The ascent began by following a stony track, but this quickly petered out to become a long climb up the steep, grassy slopes of Coinigear, which presented one false summit after another. Every time I felt I was nearing the top, it was only to find that another climb lay ahead. However, every mountain (or mountain pass) does have a top and I eventually reached the top of this one and found myself between two mountain lakes, Lough Fadda and the smaller Lough Namrat. The route up the mountainside had been very well way-marked by Pacman, but the multi-directional sign at the top was rather confusing as every element seemed to be pointing in totally the wrong direction. The reason for this became apparent when I put my hand to the sign and found that it rotated easily in the hole in which it had been planted. I turned it so that everything was pointing in the right direction, but I guessed that it would only be a matter of time before the wind would play havoc with it again.

I left the sign and followed the 540 metre high ridge of the evocatively named Foilastookeen Mountain (meaning unknown) eastwards and was greeted with a fantastic view down into an incredibly photogenic glacial valley, carved out from the mountain-scape before me. And nestling at the bottom was the beautiful Gouganebarra Lake - a long stretch of dark water running along the centreline of the valley and fringed by dark green fir trees. A very long descent down towards the lake then followed, the initial stage of which was down a sometimes very steep rocky track that had only recently been completed. The large, angular rocks that formed the path were not the easiest to walk on, but it was certainly preferable to trudging over the blanket bog that I would have had to contend with only weeks beforehand. The rocky track eventually met up with a laneway that was much easier on the legs and feet and this slowly wound its way down to meet the lakeside and then follow alongside it to reach the Gougane Barra Hotel, the only accommodation available in my final destination for the day.

I had phoned ahead earlier in the morning to see if there were any rooms available in the hotel, but unfortunately it had been fully booked – hardly surprising now that I could see at first-hand the beauty and serenity of this natural oasis hidden away in the Cork mountains. However, I was hoping that the management at the hotel might be able to do something to assist an extremely weary walker. And, oh boy, how they did! It didn't all come at once, but unfolded gradually like the petals of a beautiful flower slowly opening. I called at reception and the young man on duty, Maurice from France, was very sympathetic, but confirmed that there were no rooms available. Not even a broom cupboard – and I did ask! I then more sensibly enquired if there was anywhere I could pitch my tent and he said he would need to speak to the hotel owners about that and would do so as soon as one of them was available. In the meantime I headed to the bar/café complex in a separate building next door to the hotel and ordered my daily measure of the black stuff and captured the evidence on camera to share with the social media world. The resulting photograph showed me triumphantly holding my flag above my head and smiling broadly into the camera. However, it belied the fact that at that time I was seriously filled with doubt about my ability to complete my challenge. I was really exhausted and the soles of my feet were constantly aching. Lack of sleep from the night before and the punishing heat of the day's exposure out on the hills undoubtedly contributed significantly to my feelings of despondence. There was little doubt that so far this walk had proved tougher than anything I had ever tackled before. Had I bitten off more than I could chew this time? I wasn't quite ready to throw in the towel just yet, but I was beginning to seriously lose faith in my resolve.

When I returned to the hotel reception, Maurice was smiling broadly as I approached, which I took a good sign. He had spoken to Neil Lucey, one half of the husband and wife team that ran the hotel, and he had said that I could use a field beside the hotel to camp in. But not only that, he had also arranged for me to have access to a guest room for an hour to get showered and changed and I was also welcome to dine in the hotel's dining room later. This was absolute music to my ears. I was shown up to the guest room and after showering and doing my laundry, I was shown out to my field for the night. As I was hanging up my washing on the branches of a tree and pitching my tent, I had two very friendly lambs to keep me company. I found out that they were called Jumbo and Jet from Katy, Neil's wife, when she came out to feed them a large bottle of milk, the contents of which disappeared quicker than you could say "Jumbo Jet"! Katy told me that both lambs had lost their mums around the same time and that they were now being hand reared. "Don't worry," she said, "They'll not disturb you during the night. They're both put to bed in the big shed out back at around 10pm." As it turned out, I don't even think that two real jumbo jets in the field would have disturbed me that night. I was so exhausted after a long, hard day of walking and no sleep at all the night before. After a lovely meal in the hotel, I headed back out to my field and slept the sleep of the dead in my canvas coffin.

Chapter Three: Ghost Stories
(Days five and six - Gougane Barra to Ballyvourney)

The following morning, I couldn't quite believe it when I woke and checked my watch to find that it was 8am and that I had slept for nine hours solid. Once again the temperature had dropped during the night, but, to be honest, I think that even if the ice age that had created Gougane Barra's beautiful valley had suddenly returned overnight, I still wouldn't have felt it given my level of exhaustion. I unzipped the door of my tent and was relieved to find no sign of ice, but instead another gorgeous early morning landscape bathed in warm sunshine. I pulled on my boots and went for a little stroll to stretch the legs before breakfast. My legs were a little stiff and my feet still felt a bit sore, but they were much improved from the evening before.

There are miles of gorgeous walks around the lake and through the forests and hills around Gougane Barra, but I didn't go far. Just down to the lakeside and to the small island that gave its name to the place. Gougane Barra is from the Irish *Guagán Barra*, meaning 'the rock of Barra'. The name comes from Saint Finbar, who is said to have built a monastery on this island during the sixth century. None of the original monastery remains, although the ruins of a later monastery or church, built around 1700, are still in place to wander through. However, the real showpiece on the island was the nineteenth century oratory, which stood near to where the original monastery had been. It's famous for its picturesque location and richly decorated interior and is apparently a highly popular place for wedding photography. It wasn't hard to understand why, particularly on a day such as today when the waters of the lake were so still. The surrounding mountains were reflected almost perfectly in its mirrored surface. Without wishing to appear that I am in cahoots with the local tourist board, I have to say that Gougane Barra was a truly magical place.

And the magic didn't end at the lakeside. When I had packed up my tent and rucksack, I headed for the hotel's dining room once again for some breakfast. I left my rucksack in the corner of the room, making sure, as always, that the banner attached to it was facing outwards for people to see. I had met Neil at dinner the previous evening and had thanked him for allowing me to use the field and the hotel facilities. I had told him that I was walking the Ireland Way, but for some reason I hadn't told him why. He came to the table to take my breakfast order and then he noticed the banner on my rucksack. "You're walking for cancer research?" he asked rhetorically, before adding, "jeez, I didn't know that. You should have told us. Listen, you order whatever you want for breakfast. It's on the house. Good on ye!" So, I proceeded to order everything on the menu. No, I didn't of course, but I did have a wonderful breakfast, starting with a bowl of porridge with West Cork Whisky and sultanas – absolutely delicious – before moving on to a full Irish fry! A wonderful sleep, followed by a wonderful breakfast. It couldn't get any better, could it? Well yes, it could and it did!

As I was leaving the dining room, Neil called me over to the till and handed me back the money I had spent on my meal the evening before. "Really, you don't have to do that," I protested, half-heartedly, but he was having none of it. "Listen," he said, "you're on a charity gig. I'm only too happy to help. I wish we could have done more, but we simply hadn't a room free last night." I told him that he had been more than generous and that I had actually enjoyed a great sleep in the tent. But he was on a roll and reinforcements, in the form of Katy, had now also turned up. "Where are you walking to today?" they wanted to know. I told them that I had decided to scale back on my original plan to walk to Ballyvourney, which was twenty-eight kilometres away, and instead just go as far as Ballingeary, which was only a distance of twelve kilometres. Neil and Katy looked at each other and seemed to reach some unspoken agreement by telepathy or intuition, acknowledged only by the slightest of nods. "Tell you what," began Neil, "give me a call when you reach Ballingeary. I'll come and pick you up or I'll send someone to get you." "You can stay here tonight," continued Katy, "we have a number of rooms freed up and you would be very welcome to be our guest. You can have dinner here this evening also." "And breakfast tomorrow morning," added Neil, "and then we'll drop you back to Ballingeary to continue your walk." I was being pummelled with kindness from both sides and I was completely overwhelmed. Neil and Katy Lucey, who had been very hospitable right from the start, seemed to have gone into generosity overdrive once they had learned that I was walking for Cancer Research. "You guys are unbelievable," I said, "so, so very kind. I can't begin to tell you how much this means to me." "Hey, it's nothing really," replied Katy, "we're delighted to be able to help out." It may have seemed like nothing to them, but at that time it meant everything to me. And there was one more surprise to come. "Hang on," said Neil, "I've just thought of something." He disappeared into the depths of the hotel and a few moments later arrived back with a small daypack. "Here," he said, "transfer what you need for today into this and leave your heavy rucksack here. We'll put it up in your room for you."

I can tell you that I left that hotel that morning with the biggest spring in my step and the biggest smile on my face. A huge weight had suddenly been lifted from both my shoulders and my mind! Through the kindness of Neil and Katy, my outlook was no longer as bleak as it had been. There is a saying that I had heard repeated many times on my Spanish Camino two years previously, which simply went along the lines of, "Don't worry. Trust in the Camino and it will provide." It counselled pilgrims to not despair if things seemed to be going badly, because the Camino, or more accurately, the people of the Camino, whether they were other pilgrims, hospitalerios (hostel staff), or locals, would invariably come to your assistance and provide what you needed. I had experienced it myself on many occasions while on my own Camino. Could it be that a similar phenomenon existed here in Ireland – a country of course famously renowned for its hospitality? If Neil and Katy were representative of those involved in the 'hospitality industry' in Ireland today, then there was little doubt that Ireland's wonderful reputation was not only intact, but was positively flourishing. Neil and Katy were truly wonderful people and unfortunately, like many others, they were all too aware from personal experience of the devastation that cancer can bring. Now that they had helped get me back on track, as it were, I gave myself a rather stern talking to as I set off for Ballingeary. How could I even have been thinking of giving up on my Ireland Way walk so soon? Yes, it had been tough so far and, yes, my body was hurting a little, but I needed to remind myself of why I was doing it. And first and foremost it was to honour Jacqui's memory. What sort of an honour would it be to Jacqui to give up after only four or five days? I had been missing her acutely the previous evening as I dined alone in a restaurant filled with couples and, inevitably, memories of the suffering she had endured as cancer took its strangle hold on her body had infiltrated my mind. Without question, Jacqui had suffered much worse and for much longer than I would ever experience on this walk. And I'd still be alive at the end of it – at least I hoped so! I pulled the folded sheets of paper from my pocket and, even though I knew the words they contained almost by heart, I read through them once again and knew that I couldn't give up. I therefore resolved there and then to toughen up and complete the Ireland Way, no matter what it took.

As for the day's walk, it started with beautiful views across and over Gougane Barra and I captured some wonderful photographs of the reflections of the Shehy Mountains in the lake's perfectly still waters. The subsequent hike to Ballingeary snaked around a mixture of roads, woods and lanes and trails through fields, but thankfully no mountains. And when I say snaked, I really mean snaked. The distance between Gougane Barra and Ballingeary 'as the crow flies' is only a mere seven kilometres, but the Ireland Way route looped around the countryside in all directions for twelve kilometres before eventually bringing me to my destination. If this was the actual route taken by O'Sullivan Beare's party over four hundred years ago, I began to wonder what had prevented them from taking a more direct route. Perhaps they were trying to avoid running into forces allied to the Crown? Once again the sky was clear blue and the heat from the sun was intense. Even the sheep in the fields were seeking out whatever shade they could find under trees or behind rocks. Unfortunately, my route largely kept me under the full glare of the sun, but, thankfully, my much lighter pack and the shorter distance made it all so much more manageable than the day before. There were some nice views along the way, but I'm afraid that, after having experienced the exceptional beauty of Gougane Barra, everything else paled by comparison. Occasional sightings of electric blue damselflies and orange butterflies became very welcome along the otherwise ordinary, but nonetheless pleasant, landscape.

Three hours after setting out from Gougane Barra, I arrived into the outskirts of the village of Ballingeary to be greeted by an elderly man who was out for a slow stroll with the aid of a walking stick. He greeted me in Irish. The village was in a *Gaeltacht* area and practically everyone here was bilingual. When it became clear to him that I hadn't a notion as to what he was saying, he switched to English. He introduced himself as Con and we stopped to have a chat. He was impressed with my walking challenge, but rather sadly he held up his stick and said that he himself wasn't fit to go too far anymore. Con told me that he had just turned seventy-four and due to failing health, his doctor had recently declared him unfit to drive and had "put him off the road". He was really missing being able to drive about the place in his car and he clearly wasn't too pleased with his doctor. He leaned in conspiratorially and said, with a wink of his eye, "If you hear about a murder in the village in the coming days, just remember to say nothing to the Guards about our wee chat." I reminded him that I was from the North where, if you were questioned by the police, the advice was always, "Whatever ye say, say nathin'." We both laughed and then I asked him if he knew anything about O'Sullivan Beare. Con was able to tell me that Donal Cam and his followers hadn't actually come into the village of Ballingeary. In fact the village may not even have existed back in 1602. They had taken a more direct route towards the ruins of Augeris Church about three kilometres north of the village. I supposed the Ireland Way couldn't always follow the route of O'Sullivan Beare religiously, due to terrain and/or land ownership issues; and perhaps a need to get hikers back to civilization every now and again.

I thanked Con for his help and headed on into the village, wondering with a smile if I should report an imminent murder to the Guards. I passed the tiny Ballingeary Forge, which had been built in 1904. It no longer operated as a forge, but had been recently restored for the benefit of historians and tourists alike. A short distance beyond the forge, I came across the village shop and post office where Neil had told me I could get my Ireland Way passport stamped. Here I met Eileen, who runs the shop with her husband. Fortunately, she was just about to drive to the Gougane Barra Hotel to collect her daughter and she kindly agreed to give me a lift back, which would save Neil the trouble of coming to collect me. While I was waiting, I sat at a picnic table in the shade outside the shop and had a snack. I was intrigued to watch, over the next ten minutes or so, a string of young lads come out of the front door of the house adjoining the shop. It looked like there had been a whole football team in the house! When Eileen came out, she confirmed that that had actually been the case. There was a Gaelic football match in a neighbouring village that afternoon and the Ballingeary team had gathered in her house beforehand to talk tactics. Two of her sons were on the team and, after she collected her daughter from Gougane Barra, they were going along to watch the game.

On the way to the hotel, Eileen told me about the heavy snow that had cut off the villages in March earlier in the year. It had been right at the time that one of her sons was to be married in Gougane Barra. The wedding had been in grave danger of having to be cancelled as the roads had been completely blocked by snow. She then proudly told me of how all the locals had come out to clear the roads between Ballingeary and Gougane Barra so that the wedding could proceed. It just added to the feeling that I was indeed in a magical part of the world!

****

Following a superb stay at the Gougane Barra Hotel, including an evening meal and bed and breakfast all on the house, it was time to say farewell to the wonderful Neil and Katy Lucey. Neil had one more final surprise for me, as he handed me a copy of the Beara-Breifne Way Passport as a memento of my stay. I also took a few minutes to nip round to my previous night's sleeping quarters to say goodbye to the adorable lambs, Jumbo and Jet, who both came running across the field to me, bleating happily, once I called on them. Diarmuid O'Ceallachain was waiting for me in the car park at the front of the hotel when I got back. Diarmuid, and his partner Kate, had been following my journey on social media and had very kindly got in touch and offered to help over the next couple of days. It really seemed like the Ireland Way was starting to take on a life of its own, with hospitality running through its core. Diarmuid and I shook hands, instantly becoming good friends, and I then climbed into his car. Diarmuid told me that he was on leave from work for a week and so had plenty of time on his hands to help out. We headed to Ballingeary and then Diarmuid gave me a quick tour by road to familiarise me with the route for the day ahead. He had also brought me a day pack so I could just carry my essentials for the day's sixteen kilometre walk to Ballyvourney - once again I was spared the torture of carrying my full rucksack with me! Diarmuid then dropped me back outside the post office in Ballingeary and said to give him a call when I reached Ballyvourney.

I waved Diarmuid off, stopped to say hello to Eileen outside the post office and then set off again on the next stage of my Ireland Way. I crossed the stone arches of the bridge over the Bunsheelin River, almost immediately coming upon a sight that couldn't help but give me pause for thought. For here, by the roadside, under a little specially erected portico, was an actual famine pot that had been used to help feed the starving people in the area during the Irish famine of 1845 to 1848 - *An Gorta Mór,* The Great Hunger – a reminder of a terrible time that should never have happened. Less than fifty metres from the famine pot, I then passed the Irish-language summer school, *Coláiste na Mumhan* (The College of Munster). A sign here proudly declared that Thomas MacDonagh, one of the ill-fated leaders of the 1916 Easter Rising, had been a past pupil of the college. So, here in this small village were reminders of two highly significant events in Irish history, both of which had far reaching consequences for the island of Ireland. Although separated by more than half a century, it was not difficult to imagine that these two events were more closely related in terms of cause and effect. The route followed the path of the Bunsheelin River, first on road and then over fields, and then cut northwards, following a smaller tributary of the river. Several fields of long grass and metal stiles later, brought me to the remaining ruins of Augeris (or Eachros) Church, also known in Irish as *An Teampaillin,* simply meaning 'the little church'. The church was famous for being the site of the first encampment of Donal Cam O'Sullivan Beare and his one thousand followers in 1602. An information sign erected next to the ruins provided the following potted history:

> *On the first night of exodus from the Beara Peninsula, December 31st, 1602, Donal Cam O'Sullivan Beare rested here at Eachros Church by the Bunsheelin River. One thousand followers,*

including 400 soldiers, camped in the vicinity. Forced from their shelter in the woods near Glengarriff, the column of guerrillas and refugees had marched twenty six miles that New Year's Eve to shake off possible pursuit by Crown troops.

Following the Irish defeat at Kinsale, 1601, O'Sullivan had spent a year in rebellion against the Elizabethan conquest of Munster until the threat of starvation had forced him out. His plan was to join forces with the rebel Hugh O'Neill in Ulster. Facing a winter march of at least two weeks, the column carried rations for a single day. O'Sullivan held funds in Spanish gold, but parts of the country were on the brink of famine and his followers would be forced to raid and forage for food.

The church at Eachros was already in ruins when O'Sullivan spent the night here. He camped on holy ground wherever possible on his fraught journey north. It offered sanctuary in hostile territory and added a sense of pilgrimage to his march.

Although the context was entirely different, the concepts of sanctuary and pilgrimage were well known to me, particularly following my Camino de Santiago pilgrimage in Spain two years previously. And the need to escape from hostile forces was not unknown to me either, as the demons of loss and grieve had once tenaciously pursued me wherever I went. And like O'Sullivan Beare's pursuers, they could be shook off temporarily, but somehow they always managed to catch up again.

The ruins of the church, which dated from the thirteenth century, were fairly dilapidated and overgrown and totally overshadowed by a large ash tree, the trunk of which emerged from the centre of the church itself. The sturdy branches of this mighty tree spread out over the ruins, as if wishing to protect and shelter them from further erosion and decay. Even though I was there in the bright, late-morning sunshine, the site had a rather cold and foreboding atmosphere. My unease was compounded when the information sign also revealed that:

This site has long been used as a chillín, or burial

ground for unbaptized and still born infants, adding
a deep sense of poignancy to local memory.

I hurriedly left the ruins and its ghosts behind me and escaped over a stile into more fields that took me northwards and further away from the eerie site. However, later I would return to 'camp' close to this spot myself and experience a rather strange encounter. I crossed over a country road and from here a series of lanes and tracks took me up and round the top of Carrigalougha Mountain. In the afternoon, the temperatures began to rise again and, once I descended down the other side of Carrigalougha, I again had to endure frequent encounters with Tar McAdam! Thankfully, a lovely cooling breeze appeared occasionally to make things a little more pleasant at times, but it was sporadic and the heat was overwhelming in its absence.

As I approached Ballyvourney, I came across a sign for St, Gobnait's Holy Well and out of curiosity I decided to take the short detour required to visit it. O'Sullivan Beare and his party of soldiers and refugees stopped briefly at this shrine to pray, before proceeding with their march. O'Sullivan Beare was a deeply religious man and he consequently had a tendency to stop at religious sites, such as Augeris and here, whenever he could. St Gobnait was a medieval, female Irish saint whose church was founded beside this well when she came across nine white deer grazing nearby; a sign that had been foretold to her by an angel. Gobnait started a religious order and dedicated her days to helping the sick. She is said to have kept bees and it has been speculated that she used honey as a healing aid. She is even credited with saving the people at Ballyvourney from the plague. There were a number of cups and mugs beside the well for anyone who chose to imbibe its holy waters and I was amused to read a sign close by, which contained 'Instructions and Prayers to be Recited when making the Round'. These related to 10 'stations' that were shown on a hand drawn map that accompanied the instructions, such as a statue of St Gobnait, her grave and various points around the ruins of her church. One had to visit each 'station' a specific number of times and either walk round the station a number of times and/or repeat a number of prayers a specific number of times before jumping naked into the well. Okay, I made that last bit up. But it did seem immensely complicated and elaborate and what one got out of it, if you had the resolve to complete it, wasn't explained. Dizzy probably! The map also showed a Protestant Church right next to the ruins of St Gobnait's Church, but, perhaps unsurprisingly, none of the 'stations' were located there. Anyway, I decided not to do the 'rounds' and instead re-joined the road leading into Ballyvourney.

I crossed the bridge over the River Sullane, catching sight of a little yellow wagtail bobbing about on the rocks in the shallows as I went, and arrived in Ballyvourney at just after 4pm. I sought out the local post office to get my Ireland Way passport stamped and then stepped into O'Scanaill's Bar to have a pint while I waited on Diarmuid to come and pick me up. The locals in the bar, of which there were only three, or four if you include the barmaid, seemed to have taken a vow of silence. Even when one old-timer wanted another pint, he just plonked the glass down on the bar with a thud and the barmaid obligingly refilled it without a word passing between them. I tried to engage the barmaid in a little conversation as she was waiting for my Guinness to settle. It was hard work, but she eventually warmed to me and then became quite interested in my walk. To be fair to her, she was probably out of practice when it came to talking with the customers!

Just as I finished my pint, Diarmuid arrived to collect me and he drove me to his home, which was near Ballingeary and, surprisingly, just across the road from the field that contained the ruins of the little church at Augeris that I had stopped at earlier. Diarmuid showed me into his home and introduced me to his partner Kate and her son George, as well as to their three dogs. Diarmuid and Kate were fantastic hosts and treated me to a wonderful BBQ, which we enjoyed sitting out on a patio area out back on a warm evening with cold beers. Kate told me that they would be moving house very soon and relocating closer to Cork city. So I was very fortunate to be passing through Ballingeary both when Diarmuid was off on leave and also before they upped sticks. I was also very fortunate that they had a spare bedroom in the house and Kate had very kindly made a bed up for me and after a few drinks and some coffee it was time to turn in. I still had my blog to compose and post and it was very late by the time I actually turned out the lights. It wasn't long after my head hit the pillow that my own lights were out as well.

However, at some point during the night I woke up with a start. I had no idea of the time, but I could tell that it was well before dawn, as my room was still in darkness. I also had no idea what it was that had woken me from my deep sleep, but almost immediately I sensed that there was someone else in the room. My first thought was that perhaps Diarmuid had come in to the room to collect something. I sat up in the bed and said, "Hello.... Diarmuid? Is that you?" As my eyes slowly adjusted to the gloom, I began to make out what I thought was a figure sitting in an armchair in the corner of the room. I was convinced that I was 'seeing things' and that my eyes were playing tricks on me, but, after rubbing them, the figure started to take on a more defined shape and I felt the blood slowly drain from my face. "Holy feck! Who the hell are you?" I blurted out.

"Surely you recognise me?" the figure replied, "after all, you've been following my image for the last six days." He spoke in a calm, soothing tone that contrasted dramatically with the mad dance my heart was performing inside my ribcage. I noticed that his head appeared to be balanced on top of a strange cushion. Then, with a sudden realisation, I let out an involuntarily gasp. I could now see his face more clearly, for even though the room was in darkness, the figure appeared to have a faint luminescence, as if it was bathed in soft moonlight. And the face was indeed familiar to me, with its carefully teased moustache and neatly groomed Van Dyke. It couldn't be? Surely not? How was it even possible? "Donal Cam?" I asked hesitantly, hardly believing what I was saying, "are you Donal Cam O'Sullivan Beare?"

"The very one; at your service", he replied with a gentle bow of his head. I was weirdly relieved that the movement didn't result in his head rolling off the 'cushion'. On closer inspection however, I could now see that the cushion was actually an elaborate ruff around his neck.

"But how is this possible?" I spluttered, "you died nearly four hundred years ago!"

"Not nearly; exactly four hundred years ago", he stated matter-of-factly. "It was in 1618 that I met my end." His left hand seemed to automatically come up to gently massage his neck under his ruff, as he said this. "Perhaps if this ruff had been made of tougher material I might have survived to tell the tale", he mused, before adding, "not merely as an apparition, I mean."

"So, that's what you are then? An apparition?" I asked, still hoping that this was just a dream and that I would wake from it at any moment.

"Apparition; ghost; spirit; vision; spectre; phantom; spook; ghoul.....call me whatever you prefer", he said, becoming ever more melodramatically spooky as he progressed through his list. "But, whatever you choose to call me, know this. I am Donal Cam O'Sullivan Beare, Gaelic Prince of Beare, First Count of Berehaven and last independent ruler of the O'Sullivan Beare sept on the Beara Peninsula." His voice rose in pride as he recounted his various grand titles that he obviously still regarded with great fondness.

"Do you mind if I just call you Donal Cam?" I asked, perhaps appearing much bolder than I really felt.

"Whatever pleases you. I am here before you to serve, not the other way about", he replied graciously.

"To serve? What do you mean? How can you serve me? And, never mind that, why are you here in the first place? What in heaven's name is this all about?" Now that I was growing slightly more accustomed to this bizarre encounter in the dead of night, the questions just kept coming. "Why are you here? Why me? Did someone send you? Who........"

"I suggest you slow down and take a deep breath, young sir", he said holding a hand up to reinforce the point that he wanted me to stop with all the questions.

"I'm hardly a 'young sir' at fifty-seven years of age", even as I was speaking these words, I was fully conscious of just how ridiculous my protest was given the bizarre circumstances.

"May I remind you that I was born over four hundred and fifty years ago, so you are very much a 'young sir' to me", he said, clearly amused at his own wit. "Anyway, that's not important. I am here to help you better understand the context of the journey you are on - a journey that I completed in the dead of winter in 1603. On the four hundredth anniversary of my death, I wanted to tell someone about this epic and gruelling march north, while under almost constant attack by Elizabethan forces and traitorous locals loyal to the Crown."

"But why me?" It seemed like a perfectly obvious question to repeat at this stage.

"Well, you are following in my footsteps, aren't you? And I've seen you stopping to read about my journey on the signs along the route. Not many people do that, you know. Most just want to hurry on and get to their destination. I have seen that you are genuinely interested in what gave rise to this route in the first place. I want to help you understand it better; provide you with information that you won't find on any of the signs."

"Surely others have shown as much if not more interest before? I've already met quite a few people who seem to know quite a bit about your march – the routes, the skirmishes, the camps and the losses."

"Well, as I've already said, this year is of particular to significance to me", his hand went involuntarily to his neck once again, "and it's high time that I told my own story; in my own words. I believe you are a writer, are you not?" I nodded in response. "And, correct me if I'm wrong, but I also believe you are a pilgrim who has walked the Way of St James?"

"Yes, but that was two years ago," I replied. Then I suddenly remembered the medallion worn by O'Sullivan Beare in the picture at Carriganass Castle in Kealkill. I looked at the chest of the figure now sitting before me and, yes, there it was – the same medallion. And now I could see the red Cross of St James more clearly.

Donal Cam noticed the direction of my gaze and said, "Yes, as well as being a Prince of Beare, I am also a Knight of the Order of Santiago, sworn to protect pilgrims on the Way of St James."

"But," I said, "as I've already pointed out, that was two years ago."

"A mere drop in the ocean of time," he dismissed my point with a casual wave of his hand. "And anyway, once you become a pilgrim of Santiago, you're always a pilgrim of Santiago. And, again correct me if I'm wrong, but I believe your current pilgrimage will also take you to St James?"

"What?" I asked, somewhat puzzled, before the penny dropped. Of course! How could it have slipped my mind? My latest pilgrimage, my Ireland Way Journey, was a very personal one to me. It would end at Jacqui's final resting place in the town of Ballycastle – at her graveside in the graveyard of Ramoan Parish Church, more properly known as St James! But this was all just too much to take in. "Look," I began, "I really don't know what to make of all this. I mean, am I imagining you or are you real?"

"I am as real as you want me to be. But only you can see me and only you can hear me. So be very careful who you speak of me to, lest they think you have taken leave of your senses."

"I think I have taken leave of my senses already. I mean, why else would I be sitting up in bed in the middle of the night talking to an Irish Chieftain who died four hundred years ago?"

"I would say you still had your senses about you. You certainly sensed something at the little church at Eachros when you stopped there yesterday," he twirled the end of his moustache absentmindedly as he said this.

"Well, I certainly sensed something. Something cold and spooky."

"Welcome to my world," he said, once again bringing a theatrically menacing air to his voice.

Okay, so I was either trapped in a very strange dream or this was happening for real. Either way, I now felt strangely at ease. If I was indeed in the presence of a ghost, he seemed to be friendly enough and appeared to be here to help rather than haunt. I decided to go with the flow. After all, it's not every day you get to speak directly with a figure from history that has first-hand knowledge of events you are deeply interested in. "Okay. This is really weird, but you've got my attention. So, go on then, tell me about the events that brought you to Augeris, or Eachros, back in 1603."

"Ah, I thought you would never ask," he said with a smile. "Are you sitting comfortably?"

"Not exactly," I answered.

"Oh well, I'll begin anyway," he said, before continuing. "For you to properly understand the circumstances that led to my march in 1603, I need to go back a few years. In the latter half of the sixteenth century, there was no love lost between Protestant

England under Queen Elizabeth and Catholic Spain under King Philip. Queen Elizabeth constantly feared that Ireland would be used as a staging post by the Spanish to launch an attack on England."

"He that will England win, let him in Ireland begin," I trotted out the saying, suddenly recalling it from the depths of my memory.

"A saying that Queen Elizabeth took very seriously," Donal Cam said, before continuing, "so much so that she felt that England needed to gain complete control over Ireland if she was to prevent such a manoeuver by the Spanish. And England set about achieving this through land confiscation and resettlement and processes such as surrender and regrant. Irish chieftains were persuaded to surrender their Gaelic titles and lands in exchange for English titles and the return of some of their lands again under a royal grant. If a chieftain refused to bow to the Queen in this manner, then he was simply viewed as a rebel and he then risked losing everything by force – his lands, livestock, people, and even his life. Under Elizabeth, many Irish chieftains had succumbed to 'surrender and regrant' and acknowledged the English crown. But I wasn't one of them."

"So you became a rebel?" I asked.

"Not immediately. Munster did erupt in rebellion in 1600, but I didn't take part in it and the rebels were quickly defeated by Sir George Carew, the Lord President of Munster. A ruthless blaggard if there ever was one, although I have to admit that he was also a brilliant military strategist."

"Why did you not take part in the rebellion?" I was curious to know.

"I realised that it never stood a chance. The English forces were too powerful. I decided to keep my powder dry - wait for when the time was right and we had a fair chance of winning. And that chance came the following year when the Spanish finally sent the help that we had been seeking from them for years. Spanish ships arrived in Kinsale and Hugh O'Neill and Hugh Roe O'Donnell, who had led highly successful rebellions in Ulster, were on their way with their armies to meet them. Now I could see the possibility of a rebellion being successful and that there was a real prospect of driving the English out of Ireland for good. So I joined the rebellion and marched with my army to Kinsale to support O'Neill and O'Donnell and the Spanish to fight the English."

"So what happened?" I asked, now getting caught up in the story and almost forgetting that I was conversing with a ghost.

"The Battle of Kinsale happened. And it was an absolute disaster. It should have been an easy won victory for us, but we were let down by confusion and poor communications between our armies. The English under Mountjoy took full advantage of our disorganisation and we paid a heavy price as a result. We left twelve hundred men dead on the battlefield with another eight hundred wounded, while the English only lost about a dozen. What should have been our greatest moment of glory instead became a humiliating defeat that would have grave consequences for Gaelic Ireland. The Spanish surrendered and were shipped back to Spain. O'Neill and his army retreated back to Ulster. O'Donnell went to Spain to seek further help from King Philip. And I returned to the Beara Peninsula and tried to hang on to whatever I could."

"That can't have been easy, now that you had joined the rebellion," I suggested.

"No, not at all," he said despairingly. And then he went quiet, as if not wanting to give voice to the next words.

"What?" I prompted.

"Well, I have to admit that the first thing I did was to appeal to Mountjoy for pardon."

"Seriously? After leading your army against him at Kinsale! What was his response? Something along the lines of "Feck Off!" I imagine."

"Well, he was a little more eloquent, but it essentially amounted to the same thing. But I had to try. Not just to save myself, but to save my people. Anyway, Mountjoy refused to grant me pardon. Apparently a letter I had sent to the King of Spain prior to Kinsale pledging my support had been intercepted by English agents. The letter may also have contained some malicious remarks about Queen Elizabeth."

"Really?" I said. "That can't have helped."

"Perhaps I shouldn't have cast doubt on her claim to be a 'Virgin Queen'," he said with a smirk. "Anyway, I think it's more likely that Mountjoy refused my pardon due to the fact that I still had a well-equipped army and had declined to disband it."

"They haven't gone away, you know," I muttered in my best West Belfast accent.

"What's that?" asked Donal Cam.

"Oh, never mind. Just reminded me of a stupid thing someone said in more recent times," I replied. "Sorry for interrupting. Please go on."

"Anyway, I returned to the Beara Peninsula and set about being a thorn in the side of the English and those Irishmen who had aligned with the Crown. First of all I took Carriganass Castle off that traitorous cousin of mine, Sir Owen O'Sullivan." He emphasised the 'Sir' with distaste. "I also captured his wife and sent her to Dursey Island to be held captive. I thought that she might later become useful as a bargaining tool. I then marched with a thousand men down to Dunboy and took control of Dunboy Castle again. This castle was my main stronghold and Sir George Carew knew that only too well. In June 1602, he blew Dunboy Castle to pieces in a matter of hours. It was another disaster. Of the one hundred and forty men defending the castle, about half were killed in the fighting and the remaining half were executed after they surrendered."

"Good God! How did you manage to get away?" I asked, amazed that anyone had managed to escape the slaughter. Donal Cam said something in reply, but it was spoken so softly that I couldn't make out what he had said. "Sorry, what did you say?"

"I said that I wasn't there," he replied in a slow deliberate tone that couldn't disguise the discomfort that he felt at admitting this stark fact.

"Oh," I said, trying not to sound too judgemental, "I assumed that you were."

"I wish I had been. Things might have turned out differently if I had been there with my army. But who knows? Carew's forces were very strong and we might all have ended up being slaughtered. Anyway, I had taken my army across the Caha Mountains to Ardea on the other side of the peninsula to meet with the Spanish reinforcements that we were assured were on their way. But they never came. I later learned that there had been plans to send as many as fourteen thousand Spanish soldiers to Ireland, but that King Philip had by this stage grown weary of Irish affairs and its drain on Spanish resources and the plans were subsequently scuppered. So, while Dunboy Castle was being pulverised and its brave defenders slaughtered, I was sitting on my hands in Ardea waiting on Spanish ships that were never going to arrive. It's a fact that I can't change, but it's one that has haunted me even beyond the grave. And it was made worse by what happened on Dursey Island."

"That's where you said you had Owen's wife held captive, isn't it?" I asked.

"It is indeed. And that very fact may well have enraged my cousin when he arrived on Dursey with English forces under the command of John Bostock. Dursey was where I had planned to make a last stand in the event of Dunboy's surrender and I had stationed a small garrison of forty men there to defend the island and the three hundred refugees who had flocked over from the mainland. But I was to lose it also. First of all the attackers dismantled the fort and set fire to the little ancient church there. They then disarmed all my men and hanged them. Then they drove the refugees - old men, women and children - into a huddle and shot them down, hacked them with swords and ran them through with their spears. Some ran their swords up to the hilt through the babes and their mothers who were carrying them at their breasts. Others paraded before their comrades with little children writhing and convulsing on their spears. And finally, they bound any survivors back to back and threw them from the cliffs into the sea, over jagged and sharp rocks, and showered them with shots and stones. Their brutal work complete, the attackers then returned to the mainland, taking the five hundred cows we had kept there with them. I'm assuming that my cousin Owen took his cow back with him also!"

"Good God!" I said. "Just hearing about this level of slaughter and brutality is pretty overwhelming, I can't imagine what it must have been like to have lived through it."

"Unfortunately, such behaviour was not unusual at that time and I have to admit that there were atrocities committed on both sides. The defenders of Dunboy actually killed at least eighty of their attackers during the furious fighting. It was just a very brutal period to be alive in. You are very fortunate to be walking through such a peaceful land today."

"I'm pretty sure I would have stayed at home if it was anything like the 1600's," I responded and then asked, "so, your main stronghold at Dunboy had been destroyed and your fallback position on Dursey lost. What the heck did you do next?"

"Well, things were certainly not good, but all had not yet been lost. My *creaght*, my main herd of livestock, had not yet been captured and I still commanded a force of over one thousand soldiers. But my allies started to lose faith in the rebellion and then one of my most capable commanders, Richard Tyrell, left for Connacht and took his band of mercenary soldiers with him. I gathered my people and my remaining soldiers and headed for Derrynafulla."

"Oakwood of the blood," I chipped in, "I passed through it on my second day as I was approaching Glengarriff. It seemed so serene and peaceful."

"It seemed that way to us also; until Sir Charles Wilmot discovered our camp, that is. And once he attacked and captured our *creaght*, our situation became desperate. And just when I thought things couldn't possibly get any worse, another one of my commanders, William Burke, took his two hundred mercenary soldiers and fled to Connacht also. I was now left without enough soldiers to form an effective resistance against Wilmot and, with the loss of our sheep and cattle, I didn't have supplies with which to feed my people. I knew that I needed to lead them out of Beara and head north where I would still find allies. It was our only hope of survival. "

"So you headed for O'Rourke's Castle in Leitrim?"

"That was certainly my initial goal. If we reached there, I knew we would be welcomed by Brian Og O'Rourke and given sanctuary. Beyond that, I hoped to join with allies in Ulster and continue with the rebellion. We left Derrynafulla in a hurry, before Wilmot's army could attack our camp again. There were a thousand of us fit to undertake the march north. About four hundred were foot soldiers and thirteen were horsemen. The rest were civilians, an assortment of grooms, baggage carriers, women, old men and servants. We would be marching through bitterly cold weather and crossing over inhospitable terrain. We would often come under attack from those loyal to the crown, who had no time for rebels passing through their lands. We only had one day of rations left and, although I had plenty of Spanish gold, no one had food to sell, such was its scarcity during this time of war induced famine."

"I understand you had to leave some people behind?"

"Yes," he answered, with a terrible sadness showing in his eyes, "that was most regrettable. But some were too old, too sick and weak, or had been badly injured in the fighting. They simply wouldn't have been able to make the arduous journey ahead. I knew that they wouldn't be treated kindly by Wilmot's forces, but if we had tried to take them with us we would all certainly have perished. It was heart-breaking having to leave them behind to face almost certain death. At least they were able to help the rest of us by keeping the camp fires burning throughout the night to fool Wilmot's forces into thinking that we hadn't broken camp. It bought us valuable time while we made good our escape and for that I am eternally grateful. We left during the early hours of New Year's Eve in 1602 and marched through the night and the following day for twenty six miles until we reached the ruins of *An Teampaillin* at Eachros, where you stopped yesterday."

"And it's not far from where we are now - just a few hundred metres across the road. It took me over three days to get to it from Glengarriff mind."

"More peaceful times make for more relaxed journeys," he stated. "We were quite literally fleeing for our lives and had to keep moving. However, after twenty-six miles, we were exhausted and needed rest. We camped at Eachros that night and rose at dawn on New Year's Day 1603 to continue our journey north."

"We had only just left Eachros, when I lost my poor *An Chearc*," he added, his voice haltering slightly at the mention of what had been his favourite horse, known as *An Chearc*, meaning "the Hen". With a quiet nostalgic chuckle, he explained, "My uncle

Dermot had called him that because of his high stepping style, saying that he moved like a hen. I never really liked it, as I felt it was demeaning to my fine stallion, but my uncle thought it funny and the name eventually stuck and I became accustomed to it over time. Unfortunately, we ran into some boggy ground just north of Eachros and *An Chearc* broke his leg. I had to put him down there and then. I know he was only a horse, and God knows we would go on to suffer much greater loses, but at the time it nearly broke my spirit. At least my people weren't starving at this stage. If he had died a few days later, I would undoubtedly have had to surrender him for food as we became so desperate. Anyway, there was little time to dwell on the loss of *An Chearc* and feel sorry for myself. There were one thousand human souls depending on me to lead them to safety."

He sighed as he recalled once again the huge burden of responsibility that had rested upon his shoulders and at once he seemed exhausted by the memory. "That will have to do for now, young sir. I am tired now and we both could do with some rest. We'll continue with our discussions another time."

"Really?" I asked, "when will that be?"

"When we both feel like it," he laughed. "Good night. We will speak again."

And with that the glowing figure in the armchair slowly faded away until there was nothing left but darkness. I suppose, by rights, I should have been greatly troubled by what had just occurred and remained awake for the rest of the night trying to figure it all out. An Irish Chieftain who became a Knight of Santiago and who had died four hundred years ago had suddenly appeared before me in the middle of the night. It was truly bizarre to say the least. But for some reason, I felt quite relaxed and I quickly fell back into a deep sleep again.

Chapter Four: Wild Swimming
(Days seven to nine - Ballyvourney to Lismire)

I woke to the sound of Thin Lizzy singing about going over the Cork and Kerry Mountains and meeting with Captain Farrell counting his money. I had selected '*Whiskey in The Jar*' as the alarm call on my phone. It had seemed appropriate given my journey over the last few days. Then I remembered, as my fuzzy head started to focus, that I had indeed met someone during the night. But it hadn't been Captain Farrell counting his money. It had been Donal Cam O'Sullivan Beare recounting his story. My God, had that really happened? My memory of our encounter was clearer in my mind than any dream had ever been after waking up, so perhaps it did. Yeah, right! So an Irish Chieftain from over four hundred years ago had just turned up for a wee chat in the middle of the night? With me? How likely was that? More likely a combination of too much alcohol before bed and an overactive imagination. So, I tried to set my nocturnal reverie aside as I joined Diarmuid and Kate for breakfast and, when they asked me how I had slept, I simply replied, "Like a baby!"

After breakfast, I said my farewells to Kate and George. Diarmuid then drove me to Ballyvourney and waved me off as I started out in the direction of Millstreet on foot. Once again, he had given me his day pack to carry the bare essentials (food and water mainly) and he very kindly then drove on to Millstreet himself to leave my heavy rucksack with Eileen O'Riordan, who I would be staying with for the next night or two. I left Ballyvourney just after 9am and it was a very pleasant morning, but already starting to warm up - it was going to be another scorcher! The early part of the day presented a reasonably gentle stroll over country roads and fields and for the first time on the Ireland Way I began to feel that my 'walking legs' had returned and my feet had hardened to the challenge. The lighter pack had helped immensely of course, but I finally felt like I was at last getting into my stride. The landscapes were once again beautiful in the glorious sunshine and I had the pleasure of spotting a pheasant taking to the wing and a doe running through the woods - both creatures startled and fleeing from my sudden presence - gone before I even had a chance to reach for my camera!

It was encouraging to see that the electric fences running around some of the fields had been set in a metre or more from the boundary fence or hedge, providing walkers such as myself with a 'safe cordon' along which to walk. This not only effectively separated walkers from any livestock in the fields, but also encouraged walkers to stay to the edge of the fields and, conversely, discouraged them from tramping through the middle of farmland. Walkers on way-marked routes such as the Ireland Way are very dependent on the goodwill of farmers that allow them to walk on their land and some farmers seem to be very considerate of walkers when moving herds and erecting electric fences. However, you could be forgiven for thinking that a small minority of farmers seemed to regard walkers as a nuisance and went out of their way to make passing through their land as difficult as possible. A few kilometres beyond the 'safe cordon', I was confronted with an example of this contrariness. A fence (possibly electric, but I wasn't going to grab it to find out!) had been placed right across the route and I was faced with the choice of either high stepping over it, and risk getting roasted nuts, or crawling under and getting a bit dirty. Not wishing to sing soprano, I opted for the dirt.

Later, when the sun got up, it once again became quite punishing to walk in the hills in the twenty-seven degree heat and where shade was a very rare commodity indeed. And even when there was shade to be had amongst the trees, it was not a place to linger unless there was a good breeze to keep the flies away. I had had my fair share of midges, horseflies and other biting insects so far, but today I had to run the gauntlet of a number of small but very persistent swarms! I was doused in insect repellent, but it seemed to have very little repellent effect. I think that I was sweating so much in the heat that my skin repelled the repellent and I subsequently became irresistible to the little beggars!

I seemed to skirt round the slopes of Mullaghanish Mountain forever, negotiating wide open grassy fields, narrow woodland paths, active tree-felling operations and some very boggy stretches in the process. At times, the muddy bog water had come perilously close to spilling in over the cuffs of my boots! The route round Mullaghanish must have seemed never ending to O'Sullivan Beare and his followers also, because, as my guide book pointed out, it was around here that they came under sustained attack from the sons of Thady MacCarthy. The MacCarthy's seemed to get everywhere!

"Absolute blaggards!" a voice suddenly cried out from directly behind me, causing me to almost jump out of my skin.

"Feckin' hell!" I shouted out involuntarily, as I shot round to see Donal Cam standing there fuming. Once I had recovered from the initial shock of seeing this figure from the past yet again, I sternly said to him, "Do you mind not just appearing out of the blue like that? You nearly gave me a bloody heart attack!"

"Sorry, but I overheard you thinking about those MacCarthy's and it just made my blood boil," he replied apologetically.

"You *overheard* me thinking? Are you serious?" I protested. "Are my thoughts not even private anymore?"

"We have this..." he began, hesitating, as if searching for the right word before continuing, "....connection."

"Oh, we do now, do we! That's lovely to know. Bloody brilliant, in fact! Just flippin' marvellous," I responded in exasperation.

So it hadn't been a dream brought on by an alcohol fuelled imagination after all. Here he was again. In broad daylight! He was exactly as he had appeared the night before, except a little more ...... solid. He seemed a little more real - a little more alive! And now that I saw him standing, rather than sitting, I could see the slight twist of his back that had earned him the nickname 'Cam', the Irish for crooked. His face had now taken on a conciliatory look, rather than the one of anger when he was ranting about the MacCarthy's. I softened a little in response. "Please, please do not just appear out of the blue like that again."

"I can't help it. It's your thought's that trigger me to appear."

"Okay," I took a long exasperated breath at this point, trying to be rational when everything around me appeared totally irrational. It was a bright summer's day on an open hillside in the middle of 2018 and here I was talking to a seventeenth century dandy dressed in seventeenth century Spanish garb. "Okay," I repeated, "can you at least appear less dramatically. You know, say something quietly like "Hello Dermot, it's Donal Cam again" rather than suddenly shouting out "Absolute blaggards!" at the top of your voice."

"Okay. Hello Dermot, it's Donal Cam again," he said quietly.

"Better," I said, with a heavy hint of sarcasm. "Now, are you here for a reason?"

"Always," he replied, "I'm here to tell you about the first attack on our party by those 'absolute blaggards', the sons of MacCarthy." He pointedly dropped his voice to a whisper as he said 'absolute blaggards' and I just stared at him to let him know that I wasn't amused in the slightest.

"Hmm, anyway," he continued, doing his best to ignore my stare, "the sons of Thady MacCarthy had once been my allies. God knows I had paid them handsomely for their loyalty. Or at least I thought I had. But it obviously wasn't enough for the greedy beggars and they defected to join the forces loyal to Elizabeth. And now they were intent on showing their allegiance to the English Queen by hunting me down." He paused, as if reflecting for a moment, before continuing, "I suppose they might also have been a little miffed at me for attacking their castle at Carrigaphooca and recovering my money! Anyway, they were armed with muskets and they were like a pack of wild dogs snapping at our heels as we continued to march north. I had split my troops into two, with an advance guard to push ahead and a rear guard to protect our backs, with the civilians in between. MacCarthy's men kept rushing in and firing on my people until my rear guard soldiers chased them off, but they would then regroup and attack again. My soldiers and I were of course well used to battles and skirmishes such as this, but for our civilians it was terrifying. Can you imagine, Dermot? Being out in this wilderness in the middle of winter, running for your life over this rough ground as the sound of muskets being shot whip-cracked unseen behind you and red hot balls of lead whizzed past your head. My people were not accustomed to this at all and they screamed in terror and rushed forward in fear of their lives."

I nodded, but in truth, standing there on such a beautiful summer's day, I found it difficult to imagine just how truly frightening it must have been for O'Sullivan Beare's people to have been subjected to such an unrelenting and violent pursuit in the middle of winter.

He continued, "These relentless attacks went on for about four hours as we slowly made our way round the slopes of this mountain. Our group was starting to break up and scatter. I had to do something drastic to break the cycle of attacks and keep my people together. It would be a risk, but to allow the MacCarthy's to continue would eventually end in disaster for us all. So I commanded the advance party of soldiers to quickly swing round and join forces with the rear guard and then launch a head-on attack straight at MacCarthy's men. And it worked. It took them completely by surprise and we killed enough of their men to strike fear into the rest of them and the dogs were soon fleeing in panic."

"Good God," I offered, "it must have been such relief to have seen the back of them after four hours?"

"It certainly was. Although they had another half-hearted go at us when we camped near Millstreet later that night, along with a faction of O'Keeffe's deployed from Drominagh Castle at Cloonbannin. But they were easily dissuaded on this occasion and we sent them packing with their tails between their legs, like the cowardly mongrels they were. They continued to annoy us from afar though. My people were very tired and hungry by this stage and MacCarthy's mongrels kept howling throughout the night, making sleep well-nigh impossible for us. Unfortunately, the attacks, the cold, the hunger and lack of rest would be the pattern for the rest of our long march north. I would often question my wisdom in setting off on such a perilous venture. But it was too late now. We were already the hunted. We had to keep going until we reached safety in O'Rourke's kingdom of Breifne."

I knew that O'Sullivan Beare's intention was to lead his people to O'Rourke's castle in Leitrim, but there was something I didn't quite understand. "You were travelling up through Ireland, your own home country, which I guess was full of fellow countrymen and women. Did no one try to help you? One of their own?"

"Unfortunately, it's been a great failing of the Irish people over the centuries. We love to fight among ourselves more than we love to fight others. And Queen Elizabeth and her aides knew that only too well. They rewarded certain Irish chieftains with English titles and helped them settle old scores against their rivals. In doing so, they managed to divide and conquer great swathes of Ireland without the need to deploy much of their own resources in terms of soldiers. After the crushing defeat at Kinsale, the clans lost any remaining faith they had in the rebel chieftains and quickly aligned with the victors. From Beara to Breifne we were under almost constant attack, but rarely from English troops. No, it was mainly from local clans who had already aligned with Elizabeth or who feared retribution from the English if they were even suspected of giving me any assistance. Plus, I now had a price on my head of three hundred pounds, which was a small fortune back in those times and hard for any clan to resist during a period of widespread destitution in Ireland."

"It always comes down to money in the end, doesn't it?" I mused.

"I'm afraid so," he agreed, before adding, "I used to think it all came down to loyalty, to one's country, to one's country men and women, but that was before I learned that loyalty could be so easily bought and sold to the highest bidder."

"Well, I'm sorry to say nothing has changed," I said.

"Don't I know it, but at least in my time people were quite open about it. Anyway, we can't stand around here all day talking. It's time you were on your way again. You still have a bit to go before reaching Millstreet. I hope you have a better sleep than any of us managed during our stay. We'll talk again."

"Just remember........." I began.

"I know," he jumped in, "no sudden, loud appearances."

And with that, Donal Cam's form began to slowly fade away, as if evaporating under the heat of the midday sun. Once again I was alone and left quite perplexed at my second encounter with O'Sullivan Beare's ghost. It was like having my own personal guide appear as a 3D hologram, but one that I could interact with and ask questions of. It was truly bizarre, but I was also becoming a little more comfortable with it. I was just pleased that my conversations were well out of sight or earshot of anyone else, as God knows what they would have made of a backpacker standing on a hillside talking to himself at length. They would probably have just concluded that I had been out in the sun for too long. "*Mad dogs and Englishmen go out in the midday sun*", goes the famous Noel Coward song – perhaps it applied equally to mad Irishmen!

And it was certainly hot! I was so relieved to reach Gneeves wind farm and to see that the windmill blades were turning quite fast. This of course meant that there was a wind blowing. I stopped here for lunch in a patch of shade that was also mercifully free from flies due to the brisk cooling breeze. I then wandered through the extensive wind farm, passing right under some of the huge blades wheeling in the sky, which was quite disconcerting, and through their shadows circling on the ground, which was strangely mesmerising. It was a long walk on very dry and dusty hard-core roads before I finally left the windmills behind. I then had to cross another wide stretch of very boggy ground, but there were no worries about bog-water seeping into my boots this time. The good people of Cork County Council and Millstreet Tidy Towns had built the Coomacheo Bog Bridge. This was a wooden walkway that stretched the whole way over the bog and deposited me once again on terra firma at the other side. Mind you, I did think that Millstreet Tidy Towns had perhaps stretched their remit considerably to support this project, as I was still a good six or seven kilometres out of town, but I wasn't complaining. Anything that kept my boots out of the bog got a 'thumbs up' from me.

More open grasslands and tracks through woods ensued, before I reached a roadway, which I followed downhill for a short distance, being rewarded with wonderful views over the plains of Cork and

Kerry. It wasn't too long before I left the road again, climbing over a stile to take off over the grass and dirt tracks again on a long, hot, tiring, but very scenic loop of Claragh Mountain. Thankfully the route kept me to the lower slopes of this 452 metre high peak as I circumnavigated the mountain from its west side to east, before eventually dropping down towards Millstreet. A path through and then round the perimeter of a forest took me on another roundabout route and, just when I thought I was on the home straight, a way-marker directed me down through a field and then another one pointed me away from the town. Assuming that I was on another convoluted loop that would eventually bring me into Millstreet, I put my trust in the way-markers. I had probably covered a good kilometre before I realised that I must have joined another walking route using similar way-markers, including my normally faithful friend Pacman. I made my way back to where Pacman had fooled me and from there took the shortest route into Millstreet I could find.

I stopped in the town for a short break, having a chat with some of the friendly locals at the small tables outside a convenience store, before setting off again. It was another five kilometres out of town to Eileen O'Riordan's place, which she had informed me was near to a footbridge over the River Blackwater. On the way out of Millstreet, I called into a filling station to see if I could use their toilets. As I was waiting in the queue to ask, I was tapped on the shoulder. I turned around to see a tall, dark-haired man with an excited look in his eyes. He shook my hand and congratulated me on what I was doing. He had obviously read the banner on the back of my day pack. He introduced himself as Michael Thornton and the reason he had an 'excited look' in his eyes was because he had found a 'kindred spirit'. Michael had walked the Beara-Breifne Way in January and he was delighted to meet someone else who was undertaking the journey. When we got to the counter, he bought me an ice cream and also gave me a very generous donation! When he learned that I was on my way to Eileen O'Riordan's, he told me that she was a neighbour of his and that I would be passing by his house on the way. "Call in on your way past," he said, "I would love to hear more about your walk."

Michael headed on home and, after making use of the toilets at the filling station, I headed on out the main road. A couple of kilometres later, as I was passing the rather grand entrance to Drishane Castle, another MacCarthy establishment, I spotted a figure in the distance walking towards me. It was Michael and he obviously wasn't going to leave it to chance that I might try to slip by his house unnoticed in my eagerness to get to Eileen's. We met on the road and greeted each other like old friends and Michael then led me to Coolefield House, where he lived. There was no escaping this man's enthusiasm and, to be honest, I was delighted also to have met someone who had a great interest in O'Sullivan Beare's march. Next thing I knew I was sitting at a large table in the kitchen of Coolefield House, having a beer, meeting his family and enjoying a lovely dinner cooked by Michael's wife, Pam. I don't believe I was ever asked if I wanted dinner - it was just assumed that I would join them and I was only too delighted to avail of their wonderful hospitality.

Over dinner, Michael told me about his Beara-Breifne Way expedition earlier in the year. He grew up in Coolefield House and was raised on stories of O'Sullivan Beare and his epic march that had seen him and his followers crossing the River Blackwater at a point only two kilometres from his house. Michael had decided that he wanted to retrace O'Sullivan Beare's footsteps as closely as possible before he turned forty. So, on New Year's Eve just past, he had set off in winter weather from Glengarriff, just as O'Sullivan Beare had done over four hundred years earlier, and he had hiked his way north to Leitrim Village in only two weeks! While I was battling my way north through extreme heat, Michael had to contend with extreme cold, which would have been far tougher by my reckoning. He recounted a funny episode, added to liberally by comments from Pam, when he had camped at the ruins of the little church at Augeris. It had been bitterly cold, but he had managed to pitch his tent in the snow and snuggle into his sleeping bag and had soon fallen into a deep sleep. However, he was woken in the wee small hours by voices and lights outside his tent, which gave him quite a start as, like me, he had been a bit spooked by the place to begin with. He unzipped the tent a little and peered out through the opening, but was immediately blinded by the beams of torches pointed directly at him. Then he recognised Pam's voice and gradually realised that there was a small party of folk outside the tent. It turned out that Pam had been trying to contact him, but his phone's battery had died. "When I couldn't reach him," Pam chipped in, "I became very worried about him being out on such a cold night and perhaps with nothing hot to eat or drink." Pam knew that he had been planning to camp at Augeris Church and set off with their two children to find him and bring him supplies. Then when a farmer nearby had spotted lights in the field, he had assumed that someone was in trouble and had joined the search party also. "And all the time," Michael added with a laugh as he remembered, "I was sound asleep and perfectly comfortable in my tent until I was so rudely woken up in the middle of my slumbers!" They had all ended up in the farmer's house enjoying tea and stew until Michael chased his family home and returned to his tent for the rest of the night. Michael subsequently made it all the way to Leitrim Village without further incident, although he confided in me later that he wished he had taken more time at the end of his journey to quietly reflect on his achievement. But he was a farmer and had had to get right back to his farm, which family and friends had been looking after in his absence.

Some two hours after arriving at Coolefield House, I decided I had better be getting on my way to Eileen's and Michael, again remembering that he was a farmer, decided he'd better start milking his herd of ninety-five cows! However, before leaving, Michael gave me a photocopy of a couple of pages from a book by Philip O'Sullivan, a nephew of Donal Cam's, which told of a successful victory by O'Sullivan Beare's party at Aughrim spurred on by a rousing speech delivered by Donal Cam himself moments before the battle. I accepted it gratefully, but didn't disclose to Michael that I might hear all about it first hand from the man himself at some stage.

I left Coolefield House and made my way to the new footbridge that had been erected over the River Blackwater. This bridge made my crossing over the mellow waters of the Blackwater a very tame affair compared to what O'Sullivan Beare's entourage would have experienced in the early days of 1603. Then the waters would almost certainly have been more turbulent, and certainly colder, and the multitudes had to cross using a series of stepping stones just downstream from where the bridge was now; all the while being harassed by the MacCarthy's on one side and the O'Keeffe's, from nearby Dromagh, on the other. Once across the footbridge, I almost immediately came upon a set of pillars, each topped with a stone greyhound, at the end of a long laneway up to the O'Riordan's farmhouse. I received a wonderfully warm welcome from Eileen and her family and Lady, their friendly collie dog. Eileen had been following my journey on social media and had got in touch to let me know that she ran a B&B practically right on the Ireland Way route. After a much needed shower and a second dinner that wasn't needed, but nonetheless delicious, I sat chatting with Eileen until well after midnight, before deciding it was time to turn in for the night.

****

I decided to take a day's rest from walking before setting off on the next section to Newmarket. I'd completed my first week, which was an important milestone mentally, but I still had a lot of miles ahead of me and I felt like I could do with a rest at this stage. And Eileen's B&B was the perfect place for a little R&R. Not only was Eileen a wonderful host, but the house was in a beautiful, rural setting, with gorgeous views over the River Blackwater basin, Clara Mountain to the South and other Cork and Kerry mountains stretching into the West. Eileen also very kindly took me by car to explore the next stage of my walk, which would be mainly on road, and this proved to be very worthwhile as the way-marking on this section was rather poor in places. After having scouted the upcoming route, I have to admit that I wasn't particularly looking forward to walking it, given that there was so much of it to be done in the company of Tar McAdam and the forecast for the following day could once again be summed up in one word - hot!

****

Recipe Idea - Roast Pilgrim

- Get your hands on a well-seasoned pilgrim. Country of origin not important, but it's best if you can source locally

- Rinse pilgrim thoroughly and then leave to rest overnight

- On the morning of cooking, rub generous amounts of sun lotion into the skin and set aside for 15 to 20 minutes to dry

- Dress your pilgrim lightly and then cover any exposed areas liberally with insect repellent

- Garnish the pilgrim with any gadgets and paraphernalia of your choosing before placing in a preheated oven, otherwise known as the Irish countryside

- Turn your pilgrim frequently and baste any exposed skin frequently in its own juices

- Gradually increase the heat to 30C and leave pilgrim to bake slowly for eight and a half hours or until completely done

- Remove pilgrim from the oven and rest for a few minutes

- Serve with a pint of Guinness

And there you have it. Roast Pilgrim! Enjoy!

****

I set out from Eileen's in the relative cool of the morning, but it wasn't long before the heat of the sun turned the Irish countryside into an oven. Even my old adversary, Tar McAdam, was literally melting in the heat! And I saw lots of him today. Probably more than three quarters of today's route was on the road. Mostly on quite country roads, but some busier stretches too, where I quite often found it necessary to step onto the verge to let traffic pass by safely. I stopped at the large parish church at Derinagree, about five kilometres from Eileen's, and stepped inside to take temporary refuge from the heat of the sun. Here I learned that Derinagree is from the Irish *Doire na Graí*, meaning "oak-wood of the cattle" and, although there is little evidence now, that this area was once covered in an oak-wood canopy. And it was here, under the cover of the oak trees, that O'Sullivan Beare and his followers camped on the second night of their march and endured the racket generated by the MacCarthy's and O'Keeffe's. The woods were later burnt by Elizabethan forces so that they could no longer provide protection for outlaws and rebels and the place-name is now the only tangible reminder that remains of the once extensive forest that stood here.

I joined the roads again and paused briefly at Cloonbannin Cross, where a sign indicated that this had once been the site of

Drominagh Castle, the O'Keeffe's stronghold. No trace of the castle remained after it was first destroyed by a rival clan in 1654 and then 'quarried' for building materials in later years – an early example of recycling it would seem. A few more kilometres of blacktop brought me to a substantial monument commemorating much more recent events – that of three local men *"killed by Crown forces at Derrygallon"* during the Irish War of Independence in 1920 and 1921. More than three hundred years had elapsed from O'Sullivan Beare's time and it seemed that little had changed! Yet more tarmac followed and, in the heat of the afternoon sun, I frequently had to step around pools of molten tar to avoid building up layers of roadway on the soles of my boots.

Relief from the roadways and the overhead sun finally came when I reached the pristine Hannie's Cottage and turned down the leafy laneway alongside it towards Island Wood Park. The lane brought me right to the edge of the River Dalua, a tributary of the Blackwater, and here I stopped to consider my next move. Just as I was contemplating removing my socks and boots and wading across the shallow river, I glanced upstream and spotted a footbridge. How to reach it, however, was anything but clear. I turned and headed back along the lane the way I had come and found a gate into a field that looked like it might give access to the bridge. There were no signs to confirm this, but I entered the gate, crossed the field and found a path through the trees to reach the footbridge. Safely across to the other side, I then enjoyed a rather sublime, meandering walk through Island Wood Park.

It was still very warm, but at least I benefited from the shade of the deciduous trees in full leaf that lined the path following the course of the river. I passed a young couple swimming in the river at one point and was tempted to join them in the cooling waters, but I neither wanted to intrude on their fun nor break my stride. So I marched on through the woods, passing a sign for Mylon's Cave on the way. There's a great amount of folklore associated with the cave and one story tells of Mylon being the daughter of a MacAuliffe chieftain spirited away to the cave on the eve of her wedding never to be seen again. Apparently, young people in the district are warned that if they enter the cave with the person they love the mouth of the cave will close, imprisoning them forever. I wondered why so many Irish folktales are so sad and gloomy. Perhaps they just reflect the tragedy of real life on this island that appears to have been troubled by conflict and strife from time immemorial.

I finally emerged from the woods to enter the town of Newmarket and I called into a bar on High Street to have a delectably cold pint of the black stuff. There were a few local lads in the bar who had obviously been there for a while and they were in good spirits as a result. When they heard the barman asking me about my walk and seen him passing me a donation, they all immediately started chipping in. I had my photo taken, with two of the young and merry lads getting in on the picture also, leaning in and giving me the thumbs up. Despite my stopping for a pint in Newmarket, an act that traditionally marked the end of my day's walk, I decided to push on another few miles to Lismire in order to shorten the following day's journey. I was once again carrying the lighter day pack loaned to me by Diarmuid, as I would be returning to Eileen's for the night, but tomorrow it would be back to my own heavier rucksack. So, I headed back out into the heat of the late afternoon and onto the roads again for the final stretch to Lismire.

It was a pretty uneventful five kilometres, apart from a steep descent down one side of the valley of the River Owenanare (more a stream than a river) and the equally steep ascent up the other side. I was pretty disappointed when I eventually reached Lismire, lathered in perspiration, only to discover that the shop mentioned in my guidebook had closed the year before – I had been so looking forward to a cold drink or an ice cream. Unperturbed, I called at a house near the crossroads in the village and asked for a glass of cold water - I was still carrying water, but it had become so hot that I could nearly have made tea with it! At the house I met Sheila and Gerard Kearney, who not only gave me a glass of cold water and a bottle of water to take with me, but also stamped my passport with the official Beara-Breifne Way stamp. They said I was their very first customer, which, on reflection, was hardly surprising as I had seen no information to indicate that a stamp was available in Lismire. The name Lismire is from the Irish *Lios Machaire*, meaning 'ring fort of the plain', and the stamp featured a cow, no doubt and indication of the grazing quality of the surrounding land. I was undoubtedly entering cattle country. I didn't know it then, but cattle would come to play a somewhat defining role in my subsequent journey!

I thanked Sheila and Gerard for their kindness and headed over to the public park at the other side of the crossroads, which I noted had a stone commemorating O'Sullivan Beare's march through the village in 1603. I relaxed in the shade against a stone wall until Eileen arrived to collect me. I didn't have too long to wait and on the drive back we stopped at the nearby Kanturk Castle, a very grand fortified house built in 1601 for a MacCarthy, apparently as a defence against English settlers. Then we headed back for Eileen's home, but as we passed the River Blackwater crossing at the bottom of her drive, we noticed a few people in and around the water. We stopped and went for a paddle in the beautifully cooling shallows and chatted with the locals. I then noticed a few people further upstream, swimming near the footbridge, where the water was obviously much deeper. I discovered that one of the swimmers was Gerald O'Farrell, who I had met on the road earlier in the day and had stopped to have a chat with for a time. He was swimming with his two sons and he showed me where it was safe to access the river and before I knew it I was enjoying the delights of river swimming that I had missed out on in Island Wood earlier. It was a perfect end to my travels that day. It even made the final few hundred metres, sitting wet in the open boot of Eileen's car as it bumped all the way up her long drive while I clung on for dear life, totally worth it.

Chapter Five: Little Blackbird
(Days ten to twelve - Lismire to Galbally)

My day started with another cooked breakfast at Eileen O'Riordan's B&B. I had spent three nights there and I must admit that I already kind of felt like I was part of the family. They were so welcoming and friendly and my stay had been very comfortable, homely and great fun. And I don't know of many other B&B's that have an outdoor swimming pool at the end of their drive!

After getting a photo with Eileen and her children, Danielle and Frank, Eileen very kindly drove me back to Lismire, where I had stopped the day before. Then after a big hug, I set off down the road towards Ballyhea, via John's Bridge, Liscarroll and Churchtown. The route took me along many quiet, and some not so quiet, country roads and through pleasant, rural pastureland dotted with cattle and horses. Once again, there wasn't a cloud in the sky and at times I felt like an ant under a magnifying glass, as I made my way along the black top under the dazzling sun. "*Mad dogs and Irishmen go out in the midday sun*", I sang to myself as I went. There were frequent puddles of molten, sticky tar forming on the road's surface and, as I approached one, I noticed what looked like a piece of black plastic caught in it and fluttering in the breeze, which seemed rather strange as the air was oppressively still. I very nearly stepped on it and only just stopped in time when I realised at the last moment that it was actually a little bird flapping its wings in desperation. On closer inspection, I saw that it was a young swallow and its feet had become stuck to the tar. The poor little thing was sitting in the middle of the road and it was only a matter of time before it got run over – by a walker or, more likely, by a car. I managed to very gently prise it off the tarmac and thankfully its feet appeared to come away fairly clean. After letting it rest in the shade of a tree for a bit and giving it some water, I threw it up into the air and it flew off. My rescue was complete and thankfully a much more successful outcome compared to my futile attempts at rescuing a little Goldfinch fledgling in Spain two years before. On that occasion, the little bird had died and it had triggered a bout of depression as it brought to mind how helpless I had been to save Jacqui also. Perhaps the much happier outcome with this little swallow was symbolic of the progress I had made over the last couple of years.

Just about one hundred metres beyond the crossroads at John's Bridge, I passed over a small 'blink and you'll miss it' bridge over the River Allow. It was while crossing this narrow river, yet another tributary of the Blackwater, that O'Sullivan Beare and his followers came under attack from Captain Cuffe, who was holding the crossing, then known as the ford of Bellaghan, with a force of Englishmen supported by John Barry from the nearby Liscarroll Castle. After defeating his attackers and crossing the ford, O'Sullivan Beare's party probably gave Liscarroll a wide berth for fear of further attacks by the Barry's, but Pacman had no such worries and he led me straight through the village, which takes its name from the Irish *Líos Cearúill*, meaning 'Carroll's Ringfort'. The village was dominated by the extensive remains of a huge thirteenth century fortress, Liscarroll Castle, once the property of the aforementioned Barry family. I paused to read the information signs. Like most castles on the island of Ireland, it had seen its fair share of both legitimate and illegitimate occupiers over the years, with many lives being lost in the transition from one to the other. I wondered how they would all feel if they were to see it now, lying completely empty and abandoned.

A further kilometre out of Liscarroll brought me to The Donkey Sanctuary and I decided to call in here and see if the staff wouldn't mind me having my lunch in their outdoor picnic area. The lady in the office was very helpful and, when she learned of my challenge, she arranged for me to get my photo taken for their newsletter and promised me a free ice cream after my lunch. After my publicity shot, I found a shady spot to sit, stripped off my socks and boots to air my hot feet and enjoyed the lunch Eileen had packed for me. The sanctuary was really busy with visitors appearing by the coach load and after lunch, and after claiming my free ice cream, I had a quick tour of the enclosures where the abused and abandoned donkeys were being cared for. I was astounded to learn that this registered charity had well over a thousand donkeys in their care. I only saw a very small proportion of their 'drove' and most looked to be happy and in very good health, but one poor creature looked so shabby and dejected it would have made Eeyore from Winnie the Pooh look like a ray of sunshine. Goodness knows what the poor creature had experienced before being rescued by the sanctuary. I left a small donation before preparing to set off again. As I struggled to heave on my heavy rucksack - Diarmuid's light day pack having been left behind at Eileen's for him to collect - I have to admit to seriously considering 'borrowing' one of the fitter looking donkeys to accompany me on the rest of my journey north! Another memory of my Camino in Spain two years earlier returned, as I recalled the couple I met walking with a donkey towards Finisterre, their backs largely unburdened as the poor creature carried their heavy packs.

Aside from the staff and visitors at the busy donkey sanctuary, my encounters with other people were few and far between, but those I did meet were incredibly friendly – perhaps they were just as delighted as I was to meet another human being in such an isolated rural environment. At one point, a young man pulled up alongside me and crawled along beside in his car me for ages, with the driver's window down so he could continue his conversation with me without him or me having to stop. He was intrigued by what I was doing, but couldn't quite get his head around the fact that I was intending to walk the entire length of Ireland. "Yer not serious?" was his much repeated question, closely followed by, "well, fair play til ye", when I confirmed that I was. Before he drove off, he promised to return with a donation, but I never saw him again – he obviously wasn't serious! A little later, I stopped at a pretty little cottage by the roadside to take a photo of some large garden ornaments, one of which depicted a donkey pulling a milk cart to market. As I was composing my shot, a little elderly lady came out of the cottage to see what I was up to and then offered me a cup of tea. It wasn't that long after my lunch, so I politely declined, but happily accepted the glass of cold water she went inside to fetch for me instead.

On to Churchtown, famous for various connections to horse racing as was immediately apparent when passing through its square, which was dominated by a fine sculpture of a horse mounted by jockey Jack Moylan. I stopped for a rest outside O'Brien's Bar in the square and had a chat with a local man sitting against the pub's windowsill. He was a mine of information and told me that Churchtown was the birthplace of Vincent O'Brien, the famous Irish race horse trainer. "He was voted the greatest racehorse trainer in the world", he proudly declared. He also pointed in the direction of the village graveyard and informed me that the famous 'hell-raising' actor, Oliver Reed, was buried there. He had apparently made the village his home for the last seven years of his life. "Jaysus, he was mighty craic," said Joe, before adding, "he loved a drink, ye know, and this very pub we're leaning against was his favourite bar."

From here it was another five kilometres or so to Ballyhea, my final destination for the day. I say "or so" as I'm not really sure how far it was after the convoluted route I took – Pacman had abandoned me once again. Either way, it was a long slog in the blistering heat of the early evening and once again it was all on road. It was strange listening to the cars as they passed by, as their tyres passing over the molten tar sounded like they were being driven on very wet roads. I stopped at a house to check on directions and was invited inside and given a cold drink, which I gratefully accepted, and offered tea and biscuits, which I graciously declined. I then proceeded to walk along the hard shoulder of a very busy road, the N20, for a couple of kilometres off route to reach the Marengo B&B, which I had booked into for the night. It wasn't until I arrived at my B&B at 6pm that I noticed the note in my guidebook that said *"the lovely owners may be able to collect you from the trail; ask when booking"*. Damn! Anyway, I was given a very warm welcome by Máire O'Riordan (no relation to Eileen) and was served with the tea and biscuits I had turned down earlier – obviously not the same ones, but you know what I mean. Later, the excellent bar and restaurant next door to the B&B took good care of my drinking and dining needs.

****

Once again my host for the night turned out to be very generous and kind. Máire only charged me half rate for my B&B and then offered to give me a lift back to where I had left the trail the previous evening. It was now becoming very clear to me that, no matter how beautiful and challenging the Ireland Way route was, the one thing that made this walk so special was the amazing hospitality and kindness I was experiencing along the way. This was a route made exceptional not only by the miles travelled and the landscapes on offer, but, more than anything else, by the wonderful people encountered.

Máire dropped me off close to Ballyhoura Bridge and, after waving her off, I turned and said, "Good morning. Nice to see you again," to Pacman who had appeared once again on a way marker by the roadside. Thankfully, he was pointing me off the road and up a country lane and what followed was a lovely early morning walk between hedges, strewn with pretty white hawthorn flowers and flamboyant yellow honeysuckle blooms, and an abundance of leafy nettles, spiky thistles, towering foxgloves and a multitude of other colourful wildflowers unknown to me. The sun was still relatively low in the blue sky and it had the effect of softening the surrounding countryside with its warm, almost hazy, light. However, I suspected that this gentle start belied what lay ahead. For today I would be heading back into the mountains – in this case, the Ballyhoura Mountains, which stretch for about six miles west to east and straddle the border between counties Cork and Limerick. And it wasn't too long before my path started to rise before me and there then followed a long, hard climb up stony tracks to the peak of Carron Mountain. I later discovered that there was a less steep track that wound its way round the peak, but my feet decided, without any reference to my brain at all, that they would follow the very steep track directly up to the peak instead. It was like climbing up loose scree at some points, with two steps forward and one step back, but I finally made it to the top of this 450 metre high mountain. I then took my position on top of the stone cairn there to take in the wonderful panoramic views over Cork and Limerick and fly my flag above my head, like the conquering hero I imagined myself to be.

The route then traversed over the Ballyhoura Mountains, taking in Little Carron, but thankfully skirting round the higher peak of Seefin Mountain and finally dropping down through some woods onto the plains of County Limerick. With the exception of the short section through the trees, the mountain crossing was undertaken under the full glare of the midday sun and it was a sweltering hike. I managed to find a solitary tree (more a bush really) to sit under for a break around the midway point. I had a bite of lunch in the shade before venturing out into the furnace once again to resume my journey. It was around here that I spotted a marvellous specimen of a mountain goat, grazing nearby. It was pure white with a rather dashing beard and carrying a pair of hugely impressive, curved horns. However, despite its formidable stature, it took off suddenly as I drew closer. At first, I assumed that it had been spooked by my sudden appearance, but I soon realised that it wasn't me who had spooked it after all. I heard someone clearing his throat behind me and I turned to see another figure of formidable stature, also sporting a beard, standing on the path. It was Donal Cam O'Sullivan Beare once again.

"Thanks for not scaring the 'bejesus' out of me," I said, recalling the near heart attack inducing appearance on Mullaghanish Mountain the previous time. "Although I think you might have startled that goat."

"Ah, they're evil creatures and one of the few that can sense my presence," he replied, before adding, "I thought it was high time we had another chat."

"That's funny, I was just thinking that myself," I replied, with a knowing smile.

"Kind of spooky, eh?" he responded, also smiling. Then he asked, "You crossed the river at John's Bridge, I believe?"

"I did indeed. I crossed it yesterday on the way to Liscarroll."

"Well, it was the ford of Bellaghan in my time and it was defended by a Captain Cuffe and a small force of English soldiers. We could have dealt with them easily enough, but for the fact that John Barry had brought additional forces from Liscarroll Castle to assist in defending the ford. That was more problematic for us. We suffered grave losses during the fighting to cross the ford and I blame that traitorous scum Barry. We used to break bread together, but like many others he had bowed to the Queen and now jumped to the command of her representatives. After a good hour of fighting, we saw them all off and were at last able to cross the river, but I lost four good men in the process. It was the last time that we had the luxury of being able to pause for long enough to bury our dead. We also had a number of men injured in the fighting and we fabricated some military litters with which to carry them before setting off again. Unlike you, we gave Liscarroll a wide berth. I had no desire to encounter that scoundrel John Barry again. We managed to march for thirty miles that day, eventually setting up camp in Ardpatrick, a desolate place near woods just north of these mountains. It was the third night of our march and it was a stormy one. The guards were scarce able to keep awake through hunger, weariness and cold. It had been a tough three days of marching, but it was relatively easy compared to what was to come."

"Sounds ominous," I said.

"The mountainous areas we had passed through so far had provided us with some protection, but we now had to cross the vast Limerick plain, a much more densely populated area and with less places to hide. The following morning, the forth of our march, all we had to sustain ourselves was the watercress we plucked from the icy flow of the streams. It was better than nothing, but it did little to assuage our hunger. We broke camp before sunrise and made directly for the Slieve Felim Mountains, which were over twenty miles away. It wasn't long before we came under a sustained attack from the Gibbons."

"Sorry? Did I hear you correctly? The gibbons?" I asked with raised eyebrows.

"Not the long-armed apes, you dimwit!" he replied in exasperation. "No, these were a well-armed band of mercenaries known as the Gibbons as they fought for the White Knight, Edmund Fitzgibbon, who was loyal to Elizabeth. They set out from the White Knight's headquarters in Hospital, a garrison about ten miles north of Ardpatrick. They were joined by some natives of Limerick City and a few Englishmen and they attacked us in the manner of an undisciplined mob. But they charged at us boldly and fiercely, attacking the front, rear and middle of our party all at once. Muskets were discharged on both sides to such an extent that one party could scarcely see the other at times due to the air being clouded with smoke from the gunpowder. The attacks continued for eight hours and such was the ferocity of the fighting and the constant rain of musket balls that we had to abandon our dead and wounded where they fell. And we knew that our wounded could expect no mercy at the hands of the White Knight's mercenaries. We were severely weakened by hunger and had to endure this running battle until darkness fell and we reached Sologhod, or Soloheadbeg as it's now known."

"So you were finally able to rest?" I asked hopefully.

"Thankfully the fighting was over for the day, but now we had to contend with the ache of a bitterly cold winter's night and the hunger pains produced by starvation. We spent our forth night inside a ring-fort, the earthen banks of which at least provided us with some shelter from the wind and allowed us to light some small camp fires without them being visible to the enemy. Desperate for food we foraged for plants and dug for roots and even plucked leaves of the trees. Even so, the cold and hunger were too much for some and a number of the weak and wounded among us didn't make it through the night. We urgently needed some proper food or we would all soon be dead. Thankfully, an opportunity came the following day at Donohill and, fraught with danger though it was, we had no choice but to grasp it."

Donal Cam paused here and I instinctively knew that this was all he was going to share with me at this point. "I suppose I'll have to wait until I get to Donohill to hear what happened there?" I asked.

"Yes," he replied, before adding with a grin, "it might not be for a few days though at the rate you're going."

I responded with a mock laugh and then said, "Well, thank God I have no one chasing me. I'm in no great rush. I want to be in Ballycastle for 1st August, but I have plenty of time."

"Yes, I think even you should be able to manage that," he said jokingly. Then he continued more seriously, "Take care young sir. Until we meet again." He bowed to me with exaggerated flourish and then quickly disappeared into the landscape once again, just like the white goat had moments earlier.

"Bye," I said and then, almost too late, added, "thanks, by the way."

Bizarre though it was, it was also pretty incredible to have this ghostly guide to keep me apprised of the detail of his exploits from over four hundred years ago. But who was going to believe me? To be honest, I didn't really care. It was just such a privilege to obtain O'Sullivan Beare's first-hand account and I had now grown so accustomed to his appearances that I no longer questioned them. So when my latest encounter came to an end, I simply continued on with my journey and looked forward to our next meeting.

As I was coming off the mountains, I was rewarded with distant views of Castle Oliver on a hillside opposite. This Victorian mock castle built in red sandstone, together with the eye catching Oliver's Foley on an adjacent hillside, were obviously designed for show and they certainly managed to achieve that, even at such a distance. I proceeded on into, and through, the village of Ballyorgan and then followed a series of country roads that took me past the now derelict Castle Oliver Gate House, obviously no longer used as the main access to the elaborate castle residence. I had to sit down here for about fifteen minutes, as I had developed a worrying pain in my right hip. I really hoped that it was only temporary and wouldn't get any worse. After taking the weight off my feet and applying a little self-massage to my hip, it had improved sufficiently for me to heave my rucksack back on and begin the final five kilometres I estimated that I still had to cover. The remaining hike was through gently rolling countryside on a mix of minor roads and narrow dirt tracks and thankfully my hip held up fairly well. It was still a huge relief to reach the village of Kilfinane though. It had been a very long day's walk at ten hours and, although my right hip was okay, my feet were aching and generally my whole body felt pretty knackered. I was still faring much better than poor Staker Wallace though. A stone monument had been erected in the centre of the village as a memorial to this unfortunate Irish freedom fighter, who had been hanged in Kilfinane in 1798. His first name was thought to be Patrick, but he had been given the nickname 'Staker' following his death, when he was beheaded and his head put on a stake for everyone to see. The monument depicted Staker's head resting in the cavity of a hollowed out stone and the deathly expression on its face, like a death mask, was enough to send chills down my spine.

It was therefore with some relief that I came across another much more joyful monument in the village. Here I stopped briefly to chat to some locals, who were gathered outside O'Céilleachair's Bar on the main street. They were admiring a wooden 'totem pole' that had recently been erected on the pavement and it was easy to see why they were so taken with it. They told me that it had been carved on site by a 'chainsaw artist' from a neighbouring village to celebrate the Irish music festival, the *Fleadh Ceol*, held in Kilfinane each year. It was a striking piece and depicted a number of musical instruments, including a 'squeezebox' and a fiddle, stacked atop each other and had the words "*Craic agus Ceol*", Irish for 'Fun and Music', inscribed around its base. After posing for a few photos beside the totem, the locals invited me in to O'Céilleachair's Bar for a drink and I was only too happy to oblige. And the scene inside the pub was just as fascinating as that outside. It was an 'Aladdin's Cave' of trinkets and treasures from the past that adorned the walls and hung from the ceiling – jugs, lanterns, number plates, old photographs, a transistor radio, an old tennis racket; everything bar the cuddly toy! And they served a wonderful pint of Guinness too.

I resisted the temptation to sit on and enjoy the highly convivial atmosphere of O'Céilleachair's Bar and instead dragged myself away from my bar stool and headed the short distance down the street to check into my accommodation for the night. This was the wonderful Ballyhoura Luxury Hostel, run by Teresa and Séamus, and, after being greeted with the warmest of welcomes, Teresa gave me a tour of the superb facilities. It was unlike any hostel I had ever stayed in before and was certainly fully deserving of the word 'Luxury' being included in its name. I was shown to a male dorm, which slept about ten in a cleverly designed arrangement of bunks, and I was able to take my pick as I was the only one booked into this particular dorm. Another guest did apparently arrive later, but I was barely aware of his presence as he arrived after I had turned in for the night and had left again before I rose.

****

I woke up to Johnny Cash singing about there being nothing short of dying that was half as lonesome as the sound of a sleeping city sidewalk and Sunday morning coming down. It wasn't the most motivational song to wake up to, but I had to admit that it was appropriate given that the streets outside were pretty dead and that it was indeed Sunday morning. After a DIY breakfast in the large dining area furnished with large tables and benches hewn from solid timber, which were highly polished and most impressive, I stepped out into the Sunday morning to be hit by unexpectedly cold air! And what a blessed relief it was. At first, it was so chilly that I almost dug my fleece out of my rucksack, but instead, I embraced the chill, relishing the cold, and left my fleece where it was. I felt energised by the cold air after having struggled through the heat wave of the last eleven days. I set off on what was to be a fairly gentle walk through wonderful woods and pleasant pastures, often with great views of the Galtee Mountains in the distance. As I was following the gravel paths that wound through the forests covering the southern slopes of Slievereagh Mountain, I kept passing or being passed by a group of four cyclists. We always exchanged greetings and a bit of small talk and, at one point, one of their party, Nick, cycled alongside me for a while chatting and finding out about my hike. He told me that he lived next to the route, in the first house just beyond the forest and he invited me to drop in for a cup of tea whenever I was passing. He then sped off to catch up with the rest of his party and the group soon disappeared over the next hill.

When I later emerged from the forest and joined the country road that would lead me on to Glenbrohane, I had only a couple of hundred metres to walk before I spotted Nick and his fellow cyclists waving to me through the window of a modern looking bungalow. I waved back and made my way up to the open doorway and joined Nick, Barry, Kieran and Geraldine in a spacious and airy kitchen. They were all sat round a large dining table having a late breakfast after their cycle and they invited me to sit down and join them. I slung off my rucksack and took a seat at the table hoping to get the cup of tea I had been promised. And I did. But that wasn't all I got. I was also given a glass of cranberry juice, a bowl of fresh fruit and yoghurt and a very tasty bacon butty! Geraldine, who was Nick's wife, told me that this was a fairly normal Sunday morning for them – a good cycle in the forest to work up an appetite followed by a well-earned breakfast. They seemed fairly impressed with my intention to walk the length of Ireland and as I spoke to them about this and my previous pilgrimages, Nick suddenly leapt up from the table and went to fetch something from an adjoining room. "Have a look at this," he said when he returned a moment later, handing me a music CD and adding, with a wink, "it'll be right up your street." I looked at it and then understood the reason for his wink. It was an EP that he had bought just the month before at a music festival and it was by an Americana/Irish/Bluegrass band from Navan called Pilgrim St. It sounded like a wonderful fusion of influences, but what really caught my attention was the first track on the EP. It was simply called "My Little Blackbird".

I once again wondered at the amazing coincidences that I continued to be confronted with. For a number of reasons, I had come to strongly associate the blackbird with Jacqui's spirit and whenever I spotted one my heart would lift a little in recognition of this special link. It had always been a favourite garden bird of ours and I had experienced a number of occurrences since Jacqui had died that had only strengthened my love of the blackbird. One singing outside the hospice window on the morning after Jacqui's passing, bringing to mind the words from the hymn sung at our wedding (and subsequently at her funeral) – "*Morning has broken like the first morning, Blackbird has spoken like the first bird*". During my Ulster Way pilgrimage, I came across a seemingly abandoned coffee shop called "The Blackbird" in the village of Derrylin, which is from the Irish *Doire Loinn*, meaning 'oakgrove of the blackbirds'. And during my Camino pilgrimage in Spain, when I seemed to be following blackbirds on the route to such an extent that, when my daughter composed a song for me based on my walk, she included the line "*Keep following the blackbirds*". The very rucksack that I had taken off and discarded at the door on my way into Nick and Geraldine's home even had a little blackbird badge attached to one of the shoulder straps.

So, here I was, in this random house in the middle of, well, nowhere really, completely by accident, and I was now holding in my pilgrim hand a CD by Pilgrim St. containing a song called "My Little Blackbird". I felt myself shaking slightly. I desperately wanted to hear the song, but I feared how I would react to hearing it in the company of these kind people I had only just met. I didn't even dare try to explain the significance of the song to them, as I wasn't confident that I would be able to hold myself together. So I just said to Nick, "Ha, Pilgrim St. That's a good one. I'll have to give them a listen sometime" and I passed the CD back to him. I then thanked them for their wonderful hospitality and told them that unfortunately a pilgrim couldn't sit around drinking tea and chatting all day and that it was time I was getting back on the road again. They checked that I knew how to get to the next village okay and, before I left, Nick very kindly slipped me a generous cash donation. My encounter with the four cyclists had been truly heart-warming and, even though I had been slightly taken aback by the blackbird coincidence, it only added to the very special nature of our meeting. As I waved back to the group and continued on my way, I felt like I was basking in a warm glow that wasn't entirely due to the sun that had finally made an appearance.

Three to four kilometres of snaking roads led me through the townland of Glenbrohane and on into the village of Ballylanders, with the blue-grey shape of the distant Galtee Mountains appearing on the horizon every so often. Ballylanders is from the Irish *Baile an Londraigh*, meaning 'town of the Londoner' and the view up the long main street was dominated by the imposing ruins of a nineteenth century Protestant church that, quite literally, towered over the village. Although off route a little, I was nevertheless drawn up the street, as the ruins almost demanded a closer look. Although last in use as a church in 1880 and missing its roof, the ruins were still pretty striking, particularly the square-plan three-stage tower at the front of building, with its multiple arched windows and doors – all now open to the elements; and the animals. For, as impressive as the church ruins were, what I really loved about the place was the fact that it now appeared to be lorded over by two small Shetland ponies, one grey and one dappled white. They came strolling out through the doorway as I was taking photographs, as if they were stepping out front to proudly welcome me to their grand, if now somewhat dilapidated, residence. However, the ponies kept their distance and wouldn't venture close enough to be petted and so, after a short time of unsuccessfully trying to tempt them over, I left them in peace and headed back down the street to re-join the route for my final six kilometres to Galbally. On the outskirts of Galbally, I had another equine encounter when I came across a majestic stallion in a field beside a large farmhouse. It was almost entirely black apart from one white sock and a tiny white star on its forehead. It was a wonderful looking animal and it pranced about the field like it knew it, as if it was parading about on the equine equivalent of a catwalk. Like the Ballylanders ponies, this horse kept a respectful distance and appeared to be quite happy to just pose for a few pictures, before I pushed on for Galbally.

Galbally is from the Irish *An Gallbhaile*, meaning 'the town of the stranger' and the village has a reputation for being very welcoming to outsiders. I wondered absentmindedly if, in the past, you had arrived in the neighbouring village of Ballylanders and weren't from London, would you have been encouraged to move on to Galbally, where they weren't so particular about your background. Regardless, I would have to say that if I had had to choose between the two, Galbally would be the village I would have picked to settle in. It's an undeniably picturesque village, situated on the banks of the Aherlow River, at the foot of the majestic Galtee Mountains, Ireland's second highest mountain range after MacGillycuddy's Reeks in County Kerry. Entering the village, I looked about for a bar to enjoy my customary end of day celebration. I decided against Frazer's. It might have had something to do with the sign on the front that declared that it was both a 'Lounge Bar' and an 'Undertakers'. I'm sure it was entirely unfair, but I couldn't quite dispel the nagging thought that the proprietor might be tempted to use one part of his business to assist the other. So I settled for the Abbey Bar instead, undoubtedly named after the nearby Moor Abbey on the outskirts of the village.

After slaking my thirst, with a modest half pint on this occasion, I decided to try my hand at hitching a lift back to Kilfinane, where I was going to spend a second night in the hostel. I walked a short distance out of the village and stood by the side of the road and waited with my thumb at the ready. Galbally's reputation for being kind to strangers was immediately evident, or so I thought, when the very first car to appear, stopped to pick me up. Marie was originally from England, but had settled in the area a number of years ago. She said that she unfortunately couldn't take me all the way to Kilfinane, but would drop me at a location where I wouldn't have any trouble getting another lift. She also mentioned that she had passed me on the road out of Ballylanders, the town of the Londoner, earlier that day. However, it turned out that she drove me in totally the wrong direction and dropped me in a hopelessly remote location. Perhaps she was originally from London and had settled in Ballylanders and had now made it her mission in life to make sure that no 'foreigners' ever made their way back to her village. Anyway, I had much better luck with my subsequent lifts. Firstly, a young girl and her two friends went out of their way to bring me back to the outskirts of Galbally. They dropped me on the road that would take me directly to Kilfinane and then a very kind lady called Noreen stopped to pick me up and left me right to the door of my hostel.

Chapter Six: Close Encounters
(Days thirteen and fourteen - Galbally to near Cappawhite)

"It's a long way to Tipperary" goes the song made popular during the First World War. And it certainly proved to be the case today. I had been expecting a fairly leisurely fifteen kilometres over four and a half hours, but instead I got a very challenging twenty-four and a half kilometres over eight hours!

Firstly, I needed to get to Galbally again from Kilfinane. But Seamus at the Ballyhoura Luxury Hostel informed me that there were no taxis firms nearby. I would probably have to wait for an hour or two for one to come from Tipperary and it would cost a small fortune. So I decided to try hitching a lift again. It had, after all, worked out very well the day before – if you discounted the crazy Londoner! However, after waiting on the road to Galbally for half an hour, during which time not a single car passed me, I gave up. I couldn't get a signal on my mobile, so I called into a nearby garage to see if they might call me a taxi from Tipperary. I was resigned to waiting and paying the small fortune. However, my luck then changed big time. As I approached the counter in the office, the owner of the garage, Willie Barrett, looked up at me and, having quickly appraised my attire, simply asked, "You need help?" I explained my predicament and he came out from behind the counter and headed out to the yard without a further word. I followed dumbly behind, not really knowing if he was ignoring me or actually planning to help. He spoke briefly to one of his mechanics, who was working under the bonnet of a car, and then passed by me as he returned to his office, again without a word. I stood there perplexed, now convinced that I was being ignored, and thinking that I should now return to the hostel and get Seamus to phone for a taxi. But then the mechanic who Willie had spoken to, closed the bonnet of the car he had been tinkering with and approached me, wiping his hands on an oily rag, and said, "The boss has told me to give you a lift to Galbally." Willie was obviously a person who placed more importance on action than on words. The mechanic, who introduced himself as Michael, then drove me in one of the company vans all the way to Galbally, which was a round trip of some nineteen miles for him. However, he seemed pleased to have a break from his usual work and thankfully he was a little chattier than his boss. Not that I was complaining about Willie. Quite the opposite really. The generosity shown to me on this journey seemed to know no bounds!

Michael dropped me in the square in Galbally and then turned and headed back to work. I got my bearings and then proceeded on foot out of the village and towards the Glen of Aherlow, the valley located between Slievenamuck and the Galtee Mountains that would eventually lead me to Tipperary. As I was on my way out of the village, a jeep pulled up alongside and a man got out to speak with me. This was a local man called Pat Boyce and he had noticed my banner and wanted to know if I needed any help. I assured him that I was fine - I had my guidebook and my maps and I was making my way out to Moor Abbey in the first instance. "I can give you a lift if you wish," he suggested, more in jest than in seriousness, as he knew by this stage that walking was the key aspect of my challenge. I thanked him for his offer and headed on out of the village as he climbed back into his jeep and headed off with a toot of his horn and a wave of his hand as he passed. I followed a quiet country road that ran alongside the Aherlow River and I was only about a kilometre out of the village, when I came upon the ruins of Moor Abbey. The abbey had been established by the Franciscans in 1471 and, according to the information on one of the signs, it was the site of a brutal, but bloodless, massacre of three friars around 1570. I say 'bloodless' because one of the friars who attempted to save the abbey was beaten by English soldiers and then had his head lopped off. Cue the blood, you would imagine. However, according to the sign, "*Then a marvel was seen: for when his head was cut off, no drop of blood flowed from his body. When the soldiers saw this, they cut his body to pieces, yet no blood flowed.*" The other two friars burned to death after the soldiers set fire to the abbey, presumably to avoid any further disappointment at the lack of blood. Between the bloodless friar and Staker Wallace, it seemed that heads had a tough enough time remaining attached to their bodies around these parts.

From here, the route left the road and took off through fields and hugged the northern bank of the Aherlow River, following it upstream. Not far from the abbey, I passed through a field and noticed, with passing interest, that there were some cows grazing leisurely at the far side, well away from me. I was about two thirds of the way over this particular field when I realised that one of the cows was not, in fact, a cow. It was a rather large, cream coloured bull. And it was not grazing leisurely. It was staring straight at me and looking as intimidating as only a bull can look. I resisted the temptation to run, but I have to admit that my stride lengthened a little and my pace quickened slightly. Thankfully the bull didn't budge, but just continued to stare at me menacingly, as I made a bee line for the next electric fence. Once safely on the other side, I came across a sign, clearly aimed at walkers approaching from the other direction, warning them not to cross the field due to the presence of a dangerous bull. I had observed no such sign as I had approached the field from the direction I had come and I could only conclude that I had either missed it or that the farmer could only afford one sign and was more concerned about Southerners heading South than about Northerners heading North! It was certainly a close encounter, but unfortunately my 'close encounters of the herd kind' were by no means over.

The route continued to carry me across a series of fields, keeping me close to the river and it was rather sublime with the gentle flow of the water alongside and the views across the grassy fields to the hazy Galtee Mountains looming in the distance. I had the pleasure of following a pheasant for a considerable distance through the long grass until it eventually realised that I wasn't going to give up the chase and it took to the wing to escape this strange creature that was on its tail. There were lots of electric fences to negotiate along the way, which I had to either crawl under or step over, depending on their height in relation to my inside leg measurement. The propensity for some farmers to enclose stiles within their electric fencing was quite baffling and certainly added to the challenge involved in moving from one field to the next. A small herd of bullocks took a great interest in me passing their field, but thankfully they were on the other side of the river and so caused me no concern. But it was becoming clearer than ever that I was now in the heart of cattle country. About two kilometres past Moor Abbey, the route turned away from the river and took off northwards and uphill through a number of fields on the lower slopes of Slievenamuck Mountain. Climbing over another stile, I immediately noticed that there was a well-worn dirt track through the next field that went at an angle through the grass rather than straight up. On reflection, I should probably have realised that this track had not been worn by the passage of human feet. But show a pilgrim a path and he will follow it. After a short distance, the dirt track led me through a large gap in a tall hedge and into an adjoining field. I stopped in my tracks. This field was full of cattle. I realised that they were all bullocks and there was about twenty in the herd. I turned to go back and it was then that things took a drastic turn for the worse!

The hedge I had just come through was actually a double row of hedges and it became apparent that a few bullocks had been hidden in between them as I had passed. I hadn't noticed them, but they had certainly noticed me. As I turned to go back into the field I had just come from, a large black bullock appeared suddenly from between the tall hedges to block my escape. I needed a rod or a stick - quickly. My walking poles were secured to the side of my rucksack and would have involved taking off my rucksack to free them. No time for that. I looked around and was relieved to find a branch about four feet in length lying on the ground close to my feet. I picked it up and tried to persuade the bullock to move out of my way. But it just kept coming towards me. "Do you think I won't use this stick," I yelled at it, sounding braver than I felt. It obviously didn't think that I would and it kept on advancing. Unfortunately, my shout had only alerted the rest of the herd to my presence and I was suddenly all too aware of numerous heads lifting from where they had been quietly grazing moments before to see what the commotion was. Now, instead of one bullock advancing on me, there was a herd of twenty. I think it was at this point that I started to get quite worried. With the gap in the hedges blocked off by the black bullock, which had now been joined by a couple of his mates who had also emerged from their hiding place, I had been well and truly ambushed. There was now only one way I could go and that was to the other side of the field where I hoped I would be able to escape. I tried not to panic and run, but backed towards the other side while the herd now started to follow me en masse! I know cattle can be very curious creatures and they perhaps wouldn't get too close, but these guys seemed to be very bold indeed and some of them even began to rush at me. I had to wave the branch and roar at the top of my voice, like Mel Gibson playing William Wallace in the movie 'Braveheart'. At this theatrical performance they would stop for a moment, but then as soon as I paused my performance, they would immediately start advancing again. My heart was thumping in my chest by this stage. I really thought my time was up. I did everything I could to scare them away (except bare my ass to them William Wallace style, which I believe might have been counter-productive) but they kept coming. I banged my branch on the ground only for it to break in two and leave me with rather ineffectual stump! Thankfully, after a retreat of about forty metres, I eventually reached the far side of the field and slid down into a deep gully in desperation to escape the relentlessly advancing herd. I clambered up the other side and over a barbed wire fence to take shelter in very overgrown woodland. Here I let my heartbeat slowly return to normal as I weighed up my options. The herd had gathered along the other side of the gulley and shouldered and jostled each other to get a better view of the funny stick waving animal that had just wandered through their field and provided them with such entertainment. As they continued to stare menacingly at me from across the gully, I felt like I was in a bizarre remake of Hitchcock's terrifying movie 'The Birds', only with the birds being replaced by bullocks. There was no question of going back through the cattle to pick up from where I think I had gone wrong by following that dirt track, which I now realised had more than likely been created by hooves rather than boots. I had no option but to fight my way through the woods and brambles and other obstacles for about half an hour before I emerged and was able to find my way back onto the correct route again. If it hadn't been for Google maps, and a decent signal on my phone, I'm not sure how I would have managed!

I emerged from the dark thicket into the bright sunlight once again and paused to examine my legs. I had been wearing shorts and, unlike the bloodless friar of Moor Abbey, my legs were now criss-crossed with scratches and scores, which sprouted little trickles of blood that ran down my legs and disappeared into the tops of my socks. I struggled on up the hillside and eventually reached a laneway that turned to follow the contours of Slievenamuck and led me into the forests that covered the upper slopes of the mountain. I was meant to follow this path around the southern slopes of Slievenamuck, but multiple forks and inconsistent way-marking inevitably resulted in me choosing the wrong path at one point and I ended up dropping down into the village of Lisvernane instead, about half a kilometre off route. I was standing on a pavement in the village, studying my guidebook and map to see how best to get back on track once again, when I heard a toot and looked round to see a familiar looking jeep pulling up beside me. Pat Boyce climbed out and greeted me like an old friend with a firm handshake. "You're a bit off course," he said, as he started to pull twigs off the top of my rucksack, which I had obviously unknowingly been transporting since my fight through the thicket. "What on earth have you been up to?" I explained about my run in with the bullocks and my forced detour through the thick woods. "Ah, they're curious creatures, but they wouldn't do you any harm," he said. Easy for you to say, was what I thought, but instead I said, "Anyway, I'm just trying to figure out how to get back onto the proper route now."

It turned out that Pat knew the area intimately and he knew exactly how to get back on route, but what followed almost resulted in me suffering a hernia, as I tried to suppress my laughter at his antics. For Pat didn't just explain the way ahead to me, maybe using his arms occasionally to indicate left or right like most people would. No, Pat actually acted out the route as if he himself was walking the route in miniature along the pavement. "Walk this way," he said, as he headed up the pavement a few steps, "and you'll come to a junction about half a kilometre from here. Now, look at me. Are you watching? Turn left here." And he turned left. "Now, follow this road for about a kilometre. It swings round to the right," as he veered off to the right on the pavement. I had to follow him along the pavement to keep up with him and he kept looking back at me, repeating, "Are you listening?" and "Are you watching?" Then he stopped suddenly and I almost bumped into him. "You'll come to a sharp right hand corner in the road, but don't turn right. What are you not to do?" he demanded. "I'm not to turn right," I said. "That's right," he said, "don't turn right. If you look straight ahead," and he indicated straight ahead with his two arms stretched out in front of him, "you'll see a stile. And you climb over this stile." And he acted out climbing up one side of the stile using his arms and legs and then turned around to act out climbing down the other side. I really don't know how I kept a straight face at this point, but I think I just about managed. At the bottom of his imaginary stile, Pat turned around again so he was facing the correct way on his imaginary lane and off he set, with me once again following in his wake. "Then just keep on this lane and you'll eventually link up with the route again, which is well way-marked from then on. Have you got all that? Do you want me to go over it again?" "Pat," I responded, trying to keep the mirth from my voice, "I am never going to forget those directions. Thank you very much." "You're very welcome," he said, "and all the very best with the rest of your walk. 'Tis a great thing you're doing." And with that we parted company and Pat headed back to his jeep, which was now about fifty metres back down the road.

Needless to say, Pat's directions were faultless and I actually laughed out loud when I reached the stile and had to climb up one side, turn around and climb down the other. As Pat had promised, I eventually met up with the proper route again and Pacman returned to keep me right from there on. The rest of the journey was pretty straightforward, although very long and very hot, with temperatures climbing into the high 20's again. However, I enjoyed the fabulous views on offer while traversing the Glen of Aherlow, particularly from the Christ the King viewpoint, where a large statue of Christ stood with a hand raised in blessing over the valley below. I stopped at the picnic area close to the statue and enjoyed the uninterrupted vista spread out before me over the Glen of Aherlow and across the river to the ever present Galtee Mountains. From here, the route wound through yet more lovely forest walks until I finally dropped down from the hills and joined quiet country roads and then the very busy N24 for the final stretch into Tipperary Town. However, rather than continuing on the N24 into the centre of town, the route turned off the main road to pass under a railway bridge and then took a path round the site of the former British Army barracks that had existed here for fifty years prior to the Irish War of Independence. It was this very barracks, which operated as a military hospital during World War 1, that made the song *It's a Long Way to Tipperary* so popular at that time. The barracks were largely destroyed in 1922 and all that remained now were a water tower, the perimeter wall and a small section of the officer's quarters, which had since been turned into a peace memorial. I passed all these relics of the past, and the eerie shell of an old abandoned workhouse, before arriving in the more modern centre of Tipperary Town. Having said that, the bar I stopped at to enjoy my customary imbibing ritual, had been established over one hundred years ago in 1898. This was O'Brien's on Bridge Street and I had the pleasure of being served my pint of Guinness and having my photograph taken by Jack O'Brien, the fourth generation of the family to run the bar.

After my refreshments, and securing a few donations from other patrons of the bar, I took the short walk to the Central House B&B on Main Street and received a very warm welcome from Gerry and Dorothy Casey. The B&B was right next to a flower shop and Gerry ran the B&B while Dorothy ran the flower shop, which was called "Flowers by Dorothy", just so that there was no confusion over who did what. I was initially booked in for just the one night, but as it turned out, I would get to know Gerry and Dorothy, and Tipp Town, as it's known locally, very well indeed over the coming days thanks to some more bullocks!

****

My walk today started very late, after 11am, as I had a few things to pick up in Tipp Town - more sunscreen and insect repellent and a new pair of lightweight sandals. I picked the latter up at a bargain price in a shoe shop just across the street from my B&B. It was finally goodbye to the undersized, gaudy, flamingo-print, flip flops I had bought in Glengarriff a number of days before. I had decided to walk to Cappawhite or beyond today, depending on how I got on, and then return to the B&B in Tipperary for a second night with my lovely hosts, Gerry and Dorothy. As I was leaving Tipp Town, I reached into one of the pockets of my shorts to check that I had my folded sheets of paper with me, and felt something unusual. I pulled out a small brown envelope that I hadn't seen before and opened it to find a little card from Dorothy wishing me well, along with a generous donation. She had brought my clothes in off the line that morning and must have hidden it in my pocket then! It was yet another unexpected and wonderful act of kindness and it certainly cheered me on my way.

Clear blue skies once again allowed the sun to beat down on me relentlessly, but at least there was also a nice breeze which made things a little more comfortable. A lot of road walking to start with, but it was actually quite pleasant. Old Tar didn't seem so bad today - that melting he had got over the last few days must have softened him up a bit. About four kilometres out of Tipp Town, I came upon Jimmy White's Pub at Bourke's Cross. But it wasn't a drink I was interested in - it was closed anyway, even if I had been. No, what caught my eye was the attractive Celtic mural on the gable wall of the pub, depicting Brian Boru leading the charge against the Vikings in one of his earliest battlefield victories at nearby Soloheadbeg in the year 968. It was the start of a long campaign that would eventually see him crowned King of Ireland in 1002. This was also the location of the Soloheadbeg Ambush on 21st January 1919, which is believed to have been the first engagement of the Irish War of Independence. The ambush was staged by Sean Treacy and Dan Breen (no relation) and resulted in the death of two policemen who were escorting explosives to a quarry. Soloheadbeg was also a stopping point for O'Sullivan Beare and his followers and it is from here that he launched a daring raid on the nearby Donohill Motte in order to obtain much needed food supplies. It seemed like Soloheadbeg and the surrounding area was steeped in conflict and trouble. I prayed that I might escape unscathed. On reflection, I maybe didn't pray hard enough!

Another five kilometres of peaceful rural roads brought me through the village of Donohill, from the Irish *Dún Eochaille*, meaning 'the fort of the yew wood', and then on to the motte itself. The motte was quite an imposing ancient earth structure that towered rather incongruously above the well-tended fields and roads that surrounded it. The motte was topped with a statue of the Virgin Mary, which I presumed was a more recent addition. A stile opposite Donohill Church led me off the road and into the field in which the motte was located. I approached the base of the earth mound and gazed upwards, trying to imagine what it would have been like storming this defensive structure four hundred years ago. I sensed a presence by my side and turned to see Donal Cam O'Sullivan Beare peering up towards the top of the motte also. "So, you finally made it here, then" he said with a smile.

"Yes, I've been taking it easy," I responded, before adding, "and I also had a few unexpected detours."

He didn't react to this but, continuing to gaze up at the motte bathed in warm sunshine, he said, "It was quite different back in my time of course. It was early morning and it was the middle of winter and bitterly cold. We were starving and exhausted and the motte was heavily fortified and guarded by the O'Dwyers. We were desperate after only having had foraged leaves and roots to sustain us at Solloghod the previous night. And when we set off for here on the morning of our fifth day, our rear ranks were continually harassed by musket fire from the White Knight's forces as we went. But our hunger drove us on and it overtook the weariness and fatigue that we were all feeling. We knew that the O'Dwyer's had their winter food supplies stored here and we were determined to get our hands on it. The food was stored in a tower, which stood on top of this motte where that statue of the Virgin Mary is now. It was well guarded by the O'Dwyer's, which was only to be expected given the famine conditions that Elizabeth's forces had brought upon this land in their eagerness to break us. Our soldiers had to storm the tower."

Looking at the steep sides of the motte, which rose about nine metres above where we were standing, I said to Donal Cam, "That must have been incredibly difficult. Did you not try to buy some of the supplies? You mentioned before that you had plenty of Spanish gold."

"There was little point. At that time food was worth much more than gold, so starved was the country. And, if we had paused to ask, we would have lost the element of surprise that enabled us to take the tower. Despite coming under fire from the guards on the tower high above us, my soldiers were able to break open the main gate and overcome those defending it. Both sides suffered losses, but that was quickly forgotten as we fell upon the food and devoured all we could of the meal, beans, oats and barley. So hungry were we that we fed like cattle at the trough. The beans and grains tasted like nectar after the plants and roots we had been barely surviving on up until then. But we couldn't linger for long at Donohill, as we could so easily have been surrounded by our enemies and trapped. We ate what we could, but it was never going to be enough before I had to give the order to move out and press on with our march towards the Slieve Felim mountains."

"You still had a fair bit to go," I chipped in, realising that we were still a good seven or eight kilometres from the hills.

"Yes and we were to encounter yet another obstacle in our path before we reached the relative safety of the mountains. Thomas Butler, the Earl of Ormonde and a Protestant loyal to the Queen, had got to hear of our successful raid on Donohill and sent a large force to block our way. It was an intimidating force, made up of more of O'Dwyer's men and members of the O'Ryan clan, and we were at first quite fearful. But once again, realising that we had little other option, we threw caution to the wind and resolved to attack the enemy first. Ormonde's forces had obviously not anticipated such a move from an exhausted army such as ours. When they saw us attacking with such abandon, they were filled with the greater fear and fled their ground. We could scarcely believe our good fortune and we cheered loudly as the enemy took off."

As I listened to this, I could not have anticipated that my way would also soon be blocked. However, the outcome would not be so favourable in my case and I would be cursing rather than cheering. Oblivious to what lay ahead, I asked, "It must have given you all a great boost to have won that victory without a drop of blood being shed?"

"It certainly did, but our good cheer didn't last. On the far side of the Slieve Felim mountains, we had a disastrous episode where I lost twenty of my soldiers. But I'll come to that when you get closer to where that occurred, near Templederry. Goodbye for now, my friend."

"Oh, we're friends now are we?" I said laughing, but, as I looked towards him, it was only to catch the last glimpse of Donal Cam melting into the air. "Oh, goodbye then," I added, wondering if perhaps Donohill motte was still a place where he didn't wish to linger for too long.

I left the motte to cross the rest of the field, joining a roadway again for a short distance, before very gingerly climbing over a ramshackle wooden stile to descend into a series of fields alongside the River Cauteen. I headed for a nice new metal stile at the edge of the first field, but on reaching it, I realised that it didn't actually lead anywhere. It had obviously just been abandoned there and was presumably intended to replace the old wooden stile I had just crossed. In my view the wooden stile was well past its 'use by date' and it was high time that it was replaced by the new metal one. The route, which soon peeled away from the river, was heavily overgrown with grass, thistles and brambles in places, but passable with the aid of my walking poles, which I used to batter down the worst of it. I escaped with only a few more scratches to my legs to add to the previous day's tally. However, at the top of a hill, another stile dropped me down into a large field of grass. I stopped in my tracks. Oh no! I couldn't believe what I was seeing. Over to the right hand side of the field was a herd of about fifteen cream coloured cattle. Whether they were cows or bullocks I couldn't quite tell - until I zoomed in on them with my camera and confirmed what I had feared. They were all bullocks and quite hefty ones at that. Bollocks! was my immediate thought. Then I noticed that right in the middle of the field, about two hundred metres away from where I was standing, was a way marker. Again I used the zoom on my camera to get a closer look. And sure enough, there was little Pacmac, looking like he was casually strolling across the field without a care in the world. I'm sure that it was only the effect of the heat haze, but for a moment I could have sworn that he was waving at me to follow him! In my experience, it was highly unusual to have a way marker situated in the middle of a field. The route normally takes you around the perimeter of fields so as to minimise disturbance to crops and animals. Had the farmer deliberately moved the way marker from its proper position into the middle of the field as some sort of game of dare? However, after my close encounter the day before, there was no way I was going to dare cross through the middle of this field.

I checked my map to see if there was an alternative route to avoid going through this field all together. There was, but it would have involved adding at least an extra kilometre onto my journey. Looking back, that would have been a very small price to pay. But I didn't have the value of hindsight then of course, and instead I settled on a different plan, which at the time seemed eminently sensible. I decided to walk around the perimeter of the field, keeping to the left hand side and hence as far away from the herd as possible. In this way, I would skirt alongside the hedges and then the electric fence running across that side of the field and if the cattle came too close then I would simply slip under the wire to safety. It sounded like a very good plan to me. The herd was about one hundred and fifty metres away and they were all lying down looking relaxed and seemingly unaware of my presence at this point. So off I set, trying to keep as low as possible so that the cattle wouldn't spot me too soon. However, I had hardly left the safety of the stile before the bullocks started getting to their feet and looking in my direction. Bollocks! I stuck to my plan and continued onwards, hugging the hedge at the edge of the field as I went. The herd started to move. Shit! However, strangely they didn't come straight towards me as I might have expected. Instead, they started across the field at a gallop as if they were trying to head me off before I reached the far side. I stuck to my guns though and ploughed on, safe in the knowledge that I had only to make it to the safety of the electric fence, now only a few metres away. The bullocks had now come to a halt and were standing in a group about thirty metres away from me, effectively blocking my path. I was immediately reminded of Donal Cam's account of his path being blocked by the Earl of Ormonde's men. Perhaps, I thought, I should just charge at them, as O'Sullivan Beare's soldiers had Ormonde's men, and cheer as I watched the bullocks take off. However, I didn't even have time to discount the notion as ridiculous, before the entire herd suddenly seemed to move as one and stampeded towards me. I quickly abandoned any thought of attack and, opting for retreat instead, turned to dash the short distance to the electric fence. As I turned and pushed off on my right foot, I heard a loud pop, as if I had stood on a plastic bottle and the cap had shot off under pressure. I remember thinking to myself, "What the heck was that?" But, as soon as my right foot hit the ground again and a sharp pain shot up my leg, I knew immediately what it was. My calf muscle had popped. I yelled out in agony as I rolled under the electric fence and into the neighbouring field to safety. I sat up rubbing my calf muscle and looked up to see fifteen large beasts staring dumbly at me from the other side of the wire. I managed to stand up, but knew that my walk was pretty much over for the day - perhaps even longer! The air turned as blue as the sky above, as I cursed the bullocks and called them all the names of the day, but I have to say that they seemed pretty unperturbed. I have to admit that it only occurred to me at this point, as I stood on one side of a thin wire with fifteen very hefty animals staring back at me from the other side, that I had absolutely no idea as to whether the electric fence was switched on or not. But then in all probability, neither had they - and that was probably a good thing!

The next hour was spent hobbling painfully through fields, over lanes and along a country road until I came to a house that had cars parked outside it and looked like there might be someone in. It was a rather grand home and I hobbled up the drive and knocked on the front door. At the sound of my knocking, two large dogs appeared from round the side of the house, barking loudly. Oh no, I thought, I've escaped being trampled by bullocks only to be savaged by dogs. But thankfully they turned out to be very friendly and they were barking out of excitement rather than anger. The door opened slightly and a middle-aged woman's face appeared in the gap with an apprehensive look on her face – which, I must say, was totally understandable. I explained my mishap and this, together with my appearance, must have seemed plausible enough, because the woman, who I later found out was called Rachel, opened the door wider and told me to wait a moment, while she fetched her car keys. She then very kindly drove me to the village of Cappawhite, which was about four kilometres away by road. From there, the manager of the local Centra Store, Shane, arranged for another lady called Margaret to drive me to her home village of Donohill. However, as we were travelling and chatting, I noticed that we passed a turnoff for Donohill and I said to Margaret, "Did Shane not say that you lived in Donohill? We just passed the turnoff." Margaret simply replied, "I do, but now that I know more about you, I'm very happy to take you all the way to Tipp Town." When I arrived back at the Central House B&B, I relayed my tales of woe to Gerry and he sat me down at a dining room table and made me tea and toast. I couldn't help feeling very dejected at having had to abandon my day's walk, but at the same time I couldn't stop marvelling at all the fabulous people I had had the good fortune to meet.

****

I awoke in my B&B room and gently swung my legs out of bed to find that the lower half of my right leg was now about fifty per cent wider than my left. This was not normal! I placed my feet on the floor and slowly stood up and took a few tentative steps. I found that it was only painful if I attempted to angle my right foot either up or down. So long as I kept my foot flat, at ninety degrees to my leg, it was relatively pain free. This at least meant that I could get about, albeit very slowly as my normal stride was now reduced to a rather pathetic shuffle – left foot forward slightly, right foot brought alongside, left foot forward slightly, right foot brought alongside, etc. So, I could get about, after a fashion, but there was no way I was going to be able to re-join the Ireland Way at this rate of going. I sat down on the bed again and cursed my bad fortune. This had the potential to knock my planned schedule way off track. I had been aiming to reach Ballycastle on 1st August, the date of mine and Jacqui's wedding anniversary. In my own mind, it had just seemed so perfect that I would finish my epic walk at Jacqui's final resting place, in her hometown, on the anniversary of the day we married. This had been my plan from the outset. It had determined my starting date and my entire schedule from that point on. I had allowed a few days extra for the occasional rest day, but I had already used one of those in Millstreet and now only had a couple of days left to play with. I was hoping against hope for a quick recovery. Fecking bullocks!

After breakfast, I shuffled up Main Street and called into Kissane's Pharmacy to see if they could help. Here I met the principal pharmacist, Shane Kelly, who was extremely helpful and knowledgeable, having previously suffered a similar injury himself. He believed that I had pulled my calf muscle. He provided me with an anti-inflammatory ointment and advised me to massage this into the affected calf muscle three to four times a day. I was delighted when he said that he was hopeful that forty-eight hours might do the trick. He also gave me a stretch bandage to wrap around my calf to provide it with a little extra support should I need it when setting off on my walk again. Shane wouldn't hear of taking any payment for his time or products and once again I was humbled by the kindness and generosity of the people I met on my travels. I returned to the Central House B&B, where Gerry and Dorothy looked after me marvellously, as I resigned myself to resting up for a couple of days. Fecking bullocks!

Two days later, I called back with Shane Kelly in Kissane's Pharmacy and shared with him the disappointing news that my leg was no better. After having a quick look at it, he advised seeing a physiotherapist. "Leave it with me," he said and, 30 minutes later, I received a text from Olly Griffin, Sports Injury Therapist, to say that he could see me that afternoon! On the way to his clinic, I passed a mobility aids shop and checked out the walking sticks and Zimmer frames on display, thinking that it was always good to have a backup plan! I then hobbled the final furlong to the physiotherapist and was treated for close to an hour by Olly. He said that he had actually been following me on social media since I had arrived in Tipperary and had been considering offering his services when he had received the call from Shane. Olly was completely professional and very generous with his time and, like Shane, he wouldn't hear of taking any payment from me! However, his assessment of my injury was very hard for me to accept. According to Olly, I had suffered 'a grade two strain on the medial head of the gastrocnemius muscle located at the muscle tendon junction'. That was a very fancy and specific way of saying that I had a torn calf muscle. Grade two meant that the injury was a moderate tear, somewhere between a minor pull, which would have righted itself in a couple of days, and a serious tear, requiring surgery. According to Olly, a moderate tear, such as mine, would normally take six to eight weeks to properly heal. Fecking bullocks!

Olly sent me off again with my right leg taped up with bright blue 'kinesiology tape' from heel to the back of my knee and moving a little easier. He also strongly advised using rice. When I asked him if it should be cooked or not, he just looked at me like I wasn't half wise! 'RICE', of course, stands for 'Rest, Ice, Compression and Elevation'. The tape was to prevent me angling my foot up or down, which would only aggravate the injury and, as I had already discovered, would also cause a fair bit of pain. As I shuffled back towards my B&B, I considered my seemingly hopeless situation. I just couldn't face being out for six to eight weeks. I decided to seek a second opinion. Not that I didn't trust Olly's verdict, but more because I stubbornly refused to concede defeat. And Olly had advised me to use rice. So, I put a call into Noel Rice, my physiotherapist in Belfast, and explained what had happened. Noel obviously couldn't diagnose my injury down the phone, but he suggested staying in Tipperary for a few days more to see if there was any improvement. This I decided to do, clinging on to the desperate hope that my leg would heal sufficiently in two or three more days and allow me to continue. Thankfully, Tipperary Town was not a bad place to be convalescing in and I enjoyed shuffling about the streets, seeing the sights, visiting the cafés and chatting with the friendly locals.

Later that day, I sat in the grounds of St Michael's Roman Catholic Church to relax with a book. I thought I had chosen a nice quiet spot, but a pickup truck soon pulled up and parked nearby. The driver's window was down and I was both simultaneously disturbed and intrigued by the loud phone conversation the man in the truck was having with, as far as I could determine, a woman in Nigeria. His side of the conversation veered wildly between measured and reasonable one moment and angry and exasperated the next and involved a lot of language that wasn't exactly appropriate for our consecrated surroundings. I had no idea what the argument was about, but at one point, after a particularly heated exchange, he suddenly changed tact and I heard him saying to the woman, "Wait 'til you hear this." And he then held the phone out the window of his vehicle and, right on cue, the bells of St Michael's started ringing out the six o'clock Angelus. After a few moments he brought the phone back to his ear again and I imagine that the woman then enquired as to what she had been listening to. He then lost it again and started yelling down the phone, "'Tis the bloody bells woman. Are ye feckin' deaf or what? Jaysus, it's the feckin Angelus." He was obviously making no allowance for the fact that this woman was probably in a different time zone and may well have had no idea what the Angelus was anyway. It was highly entertaining in a strange sort of 'car crash' way, but, after his rant continued unabated, I decided to find somewhere quieter than a church to continue with my reading. Unfortunately, I had to pass his pickup to leave and, just as I did, the phone conversation came to an abrupt end. He cursed about the useless feckin phone signal in Nigeria, although I strongly suspected that the woman had simply had had enough of him and had hung up. "Hi there," he said to me as I passed. Shit, I thought, as he climbed out of his vehicle and introduced himself, before adding by way of explanation, "That was my ex. She's Nigerian and has gone back home and taken the kids with her." I couldn't for the life of me wonder why. Realising that I was from out of town, he then totally forgot about the subject matter that had so exercised him for the last ten minutes and engaged me in a long conversation about the history of the town and places I should see. He was actually very friendly - in a 'Jekyll and Hyde' sort of way - and had quite a local knowledge, but I'm sure you will understand why I have chosen not to reveal his name.

Over the next couple of days, I explored more of Tipperary town and visited some of the places the man from St Michael's had told me about. I explored the other main church in the town, St Mary's Church of Ireland, and its graveyard. Here I found the ancient, lichen covered, but beautifully inscribed Emmet headstone, marking the burial place of Christopher Emmet, grandfather of the celebrated Irish Patriot, Robert Emmet. I then strolled around the extensive parklands alongside the Old Monastery Road and, from its elevated position, enjoyed superb views over the town, with its prominent church spires, to the Galtee Mountains in the distance. It was in this park that I came across a large area enclosed within a low stone wall. This was St John's famine graveyard. The beautiful setting, on a gently sloping hill facing the Galtees, bathed in warm sunshine that served to highlight the sparse scattering of headstones, belied the awful truth that lay beneath the soil here. In 1847, during the Great Famine in Ireland, it was felt that the town's church graveyard could not accommodate the volume of deaths and so this new famine graveyard was opened. A sign at the site recorded the shocking fact that, in the eight month period between October 1849 and May 1850, around fourteen hundred people were buried here, including five hundred children. The relatively small number of headstones in the graveyard clearly did not come close to representing the staggering number of souls interred here during this darkest period of Irish history. Despite the heat of the sun, I shivered at this stark reminder of the immensity of the tragedy that was replicated throughout the island and which saw Ireland's population reduced by one quarter, due to both starvation and emigration. So devastating was the famine, that Ireland is the only country in Europe with a lower population today than in 1840. And it was a famine that was avoidable and should never have occurred – the potato crops may have been destroyed by blight, but the quantities of grain and other food supplies exported from Ireland at the time was truly shameful. Hunger and death on a massive scale caused by the greed and lifestyle of a privileged few. And this all happened when Ireland was a fully constituent part of the United Kingdom of Great Britain and Ireland, following the Act of Union in 1800. It was chilling to learn that, at the time of the famine, the assistant secretary to Her Majesty's Treasury, Sir Charles Trevelyan, wrote that the famine was an "*effective mechanism for reducing surplus population. Judgment of God sent the calamity to teach the Irish a lesson, that calamity must not be too much mitigated… The real evil with which we have to contend is not the physical evil of the Famine, but the moral evil of the selfish, perverse and turbulent character of the people.*" For many Irish people, the famine, *An Gorta Mór*, The Great Hunger, is not thought of as a natural disaster caused by potato blight, but a man-made disaster caused by British colonial attitudes towards the Irish at the time.

Seeking out something a little more cheerful, and somewhere I could rest my injured leg for a bit, I walked on round the park's pathways and found a park bench where I could sit and relax in the sun. I was certainly able to get about, but it was at a snail's pace and, of course, I was carrying no rucksack while strolling around Tipperary at my leisure. I was starting to realise that there was going to be no quick fix. My injured calf wasn't going to be right in a few days. I was beginning to accept that I would probably have to return home to recuperate for a few weeks until I was fit enough to walk again. I remembered having to take a few weeks out of my Ulster Way walk three years earlier, due to painful shin splints, so it's not like I hadn't experienced an unplanned interruption to my walking plans before. The Ireland Way would still be here for me when I got back and, rest assured, I would be back to complete my walk. But it was still a very bitter pill to swallow. Feckin bullocks!

That evening, I received a message from Stephen Bell, aka Wildfoot. Stephen was also walking the Ireland Way and he was now in the village of Upperchurch, about thirty kilometres north of Tipperary. He had started his journey well after I had started, but he had already overtaken me. I would like to say that this was entirely due to me being laid up in Tipperary for days with my injury, but the fact was, Stephen was moving at a terrific pace and would have overtaken me anyway, whether I had been injured or not. However, the most remarkable aspect of Stephen's Ireland Way walk was the fact that he was undertaking it barefoot! I felt like a right wimp by comparison. Anyway, we had been following each other's progress on social media and Stephen let me know that his partner was down to stay the night with him in Upperchurch and that she would be driving back to Belfast the following morning. A lift home was duly arranged.

The following morning, I said farewell to Gerry at the Central House B&B, who had been expecting to put me up for just one night and had ended up looking after me for six! He and Dorothy had been so hospitable and they also refused any payment for the extra days! Before I left, I had a wonderful surprise when Robert Pratt and Yvonne Larmour unexpectedly called in to say hello. This Australian couple, who lived and worked in China, were also walking the Ireland Way and, as with Stephen Bell, we were also following each other's progress. They had learned of my injury and, as they were on their way through Tipperary, they had sought me out and called in to wish me all the best. It was a wonderful gesture and I was delighted to meet them in person at last! Robert and I had hoped to have a Guinness together if we ever met, but that would have to wait to another time. I was also very fortunate to run into Sister Charlotte again. She was originally from Cushendun on the North Antrim coast, but now resided next door to Gerry and Dorothy and I had had the good fortune to enjoy her company for a few hours one evening. A more gentle, caring and fun loving soul you would be hard pressed to find. So, all in all, I had a terrific send off from Tipperary Town that morning. Dorothy drove me to the very pretty and tranquil village of Upperchurch and here I met Stephen Bell's partner, Agnieszka Lukaszek, or Aga for short. Aga had driven down from Belfast the previous day to bring Stephen fresh supplies and had very kindly agreed to ferry me back home. She was an equally amazing person and was great company on the long drive north. She and Stephen ran the Wildfoot Centre near Lisburn and offered clients a holistic approach to health; embracing fitness, strength, balance and nutrition.

Returning home was certainly good for the body. My leg needed rest to heal properly and a few complimentary physiotherapy treatments from Noel Rice of Belfast Physio and Sports Injury Clinic also helped considerably. Noel had also provided free treatments during my Ulster Way walk three years before and so was very familiar with my hiking challenges. However, while my body slowly recovered and became stronger again, my mind did not fare so well and my mental resolve weakened. I had lost the momentum I had begun to build up on my walk and the enforced break was not easy to cope with. And the longer I was away from the walk the less enthusiastic I was becoming about having to return. It had certainly been very rewarding in terms of sights seen and people met, but it had been a tough journey and I felt that it was going to be difficult to embrace it fully again.

However, just less than four weeks after my injury, I was on my way back by bus and train to Tipperary Town. I felt that I was physically ready to restart my walk, although I would need to take it easy for a few days. Undoubtedly, I was feeling quite apprehensive about starting again. Why would anyone in their rights minds voluntarily choose to leave their home and travel hundreds of miles away via public transport, only to turn around and start walking back? And why would any sane person shun the comforts of their own home to deliberately spend the next four weeks carrying their belongings on their back, hauling them from place to place, in all sorts of weather and often uncertain of having a proper place to spend the night or somewhere to get food? But there were a number of reasons that had forced me to set aside my own personal desire for a comfortable life and set off again on this challenging journey. Firstly, I didn't want to be thought of as a quitter. I was still pretty determined to finish what I started. No feckin' bullocks were going to prevent me from completing my challenge! And, I have to admit that I derived a certain satisfaction from the challenge and the feedback and interaction with people that came from sharing it on social media. Also, I was undertaking this walk in memory of my late wife, Jacqui. This walk was a means of keeping her memory alive. Not for me. I needed no such means. But for others, including many who were never fortunate enough to have met her. However, my main motivator for putting myself through this self-inflicted endurance test was the hope that it would help prevent or lessen the suffering of others by helping to fund cancer research. It undoubtedly provided me with great motivation to believe that the terrible disease that had claimed Jacqui's life could maybe someday be beaten and we would all be free of the awful scourge that blights so many lives.

As I approached Tipperary Town, grey clouds closed in over the sky, blocking out the sun, and it wasn't long before the rain followed. Ireland's heat wave had finally come to an end and the parched fields of the surrounding countryside undoubtedly welcomed the much needed moisture. Normal Irish summer weather had returned to the island. It would certainly make for cooler walking conditions than I had experienced during the first fortnight of my walk, although I was hoping that not too much wet weather lay ahead. I was also hoping that my right leg would hold out for the next seven hundred kilometres. I was now wearing a support sleeve around my right calf and was carrying a short yellow foam roller in my rucksack to 'roll' my calf muscle over, back and forth, twice a day as directed by Noel Rice. Hopefully these measures, together with a more measured approach to distances, would see me through. Only time would tell.

Chapter Seven: Back on Track
(Days fifteen and eighteen - Near Cappawhite to Ballingarry)

I had returned to the Central House B&B in Tipp Town and, after a comfortable night, Gerry served me up a hearty breakfast and then arranged for a friend of his, Sheila, to give me a lift to my starting point for the day. Dorothy was away for a few days with her sister, but she very kindly phoned me to wish me all the best for the rest of my journey. With the help of my maps and advice from a few locals along the way, I was able to guide Sheila back to where I had sought the assistance of Rachel almost four weeks previously after my unfortunate incident with the cattle. I waved Sheila off and turned to say hello to Pacman who was by the roadside, waiting patiently on my return. It was true after all; the Ireland Way hadn't gone anywhere. My few weeks off due to injury were no more than a blip in the grand scheme of things.

It was raining lightly, but persistently, and I was wearing my wet gear, which subsequently remained on for most of the morning. My view was pretty blinkered by the hood of my jacket as I proceeded along the country roads and lanes towards Cappawhite, although it hardly mattered as the landscape was hardly worth looking at anyway in such dismal weather. Early on, a laneway brought me through the grounds of a private residence with numerous outbuildings, which was rather unusual as the Ireland Way normally avoids such close proximity to dwellings. I was at first very reluctant to pass through the grounds, not because they appeared private, but because they were being patrolled by two rather large Rottweiler dogs; one lean, one heavy. I removed a walking pole from my rucksack and hesitantly advanced, ready to use the pole for defence if required. The heavier one stayed well back and appeared disinterested. The leaner one seemed quite pleased to see me and dashed around the grounds excitedly, but seemed too nervous to come close. However, as I proceeded, the leaner Rottweiler became gradually bolder and when I reached a hand out, it came right up and first sniffed and then licked it. "Good boy," I said, happy that it was clearly a friendly animal. However, it very quickly got too friendly and next thing I knew it had its front paws up on my chest and was slobbering all over my face. "Get down," I commanded firmly. It totally ignored this and continued to drool all over me. Meanwhile, I hadn't noticed that the heavy Rottweiler had sneaked round behind me and it seemed to take great exception to his pal getting too friendly with me. It started growling loudly and clearly wasn't happy at all. I shoved the slobbery one away from me and held up my walking pole threateningly and shouted at them both to stay. I then backed away slowly. The heavy one started barking angrily while the leaner one just seemed confused. Thankfully they stayed put for long enough for me to put a comfortable distance between them and me, although the leaner one did then begin to follow me for a while, as if he couldn't understand why I wasn't his friend anymore. It wasn't a great start to my first day back on the Ireland Way, but I was thankful that it hadn't become any nastier.

I followed the winding paths that led me through Greenfield Nature Park and eventually into the village of Cappawhite, for the second time on my Ireland Way journey. Cappawhite is where the last recorded faction fight took place. Faction fighting was a brutal method of settling disputes between rival gangs in Irish towns and villages during the nineteenth century and often involved the murderous wielding of 'shillelaghs', the Irish blackthorn stick. But the practice was stopped in 1887 when the Russian Buckley, so called because he was "*as big as a Russian*", was killed in the final fight. "*The Fair of Cappawhite is no place for a man with a thin skull*", was apparently the defence put up by another character accused of murder after a Fair in Cappawhite. Keeping an eye out for crazy men with blackthorn sticks, I hurried on out of the village. I almost immediately started climbing into the Red Hills of Slieve Felim and then followed paths over the mountains and between the windmills and forest trees for about eighteen kilometres before dropping down towards the village of Milestone.

I stopped by the side of a road on the edge of the village for a short time, resting on a low stone wall, before climbing over a stile to enter the first of a series of fields. I was in an area known as 'the Golden Vale', which stretches from Tipperary to Limerick and which is known for its rich, rolling pastureland. It is reputed to be the best land in Ireland for dairy farming. So, I realised that, if I was passing through fields, there was a significant chance that I was going to encounter cattle again at some point. And it wasn't long before I did. The route took me right up to a field with a large mixed herd of cows, calves and bulls. Once again Pacman signalled me to follow him through the field. No way! I had learned my lesson. I proceeded to skirt around the field, which wasn't at all easy as it involved getting over or through hedges and fences that weren't meant to be got over or through. And all the while, the herd followed my progress very closely from the other side of the boundary of their field, pushing and shoving at each other to get a better look. They seemed to want to get at me as much as I wanted to stay clear of them! Among the herd, there was one particularly fearsome looking animal – a large brown bull, with a mucus covered chain dangling unattractively from its nose, that roared at me almost constantly. At the other end of the spectrum was a little white calf with the most adorable face and big brown eyes that just seemed filled with curiosity. At one point, I had to climb over a barbed wire fence and drop down into a very long stretch of sand that ran adjacent to the herd's field. I soon realised that I was actually on a circuit used for training race horses. Preferring to take my chances with horses rather than cattle, I hurried along the sand track for a couple of hundred metres before I was able to climb out again and into a neighbouring field clear of any animals whatsoever. Phew!

Back on route, I was eventually led into a beautiful grassy valley, which, from my map, I could see was next to the wonderfully named Knockcurraghbola, from the Irish *Cnoc Corrbhuaile*, meaning 'hill of the mountain dairy'. I obviously wasn't out of cattle territory yet and the presence of numerous electric fences seemed to back this up. However, I could see for quite a distance along the valley in the direction I was headed and, as far as I could tell, it appeared to be cattle free. I relaxed a little - perhaps a little too much! As I was negotiating my way over one of the many electric fences from one field to the next, I had a little tumble. The fence wire was quite high and I had to really stretch my left leg up to step over it. My left foot touched the ground and I was now straddling a wire with I don't know how many volts running through it. This, as you can probably imagine, was quite a critical stage in the process! Using my walking poles to steady myself, I then lifted my right leg high to swing it over the wire also. Unfortunately, I swung my leg a little too fast and I then felt the momentum of my rucksack take over. It seemed to happen in slow motion, but I couldn't arrest the sideways motion of my rucksack and I then found it pulling me backwards and then downwards. I toppled over completely and landed on my back on top of my rucksack. I came to a rest and assessed my situation. No injury and no damage done thankfully - my rucksack had cushioned the fall. I breathed a sigh of relief. But then things became rather farcical. When I went to get up, I found that I couldn't. I leaned to the right - no good! I leaned to the left - no luck! Try as I might, I just couldn't get enough momentum to roll over onto my front. Lying on my back, with my heavy rucksack under me, I now felt that my transformation into a slow tortoise was complete! I lay there trying again and again to get over onto all fours, but only managing to get more exhausted. I undid the chest and waist straps of my rucksack, but found that I couldn't wriggle myself free of it. It felt so ridiculous and I couldn't help laughing at the hopelessness of the situation. I stopped struggling for a minute and thought seriously about my predicament. I finally came up with a solution. Using my feet I swivelled myself around so that I was lying perpendicular to a slight downward slope in the field. This provided me with just enough extra momentum to roll down the slope and get onto my hands and knees and finally onto my feet. Sometimes it was a blessing that the Ireland Way route was so remote and that there was no one around to witness one's less elegant moments! I brushed myself down and continued with my journey as if nothing had happened.

I headed on along the shallow valley, enjoying the pleasant landscape, particularly now that the sunshine was occasionally managing to break through the grey cloud cover. It was a simple joy to watch the shadows of the clouds rushing over the sunlit, patchwork fields on the hills beyond. Three fine looking horses, standing in a neighbouring field, watched me passing by with interest. White butterflies danced ahead of me as I walked through the long grass and, quite suddenly, a family of wrens erupted out of a hedge and provided me with an unexpected, but delightful, surprise. I was only about two kilometres from Upperchurch now and would soon be leaving the fields behind for the day to join the final stretch of roads into the village. I was crossing the last field and my route looked clear of cattle. The boundary between this field and the one next to it was marked by a row of pine trees. I assumed that there would also be a fence line running through the trees, but, when I got closer, I could see that there wasn't and that movement between the two fields was unimpeded. At the same time as noticing this, I also noticed a herd of about a dozen bullocks grazing in the neighbouring field. I froze! What to do now? I could either, keep going and hope that they didn't notice me, or slowly backtrack and look for an alternative route. However, before I even had a chance to decide for myself, some of the herd spotted me and headed straight for me. What is with me and these feckin' bullocks, I thought. A bellow from one soon had the rest of the herd's attention and, once again, I was in a situation that I had absolutely no desire to be in. Trying not to run, I smartly retreated back up the field the way I had come and climbed up onto a raised, earthen mound that ran along the upper side of the field and, along with a hedge on top, formed the boundary of the field on that side. I felt relatively safe up there and, sure enough, the cattle made no attempt to climb up, but simply gathered around to stare up at me from below. I suspected that they knew that they had me trapped. And they had. The other side of the earthen mound dropped down into a deep ditch that was filled with gorse and brambles and it was totally impenetrable. "Feckin bullocks!" I shouted in total frustration at having my journey interrupted by cattle once more. I considered phoning for help. But who on earth do you phone in such a situation? The Garda (police)? Can you be held against your will by cattle and is it a crime, I idly wondered? But I'm sure that the police probably had more important things to deal with, like real crime. Mountain rescue? But, I was no longer in the mountains. The Irish Society for the Prevention of Cruelty to Animals? But it was the animals that were being cruel to a human, not the other way round. Anyway, even if there was someone I could phone for help, what would they think if they knew that a fully grown man was afraid of a few cattle? I decided that it was time to 'man up'. I attached my flag to one of my walking poles and proceeded to march through the herd, waving the flag about me and hollering at the cattle as I went. They followed close behind for the hundred metres or so that I had to go before I ducked under an electric fence. Even then, they continued to follow me alongside the electric fence for the next hundred metres until I reached a lane and they could follow me no further, as their way was barred by a gate. They seemed very put out by this and the noise that followed me down the lane was nothing ordinary. It felt like they were shouting after me, "Come back, you coward. What are you? A man or a mouse?" I was quite happy to scurry, mouse-like, on down the lane.

Ten hours after leaving Cappawhite, I finally arrived into Upperchurch and checked into the Hillview B&B. At thirty-two kilometres, it had been a very long walk and I had travelled much further than I would have preferred, particularly on the first day back after my injury. But, there were no accommodation options between Cappawhite and Upperchurch and, although I still had my tent, which I could have pitched anywhere, I preferred to walk a bit further to secure a proper roof over my head. And, of course, there was the added bonus of Pa's Bar attached to my B&B that served a very decent pint of Guinness. It was great to take the weight off my feet after such a long trek. My soles had complained bitterly for the last few kilometres and still ached a little. However, my right leg had held up very well. I had experienced no discomfort at all in the calf muscle and for that I was very thankful.

****

I woke to a beautiful morning in Upperchurch and, after a modest DIY breakfast, I stepped outside to better take in the unique ambiance of this quaint little village. As the name suggests, the village is centred round the church, a Roman Catholic edifice built in the early 1800's, which dominates the settlement with its pretty Romanesque style facade. But it is the remoteness and tranquillity of the village, resting snugly within the rolling hills of Slieve Felim, that really makes the place, if not unique, then certainly the embodiment of idyllic village life in rural Ireland. I made my way to the post office to post my room key from the Central House B&B back to Gerry Casey in Tipp Town. I had discovered it in my jacket pocket when I was getting my gear ready that morning. I chatted with a few of the friendly locals both inside and outside the post office and was delighted to run into an elderly gentleman called Jim again. I had met him in Kinnane's Bar across the street from where I was staying and he had rustled me up a very tasty pizza for tea, as Pa's Bar didn't serve any food. Jim waved me on my way, as I picked up the road heading north out of the village to begin my day's trek. The next eleven kilometres were both on and off road and it was like being on a slow roller coaster, as a series of undulating hills took me gradually towards the village of Templederry. Sunshine and showers and pleasant rural landscapes were the order of the day and I had lots of encounters with wildlife of all shapes and sizes, including bleating goats, fluttering butterflies, prancing horses, busy bees but, thankfully, absolutely no cattle!

It was a tough, but pretty uneventful hike, apart from the unnecessary battle I had trying to find my way through a thicket near a place marked as Knocknagarve on my map. Here, just before a road junction, a way marker and a stile took me off the road and onto a vague path that then followed alongside the adjoining road. Fair enough, I thought, the route is keeping me off the road – that's a good thing. But after walking for a couple of hundred metres, the path started to become very overgrown. I persisted for as far as I could, my walking poles now deployed as beaters to fight my way through the brambles and nettles. However, I gradually reached a point where further progress would have been impossible without a machete or a chainsaw and I had to give up and make my way back to the stile. I then followed the road that ran right alongside the overgrown track, which I had just wasted so much time trying to fight my way through. A little adjustment to the route was clearly required here. I learned that Knocknagarve was from the Irish *Cnoc na nGarbh*, meaning "the rough hill". It was indeed very well named.

Later, as I was walking down a quiet rural road on the outskirts of Templederry, I spotted the top of a man's head bobbing along above the hedge of a nearby lane. At first I thought that it might be Donal Cam coming to share the next instalment of his story with me. But it turned out that the head belonged to someone who was very much alive. The lane joined the road and it so happened that we both reached the junction at exactly the same time. The man was a local farmer called Joe who had just been out checking on some of his cattle in a neighbouring field. We walked alongside each other for a while chatting about the weather and what impact the heat wave had had on farming. Depleted winter supplies of fodder was the main impact, as farmers had had to supplement the meagre grazing on offer in the parched fields with supplies normally held over for the winter. The worry now was that farmers might not have enough winter supplies to last and would have to buy in extra, which would obviously come at a cost. I then thought that I should take advantage of my chance encounter with a cattle farmer and I asked Joe about how best to walk through a field of cattle. I had kind of expected his first answer, which was, "Don't." But he then went on to say what to do if you had no choice. And I then learned that waving my flag and shouting as I walked through the field was totally the wrong thing to do. Apparently the cattle think that this is great fun and believe that you want to play with them. It only serves to get them excited – and when they get excited, they become unpredictable. The best thing to do is to walk unhurriedly and quietly through the field, keeping an eye on the beasts but not attempting to engage with them in any way. I wish I had known this before setting off on my Ireland Way. By this time we had reached Joe's house and he asked me if I fancied a cup of tea. I had been planning to stop for a break in Templederry anyway, so I took him up on his offer and followed him into his bungalow, where I was introduced to his wife Teresa and his two daughters. As I had found out when I had met Nick and his cycling group on the way to Galbally a number of weeks back, a 'cup of tea' in Ireland does not simply mean 'a cup of tea'. It was at least an hour later before I was waving goodbye to Joe and his family, having enjoyed a very tasty omelette with new potatoes, followed by cheesecake and a mug of coffee! And, luckily, the heaviest downpour of the day had occurred while I was inside enjoying the hospitality!

The onward thirteen kilometre walk to Toomevara started off well, with a very pleasant path following close to the banks of the Nenagh River for the first half. I came to a bridge over the river and stopped to study the map. I could either follow the official route marked on the map, which would take me on a long five kilometre loop, or cross the bridge and follow the road and get to the same point after only one kilometre. My resolve started to weaken. Four kilometres of a difference – that was at least an hour and a half of walking. My right calf muscle was still holding up very well, but the soles of my feet were beginning to feel quite sore. My resolve weakened yet further. I looked in the direction of the official route and saw a herd of cattle grazing in the second field I would be required to pass through. What remained of my resolve disappeared in an instant. So, for the first time on my

Ireland Way challenge, I took a shortcut. It played on my mind for a time. Was this cheating? Will I be able to claim that I had walked the entire Ireland Way if I deliberately skipped a bit out? However, this self-reproach did not last for long. The remainder of the journey was on rural roads and quickly became a real slog and my feet felt each and every step. I was so glad that I hadn't made things worse by adding a seemingly pointless loop onto my journey and having to pass through at least one field of cattle in the process. And I had more than made up for my shortcut through all the accidental detours I had already taken – and undoubtedly there would be more detours to come! I passed a wooden sign by the roadside, the top half of which was broken off and missing and the remaining bottom half simply reading "*Castle*". I looked through a tumbled down gap in the stone wall behind the sign and, sure enough, there in a field were the overgrown remains of a castle tower. Less than one hundred metres further up the road, I came to Latteragh Graveyard and the ruins of Latteragh Parish Church, which were a short distance in from a layby at the side of the road. Another wooden sign, unbroken this time and fixed to a wall, read "*St Odhran's Monastery and Graveyard*". I paused here to rest my sore feet for a while. As I was leaning against the wall, looking over towards the ivy shrouded ruins of the church resting among the ancient tombstones, I heard the familiar voice of Donal Cam beside me.

"So you decided to come back then," he said, in a slightly mocking fashion. "I thought that maybe you had 'given up the ghost'," he added, laughing at his own wit, as he was prone to do, before asking, "what on earth happened?"

I had been anticipating running into Donal Cam since passing through Templederry, so his sudden appearance did not come as a complete surprise. "Well, remember you told me about your path being blocked beyond Donohill by the Earl of Ormonde's men?"

"I certainly do," he replied, "and I also remember telling you of how we attacked them and scared them off."

"Well, I had my path blocked just beyond Donohill also. Not by an army of men, but by a herd of bullocks. And instead of me attacking them, they attacked me! In my efforts to get out of their way, I tore the calf muscle in my right leg. I had to stop walking for four weeks to allow it to heal. But now I'm back and determined to finish my challenge."

"That's the spirit," said Donal Cam.

"No, you're the spirit," I quickly responded.

"Oh, very droll," he said with a groan.

"You have taught me well, my Prince," I said and gave him a slight bow and a broad grin.

"Enough, enough," he cried, pretending to be affronted. "Anyway, it's good to see you back on the road. The last time we met, I finished by telling you that we had a disastrous episode close to here." I nodded and he continued, "It actually happened on the other side of Templederry, as we were coming off the Slieve Felim mountains. Although we had successfully raided the food stores at Donohill and managed to eat and take some of the beans and grain with us, many of our party were still bitterly pinched with hunger. As we were coming down off the hills it was growing dark and we spotted the glow of fires off to one side. Thinking that they might be the camp fires of unarmed locals and that there might be booty and food to be captured, I decided to send two of my Connacht captains, Thomas Burke and Daniel O'Malley, with sixty men to investigate and carry out a raid if possible. They veered off towards the camp and the rest of us continued down the slopes towards the plains of the Nenagh River. Unfortunately, Burke and O'Malley stumbled upon, not a camp of unarmed natives, but a camp of well-armed enemy soldiers. Who they belonged to - the White Knight, Ormonde or another lord loyal to the Queen – I don't know, but my scouting party got too close before they realised the danger they were in. The military encampment had posted guards around the perimeter of the camp and Burke and O'Malley's men were spotted as they approached. The guards quickly alerted the rest of the camp and the enemy soldiers launched a ferocious attack on my men, who were taken completely by surprise. The first I was aware of it was when the sound of enemy muskets being discharged rang out around the hills. My raiding party carried no muskets, only swords, pike and daggers, and I knew immediately that they were in great peril. I called the rest of my fighting men together and we rushed to help our comrades. We met Thomas Burke and his men fleeing from the camp towards us. Thomas said that he had been captured by the enemy and stripped of his weapons, but had managed to break free and escape. He urged me and the rest of our rescue party to turn back immediately, saying that there were far too many of the enemy to engage with. So our rescue party and the remnants of the raiding party returned to re-join the civilians we had abandoned and we made haste towards the Nenagh plains. Thankfully the enemy must have considered it unwise to leave their camp and pursue us in the darkness, but we lost twenty men, including Daniel O'Malley, in that disastrous raid. Eventually we were able to make it to the relative safety of these ruins of St Odhran's Church here in Latteragh."

"You seem to have been drawn to churches and other holy sites on your exodus," I suggested.

"My faith has always been very dear to me and I suppose I also had the hope that such sites might provide my people with some protection; some sanctuary from our assailants. It wasn't to be the case on this occasion, however! Did you notice the castle ruins across the road a little way back?"

"I did, although the sign was in as bad a shape as the castle," I replied.

"It was Latteragh Castle and although the church was in ruins when we sheltered here, the castle was not. It was a well garrisoned fortress belonging to the de Marisco family and its inhabitants were none too friendly towards us. Thankfully, they didn't launch an all-out attack, but they annoyed us the whole night by firing at us from the castle ramparts and by occasional sallies of the garrison. The church was small, but its ruined walls provided us with some shelter from the weather and the muskets. We couldn't let down our guard though and I posted sentries to patrol the perimeter and we kept our swords drawn and our own muskets ready. As well as the enemy in the castle, the sentries reported that another larger enemy force had gathered not far from our camp and we feared attack from them throughout the night. But it wasn't until we were breaking camp at dawn the following morning that the enemy really sprang into action. A storm of red-hot musket balls blazed upon us as we were leaving.

This was becoming a daily salutation with which the enemy honoured us; a farewell as we drew off in the morning; a greeting as we turned up at night. Throughout the whole day, my rear column was continually engaged in fighting and some fell on both sides. Yet again, we simply had to leave our men where they fell as we rushed ahead of the attacking Royalists. Needless to say, we were at a great disadvantage, being a party of weary and wounded soldiers and civilians against a fresh and staid enemy. Nevertheless, the enemy forces remained cautious; canny even. Whenever we halted and turned to face them, the enemy fled, but as soon as we advanced again they quickly pursued and rained down missiles upon us. It was only when darkness fell again that the fighting, at last, came to an end for the day. By that stage we had reached an abandoned monastery close to the O'Kennedy's tower house at Lackeen. The O'Kennedy clan neither harassed nor helped us on our journey and I could live with that. Here we found some peace for a few hours, before setting off north again on 6th January to face what was to be our greatest opponent yet – the mighty River Shannon!"

"Was there no bridge across the river?" I asked in all innocence.

"There was a ford at Shannonbridge, but it was much further north and I reckoned that it would have been heavily guarded anyway. The Shannon was mainly crossed by ferry and at this stage we still hoped to be able to hire or steal a few boats to make our way across under the cover of darkness. However, when I sent a few scouts ahead to commandeer some boats, they reported back that the Queen's sheriff, Donagh MacEgan at Redwood Castle, had had all the boats removed and had threatened all the ferrymen in the area to ensure that no-one would help us. When we got closer to the banks of the Shannon, we concealed ourselves in the thick and secure wood of Brosna and tried to figure out our next move. We seemed to have landed ourselves in a very tight corner, hemmed in between MacEgan's forces and the wide River Shannon, with no means of crossing. Everyone's heart was filled with a great despair."

"My God," I exclaimed, "it must have seemed like the end of the road."

"It did, for a time," Donal Cam said sadly, but then winked as he added, "but we weren't finished yet. And that was largely thanks to my uncle, Dermot O'Sullivan, who at a stroke came up with a solution that would allow us both to cross the Shannon and also help satisfy our soldiers' need for food. My uncle Dermot was a truly remarkable man."

"What's in a name, eh?" I asked, jokingly.

"Ha, my uncle was nearly in his seventies and a fearless warrior," he proclaimed proudly.

"Well, I'm in my fifties and a fearless walker," I countered.

"There are some bullocks in a field near Donohill that might disagree," Donal Cam said with a guffaw.

"Feck off!" I said, pretending to be offended.

"Only jesting," he replied. He went to slap me on the back in a jovial sort of way, but his hand simply passed through me.

We both laughed at this and then I asked, "Well are you going to tell me of my namesake's bright idea, or not?"

"Oh, I certainly shall, but all in good time. Let's wait until you cross the Shannon yourself."

"Okay, but if you don't mind, I'm going to use the bridge at Portumna. It's a bit of a diversion, but I think it will be worth it to keep my feet dry."

"Seems like a bright idea also. Maybe there is something in the name," he said, smiling again and, as he began to fade away, he added, "I'll see you on the other side."

"I hope you're still talking about the river," I said, but he had already gone. I pushed myself off the outer wall of Latteragh graveyard that I had been leaning against and set off once again.

I still had another seven kilometres to go before I reached Toomevara and, by the time I got there, I could go no further. My calf muscle had continued to give me no bother at all, but the soles of my feet were a different matter. They felt like someone had been repeatedly beating them with a big stick for several hours. I called into the Tipperary Inn to ask if there was anywhere in the village that offered B&B (or even just B), but there wasn't. However, the owner John said I could pitch my tent on a patch of ground behind the premises and use the facilities in the bar. It was another twelve kilometres to the next village of Cloughjordan, so I was happy to accept his offer, even though I wasn't that keen on getting under the canvas again. John showed me out back to a grassy area beside some outhouses and left me to pitch my tent. It was a lovely evening and so, once I had everything set up, I relaxed with a cup of coffee while sitting in the shade out of the sun and allowing my feet to rest. Later I made my way back to the bar for my customary pint and enjoyed a nice dinner there also, while chatting with some of the locals and accepting their generosity in the form of drinks and donations. I could so easily have sat on and enjoyed the craic, but I reluctantly dragged myself away, before it got too late or I became too merry, and headed out to my airbed for the night.

****

Maybe I should have stayed up drinking into the wee small hours after all. I had endured another restless night under the canvas. I wasn't sure why. I had certainly been tired enough, comfortable enough and warm enough, but nevertheless sleep had eluded me. I was going to get up and move on at about 5:30am, but then the rain came on. Nothing heavy, but sufficient for me to stay put and await its passing. I eventually got on the road two hours later under very grey skies that remained obstinately overcast for the duration of today's short walk. However, it stayed dry and fairly cool and so walking conditions were quite comfortable.

A pleasant but unremarkable journey ensued through fairly flat countryside that took me over farm lanes, empty fields and rural roads. However, my right foot became rather sore after a few kilometres and this convinced me to cut today's walk short. So rather than walking the planned twenty-four kilometres to Ballingarry, I decided to stop after only twelve kilometres in Cloughjordan and check into the Django Hostel in the Cloughjordan Ecovillage. I arrived at just after 11am and was warmly welcomed by Pa Finucane, the hostel manager, who gave me a quick tour of the facilities and showed me to my room. It was so nice to get in early, get the boots off and have a refreshing shower after having camped out the night before. I later discovered the lovely little *Sheelagh na Gig* bookshop/coffee shop in the village, which was the perfect place to relax and rest my weary feet for a few hours. Here I discovered that Cloughjordan was from the Irish *Cloch Shiurdáin*, meaning 'Jordan's stone'. The story goes that Geoffrey de Marisco, who was a Norman Knight, travelled to the Holy Lands to take part in the Crusades in the thirteenth century. He is said to have brought back a stone from the River Jordan, which he built in over the doorway of his castle in this very village and it was from that stone that the village got its name. This was the same de Marisco family that had owned the castle at Latteragh, where O'Sullivan Beare's party had been harassed throughout the night in January 1603.

****

The following morning, I woke to the realisation that it was the first day of August. Nothing special about that, you might think. It was just another date. Just another day. Just another twenty-four little hours. Except that it wasn't. It was a very special date for me. For it was on this very day, thirty-one years before, that Jacqui and I had both said "I do" and agreed to love one and other "till death us do part". And we did. For twenty-eight wonderful years. And then cancer visited us and wreaked havoc on our lives, ending Jacqui's life and changing mine forever. When I had started my walk back in June, I had hoped to finish on this very day, the anniversary of our wedding. But that plan had gone totally awry in a field north of Tipperary Town thanks to a herd of bullocks.

Initially, I had been really disappointed to have had my carefully planned schedule disrupted in such an unceremonious fashion. But since then, I had tried to convince myself that, actually, the date wasn't really that important. Any date, after all, is just an arbitrary moment in time, labelled by us humans in an attempt to bring some order and structure to the infinite spinning of this planet we call home. So, I continued to tell myself that the timing of my finishing was not really that important at all. It would have been nice to finish on our special date, but ultimately it wasn't critical. Jacqui certainly wouldn't mind! But the place - now that was an entirely different matter. The place, Ballycastle, where the Ireland Way ends, was the very reason why I had chosen to do this particular walk. The challenge had always been about walking to Jacqui's hometown - to her resting place, under the watch of Knocklayde Mountain and Fair Head. And that was what I still intended to do, no matter how long it took me – both me and the folded pages in my pocket, which I still carried with me like some sort of comforter.

So off I set from the Django Hostel and wound my way through the unique houses and garden allotments of the Cloughjordan Ecovillage. Pa had filled me in on the concept behind the eco-village the night before. This was the first and, to date, only ecovillage in Ireland and was established in 2010 as part of the Global Ecovillage Network aimed at promoting and encouraging sustainable living. The Cloughjordan Ecovillage is situated on sixty-seven acres within the older village of Cloughjordan itself and includes one hundred and thirty low-energy homes, a solar and wood powered community heating system, land for growing food and trees, an enterprise centre and community buildings, including a hostel for visitors such as myself. It was a highly admirable project and appeared, from what I could see, to be a great success. The interestingly designed houses and the variety of crops being produced certainly made for a pleasant start to my day's walk, even though it was under a blanket of grey cloud cover. The sky threatened rain and, after about an hour, it delivered good on its threat and the rest of my walk was through constant and sometimes very heavy rainfall. But, I didn't mind that much. I had my rain gear on and it was a relatively short walk of thirteen kilometres today. And given the significance of the date, the weather seemed appropriate and perhaps matched my mood more than I was prepared to admit.

Most of the route between Cloughjordan and my destination of Ballingarry was on road, except for a couple of kilometres of lanes and tracks through Laghile Wood and a kilometre through a number of fields. It was almost inevitable that I was going to run into some cattle and, sure enough, it wasn't too long before I spotted a herd of twenty-five or more bullocks. I picked up a large branch off the ground to carry with me as a precautionary measure. I had forgotten to take my walking poles with me as I was leaving the hostel that morning and I felt a little vulnerable without them. I then proceeded through the field. The herd followed me all the way across the field and even rushed at me a few times. However, having listened to the advice of Joe, the farmer from Templederry, I remained as cool as a cucumber and just strolled casually on, gently chasing the cattle back whenever necessary. The branch also made crossing the electric fences a little easier, as I was able to use it to push the wire down a bit before stepping over. It helped prevent any nasty, unwanted shocks.

When I emerged out of the fields to join the roads again, I stopped in the rain for a time to watch in almost total mesmerisation, as a flock of swallows swooped and turned in the shelter under the canopy of a very large ash tree. I suspected that the insects, on which the swallows were feasting, were also sheltering from the rain under the tree's canopy. Just over two kilometres of country roads brought me first past Ballingarry Church and then into the village itself. By the time I reached my destination for the day, the rain had finally eased and I was fortunate to be able to hitch a lift with a Brazilian man into the town of Borrisokane. From here, I believed that it would be easier to pick up a lift back to Cloughjordan, where I was planning to stay a second night in the Django Hostel.

While in Borrisokane, I stopped for lunch in The Country Kitchen. The owner, Michelle, proudly told me that she had read about my walk. When I went to pay for my lunch, Michelle wouldn't take anything from me and instead she handed me a very generous donation. I then walked out of town a bit on the road heading towards Cloughjordan. I was glad that the weather had improved because I was left standing by the roadside for half an hour or more before a gentleman finally stopped to pick me up. He introduced himself as Liam Hafferty and told me that he had stopped because he had recognised me from the Tipperary Inn in Toomevara when I had been there a couple of nights before! It seemed like I was becoming famous in this part of the world! Liam drove me all the way back to Cloughjordan and also gave me a donation when he dropped me off, practically at the door of the Django Hostel.

I stepped into the wonderful hostel once again at the same time as Pa, who had just returned from walking his dog – a large, hairy and very friendly cross-breed called Django. I felt that it was time to ask Pa about where the name Django had come from, given that both the hostel and his dog bore the unusual name. I had only heard it used before in relation to a 2012 Tarantino Western, 'Django Unchained'. However, Pa informed me that it had nothing to do with the western, but was after Jean 'Django' Reinhardt, a very talented French jazz guitarist popular in the 1930's and 40's. Pa played guitar also and greatly admired the music of Django Reinhardt, which was subsequently reflected in the name of his hostel and his dog. I asked him if he had called anything else after Django, but he just laughed and instead told me that he and a few friends would be getting together later in the hostel to rehearse for a gig coming up the following week and that I was very welcome to listen in if I wished. So, after visiting the local chip shop for the second night running to acquire another unhealthy tea, I joined Pa and his eclectic group in the sitting area of the hostel. Here I enjoyed being serenaded by the unusual but very harmonious sound of guitar, ukulele and double bass, accompanied by the smooth voice of the group's female lead singer, as they played the Beatles 'Come Together' and other classics. It was thoroughly enjoyable and a very soothing way to end my day of mixed emotions.

Later, before going to sleep, I recalled the words I had written on this day one year before.

Happy Anniversary

Though we didn't make the thirty years
I don't want it marked with any tears
We can't exchange gifts made of pearl
Instead I'll remember the green-eyed girl
Who captured my heart all those years ago
And made me happier than you'll ever know
So here's to us, even though you're gone
For in truth, life is short and love is long

Chapter Eight: Shannon Crossing
(Days nineteen to twenty-one - Ballingarry to Aughrim)

After two nights in the superb Django Hostel, it was time to leave Cloughjordan. I said farewell to Pa and also Brian, a long-term guest at the hostel and volunteer at the ecovillage, and received generous donations from them both. I had arranged a taxi the previous evening and Pat showed up right on time and drove me to Ballingarry and dropped me at the location I had walked to the previous day. Pat only charged me half fare when he learned that I was walking for cancer research.

From Ballingarry, five kilometres of a straight, flat, country road brought me to the edge of the village of Aglish. Here, the route turned sharply east, before turning north again and following another six kilometres of rural roads to the substantial ruins of Lackeen Castle, a sixteenth century tower house that was once a stronghold of the O'Kennedy clan. I recalled that Donal Cam had told me that it was close to Lackeen Castle that he and his followers had camped before moving on to cross the River Shannon. Folklore also tells of an O'Kennedy from Lackeen Castle who was one of the few men to have ever caught a 'Pooka', a fairy shape shifter, capable of assuming a variety of terrifying forms. Apparently the Pooka cursed and swore the whole way back to the castle and shouted "*If you dare to bring me into your castle, I'll burn you all with my breath and you'll be truly gone to the blazes!*" O'Kennedy's servant, fearing the unnatural powers of the Pooka, pleaded with his master to set the creature free. Eventually O'Kennedy listened to the advice of his servant and let the Pooka go, but first made it promise that it would harm no breed, seed or generation of the O'Kennedy family. Apparently, over the years many people have seen the shapes of otherworldly goats lurking about Lackeen Castle. I saw only a few small calves wandering around the grounds looking entirely innocent, although I have to say that the grey stone of the imposing tower house made for quite a foreboding image under the grey clouds that ominously darkened the sky above.

A short distance beyond the castle, the route required me to leave the road for the first time today and pass through a number of fields. Checking my map, I could see that I could easily avoid the fields by staying on the road and that I would meet up with the route again after about a kilometre and that it was roughly the same distance either way. However, I was feeling more relaxed about potentially walking through fields of cattle now and so I followed the official route and climbed over the stile into the first meadow. There were no cattle, but I passed a single gable wall of stone standing alone, about four metres above a thicket in which it was partially hidden. It had a single narrow arched window in its centre, which marked it out as clearly having been a church of some sort. Given its proximity to Lackeen Castle, I presumed that this was where O'Sullivan Beare had camped with his followers. A couple of fields further on and I had my own followers. A large herd of Friesian bullocks followed me the whole way across a long meadow, as if I was some kind of Pied Piper of the bovine world. There were at least thirty in this herd – they seemed to be getting larger every time! As I proceeded across their territory, they became bolder and came closer, particularly any time my back was turned on them. They reminded me of how Donal Cam had described his attackers between Latteragh and Lackeen, "*Whenever we halted and turned to face them, the enemy fled, but as soon as we advanced again they quickly pursued.....*" They even encircled me at times, but I just kept moving forward and they, thankfully, continued to move out of the way. When I finally reached the metal stile at the end of the field, I climbed onto it and sat at the top to see how close the cattle might actually come. They all remained very wary of me and kept a couple of metres back, except for one bold fellow who eventually came close enough to sniff my outstretched hand.

I emerged from the fields again and, after following a long, grassy path though Lorrha Bog, I arrived into the small village of Lorrha itself. I stopped here at St Ruadhán's Heritage Centre and Tea Room for a very welcome rest and a pot of tea to have along with my own meagre food supplies. Despite all the road walking, my feet were not as sore as they had been in previous days, but I nevertheless relished the opportunity to leave my boots at the door of the centre and relax in my sock soles for a time. I was the only visitor and Bridget, the lady looking after the centre, insisted that I make myself comfortable. On enquiring about the centre's name, Bridget informed me that it was named after Ruadhán, a Christian abbot, who founded a monastery in Lorrha in the year 540, although the ruins of St Ruadhán's Abbey date from around the eleventh century. She then went on to tell me proudly that St Ruadhán's was only one of three abbeys in the village, as there was also a twelfth century Augustine Abbey and a thirteenth century Dominican Abbey. I enjoyed relaxing in the centre and chatting to Bridget to such an extent that, by the time I had finished my tea and pulled on my boots again, I no longer had the time nor, I'm ashamed to say, the inclination to explore Lorrha's undoubted rich ecclesiastical history. And the route unfortunately turned me away from the village before I could get a glimpse of even one of its three abbeys.

About one kilometre out of Lorrha, I came upon the overgrown remains of the stone abutment of an old railway bridge. This was one of the few remaining visible clues to the fact that, between 1868 and 1878, the Parsonstown and Portumna Bridge Railway ran through here. Bridget had also told me a little about this railway over my tea break in Lorrha and had said to look out for the old abutment. It became known as "The Stolen Railway" and has been described as Ireland's biggest commercial railway failure, apparently making a huge loss and closing after only ten years of operation. Some of the rails were successfully sold off at auction, but practically everything else that could be taken – the remaining metal rails, the wooden sleepers, the stone ballast and even the station building in Portumna – was stolen by locals far and wide and used in farm lanes and buildings, hence the name "The Stolen Railway". At this point, the Ireland Way route was supposed to leave the road and follow the bed of the old railway line for a time, but that way was blocked and so I continued to follow the road instead, which took me in a northwest direction. Ever since passing Lackeen Castle, my direction of travel had been more westerly than northerly, as the route veered towards

Portumna and the bridge that would see me safely over the River Shannon. Donal Cam and his followers had little choice at this stage but to keep heading north and finding some other means of crossing the wide expanse of water that stood between them and County Galway. I soon joined the busy R489 and later the even busier N65 into Portumna, catching the occasional glimpse of the mighty River Shannon to my right as I proceeded. On the outskirts of Portumna, I finally crossed over the wide river via the 'swing bridge' that pivots open at certain times of the day to allow larger boats to pass along the navigation channel. Thankfully it was closed to boats and open to cars and pedestrians when I arrived. From here it was still over a kilometre into the town centre.

It had remained very overcast but dry for most of the day, but it started to rain just as I came into town. I quickly pulled on my black cape to deflect the worst of the rain and made my way to The Cottage Store on St Brendan's Street, which was run by Celine and Gerry Byrne. Celine had been following my progress on social media and had offered to help - and help she certainly did! In fact, she and Gerry really pulled out all the stops to ensure that my stay in Portumna would be a memorable one. They had arranged wonderful free accommodation for me, treated me out to a lovely meal in a French restaurant and, knowing my fondness for Guinness at the end of each day's walk, brought me to a great little local bar and ordered me a pint of the black stuff. Here they introduced me to a few of the locals, including Jim Hynes, a reporter for The Connaught Tribune newspaper, who was very interested in covering my story!

****

I woke the following morning feeling both refreshed and truly blessed. The apartment I had stayed in, courtesy of Johanna, a friend of Celine and Gerry's, was wonderfully spacious and comfortable. I reflected on the kindness, generosity and hospitality that had been shown to me over the time that I had been walking the Ireland Way. People, who I had never met before, simply reached out to me and offered their help in whatever way they could. It was truly humbling and I was really touched by the level of love and support that people had for me. I liked to think that Jacqui's great capacity for love was somehow continuing to manifest itself through the love shown to me by others. Perhaps such a love never really dies, but continues on as a sort of life force, coursing through our collective beings and giving succour to whoever needs it. I was very thankful to have known Jacqui and to have had her love for so many years. I desperately missed having her around, but it was comforting to imagine that somehow her love still found its way to me.

I made my way from the apartment, which was just off Clonfert Avenue, and walked the short distance to meet Thomas Kelly in Blas Restaurant. Thomas was another good friend of Celine and Gerry's and Celine had arranged for me to meet him over breakfast. Originally from Belleek in Northern Ireland, Thomas had lived and worked in California for many years before deciding to retire and settle back in Ireland. His family had connections to Portumna and when he visited to check it out as a possible place for his retirement, he fell in love with the place and its people. After spending less than 24 hours here myself that was something I could already entirely understand. The wonderful owner of Blas Restaurant, Majella Foley, served me a great breakfast, which was on the house. As I ate, Thomas told me a little more about the town, about its seventeenth century castle, its forest park, the Irish Workhouse Centre and the fact that the town marked the point where the River Shannon opened out into Lough Derg. We were soon joined by Celine and reporter Jim Hynes. It was a very sociable and friendly gathering and I also picked up a few more donations into the bargain.

Celine then gave me a lift to the Irish Workhouse Centre on the outskirts of town to get my Ireland Way passport stamped. Here I also had a quick look at an Irish Famine Exhibition, called 'Dark Shadows'. The incredibly haunting figures, some life size and all carved from black bog oak, certainly brought home in stark relief the despair and horror of that dreadful period. The figures depicted were not so much of people, but more of shadows of people. The display brought to mind once again the shocking statistics revealed to me at St John's Famine Graveyard in Tipperary. We returned to town, where I collected my rucksack from the apartment, and then Celine and Thomas dropped me at the starting point for the day's walk, not far from the swing bridge I had crossed the evening before. After hugs and handshakes, they waved me off and I began the next leg of my journey along the northern bank of the River Shannon. From here, the route essentially followed the top of a grassy embankment that ran, almost uninterrupted, for sixteen kilometres to a small marina near the village of Meelick. The rain from the previous evening had disappeared, leaving a cloudy, but nonetheless bright and warm morning that made for easy going along this flat and pleasant section. It was quite a delightful riverside walk and more than once I paused to wave back to the boat people casually cruising up river or to admire the graceful swans even more casually drifting downstream. I came across a family of swans at one stage and it was a real treat to see the two magnificently regal white parents watching over their brood of five terribly awkward grey 'ugly ducklings'. Often the reeds and bulrushes were growing so tall on the riverbanks that the water of the river was not visible, creating the illusion that the boats were sailing through fields of long grass. At other times I had an uninterrupted view across the wide expanse of the river to the far bank. I couldn't quite grasp how O'Sullivan Beare and his followers had managed to cross it back in 1603, when the river was much wider and it was in the depths of mid-winter.

I was standing, dreamily watching a large cruiser powering upstream, its wake disturbing the calm waters in its path, when a voice beside me said, with a sigh, "Ah, if only we had had one of those back then, things would have been so much easier." I had had a strange feeling that Donal Cam might make an appearance around this time and I said as much to my intermittent companion, as we both continued to watch the boat round the next bend of the river. I was, after all, close to the place where he and his remaining followers had struggled ashore after facing one of their toughest challenges to date. It was also, to my mind anyway, one of the most amazing tales of tenacity and ingenuity associated with the whole O'Sullivan Beare saga. Turning to face him, I said, "Why don't you tell me all about it." He looked at me for a moment, as if weighing up something in his mind, and then he replied, "I think I can do much better than that. I can show you." And with that the sky darkened, the temperature dropped dramatically and the river banks drew away from each other so that the stretch of water between them became even wider.

Suddenly I was in a wood on the opposite bank of the Shannon and all around me were the most wretched looking souls, sitting or lying in filthy looking rags and looking totally despondent. I only realised that my companion was still by my side when he said, "By the time we had reached the Redwood bank of the river, our numbers were depleted by hardship, hunger, and by constant attack. Every heart was filled with giant despair." I became aware of a chilling sound coming from beyond the trees. It sounded like a number of horses in great distress. Donal Cam noticed the questioning look in my eyes and said, "Come and see." I followed him through the woods in the direction of the blood curdling noise and, as we drew nearer, it suddenly dawned on me what was happening. A number of men were desperately holding onto the reins of about eight horses between them. The horses were clearly frightened and struggling to get free of their captors, whinnying anxiously and pulling back and forth against their reins; ears flicking and the whites of their eyes clearly showing. And a short distance away in a clearing, the reason for their distress was all too apparent. For here lying sprawled in a hollow, and in the most grotesque arrangement, were the bodies of at least three horses in a thick porridge of blood and dirt. As I watched, a forth animal was having a knife drawn across its neck as it kicked and reared and whinnied in terror against the men restraining it. An unbelievable eruption of blood gushed from the horse's neck, adding to the gruesome porridge below, and its legs suddenly buckled as it folded in the most ungainly fashion to the ground beside the other carcasses. Its legs continued to spasm for a time, but gradually its hopeless fight to cling onto life dissipated and the beast became still, while the blood continued to flow from its ghastly wound. In agonising contrast, the remaining eight animals fought and reared even more wildly, and then yet another one was dragged forward to the slaughtering pit. "I have watched this scene replayed so many times over the centuries and yet it still chills my blood," Donal Cam said sadly, leaning in close to my ear to be heard over the pitiful noise. "I believe this place is now known as *Poll na Copall*, 'the hole of the horses', and it still sickens me to the pit of my stomach. Come," he went on, "we've seen enough of this horror." He headed back through the woods and I stumbled after him and finally managed to find my voice. "What the hell was that all about? Why were they killing the horses?" Donal Cam charged on in front of me and, without even looking back, he growled, "You'll see soon enough."

We emerged from the trees at the edge of the wood, now only a short distance from the bank of the river. Here a team of about ten men were hard at work hacking and shaping at the trunks and branches of felled trees. Others were securing rough planks of wood together with thin willow branches to form a large skeletal frame about eight metres long. "They're building a boat," announced Donal Cam, with a distinct air of pride in his voice. "My people were trapped here in a seemingly impossible position. The Sherriff MacEgan had threatened anyone coming to our assistance, or even allowing a boat to fall into our hands, with immediate death. As a result we were marooned on this side of the Shannon. But then my uncle, Dermot, came up with the idea of building a boat. Luckily we had a boat builder in our party, who was skilled in the construction of currachs, and under his direction we were able to construct this boat frame. The horses you saw being slaughtered in the woods were to provide the skins necessary to cover the frame. They also provided much needed meat to keep my people alive, although I myself could never stoop to eating horse flesh. It really pained me to order the animals slaughtered, but I had no choice. If the horses hadn't been sacrificed, we would surely all have died at the hands of Donagh MacEgan." I could see how, even now, after all the years that had passed, Donal Cam still felt it necessary to justify some of his actions. I suppose that great leaders are often filled with doubt over the life and death decisions they are forced to make; they wouldn't be human otherwise. It was bizarre to see another Donal Cam O'Sullivan Beare striding about the works, providing encouragement and even lending a hand on occasions. This O'Sullivan Beare was very different from my dandy companion. He was pale and gaunt, dressed in grubby garments and looked like he hadn't slept in days, which he probably hadn't. My companion and I were merely observers from another time and, while we could see these renegades from more than four hundred years ago, they were clearly unaware of our presence. Another group of men were busy constructing a second, much smaller boat. It had a circular bottom, like a shield, with high sides and looked more like a coracle and, even to my untrained eye, looked totally unsuitable for crossing a wide and fast flowing river. "God help them," sighed Donal Cam - not for the first time I imagined, "that's the Connacht men's effort, under the direction of the O'Malleys. A proud seafaring clan, but they hadn't a clue when it came to rivers. Doomed to failure, I'm afraid."

"Two days it took us to construct our boats and in that time MacEgan stayed hidden in Redwood Castle, not far from here," continued my guide. "He certainly couldn't have failed to notice that we were here, what with us cutting down trees, burning fires and butchering our horses. For a time, I believed that he might have been content to leave us be. He had done his duty by his Queen and ensured that we were offered no help by the locals. Perhaps he would turn a blind eye to us, his fellow Irishmen, struggling to find our own way across the Shannon. But I now know that the cowardly blaggard was simply biding his time and waiting for an opportune moment to strike."

Suddenly, the scene before me changed. It was as if someone had pressed the fast forward or skip button on our replay of history. Night had fallen, but there was just enough light from the quarter moon to see by. Both boats, now finished and covered with the horse hides, were being carried on men's shoulders down to the river's edge. It was bitterly cold and the breath of the men misted before them as they struggled to carry their heavy loads into the muddy shallows of the Shannon. The boats were set in the water, amongst the reeds, and about thirty of O'Sullivan Beare's soldiers climbed into the bigger boat and pushed away from the bank. The few remaining horses were also led into the water and they swam behind the bigger boat, their reins tied to the stern. Ten of O'Malley's men crowded into the smaller round boat and they too pushed off, but almost immediately it started to spin in the current. The Connaught men tried desperately to control it with their paddles, but the boat was swept away in the strong current. Panic ensued and the boat suddenly overturned and the ten men, weighed down by their heavy cloaks, all quickly disappeared beneath the surface of the dark, icy waters never to be seen again. The shape of the currach type vessel allowed it to fare much better and, after a time, the oarsmen managed to row it successfully over the quarter mile wide stretch of water to reach the opposite bank. The soldiers disembarked and the boat was rowed back to pick up another group. This was repeated many times and by daybreak most of the soldiers were on the far bank. "I had judged it best to ferry the majority of my soldiers across first," said Donal Cam, with a heavy heart, "leaving just a handful of fighting men behind to protect the civilians, until they too could be transported across. It was what that coward MacEgan had been waiting for."

The air around me suddenly erupted with the sound of musket fire, the whistling of lead and the screaming of the civilians. O'Sullivan Beare's people had been patiently waiting with their belongings to be ferried across the river, but they now scattered as Donogh MacEgan and his troops attacked them without mercy. The troops fired into the crowd and used brute force to drive the terror stricken women of the group towards the river, hoping to drown them in the swirling waters. O'Sullivan Beare's rear guard, who up to this point had been keeping well hidden, suddenly rose up and mounted a counter attack on MacEgan's men. O'Sullivan Beare's men had the element of surprise and it was clear that their sudden appearance had caught MacEgan's troops totally off guard. I saw at least fifteen of MacEgan's men fall, including what I took to be their leader, who looked totally shocked as a pike was thrust through his chest so forcefully that it exited out his back. Almost as quickly as the attack had been launched, the remaining troops were beating a hasty retreat, many of them gravely wounded. It was a loud, bloody and terrifying encounter that lasted less than fifteen minutes, but resulted in so much gun smoke, death and panic. And that panic was exacerbated greatly when local tribes, alerted by the sound of gunfire, appeared on both banks of the river. O'Sullivan Beare's rear guard soldiers and the civilians, who hadn't already perished in the river or taken flight, rushed to crowd into the boat and I watched in disbelief as it quickly sank under the weight and panic of its would-be passengers. Fortunately, the boat was in shallow water and the soldiers were able to float it again and make their way across to the far bank. Some civilians also made it over in the boat, while others managed to swim across the river and yet others had to flee from the natives and hide themselves.

"It was an unfortunate ending to an otherwise very successful venture," said Donal Cam, as we watched the last of the civilians wade and stumble through the reeds on the opposite bank and pull themselves ashore, with the help of others in many cases. "I've never forgiven MacEgan for his ruthless attack on what he thought to be defenceless civilians. It's of some comfort to know that Thomas Burke, who led my rear guard, drove a pike through MacEgan's heart. I have to admit that I get some pleasure out of seeing the look of surprised shock on his face again at his unexpected skewering." After he had obviously savoured the memory for a moment, he added, "I ordered that our boat be broken up lest it should prove useful to the enemy. But, even now, we weren't able to rest."

And suddenly I was back on the Galway side of the river myself and back in the present. "Feckin' hell!" I cried out, as I tried to steady myself after my sudden relocation in time and space, "That was pretty damned scary."

"Not half as scary as being in the thick of it at the time," Donal Cam said. He was still by my side and he continued with his account, but now from the present looking back, rather than being present in the past. "As I was saying, even when we reached this side of the river, we weren't able to rest. By crossing the River Shannon, we had finally escaped Munster, but unfortunately Connacht was no more welcoming of our presence. The local O'Madden clan assembled a crowd of natives and they fired on us as we continued our advance from the banks of the river. We were exhausted after the river crossing and all we wanted to do was to lie down and rest. But we had no choice other than to keep moving, defending ourselves in skirmish after skirmish with the O'Madden's. I divided my remaining soldiers into two parts, each part in turn withstanding the enemies' assaults, and, by the time we reached Magheranearla just before midday, we had eventually managed to shake off our attackers. We came across a small village, in truth no more than a collection of huts, which had been abandoned by the inhabitants, who had probably fled upon hearing of our approach. We gathered up sacks of wheat, beans and barley and refreshed ourselves on the grains and by drinking beer. This kind of food and drink seemed to our parched palates and hungry stomachs like nectar and the greatest of delicacies. We marched on for another while, but by the time we reached St Iomar's Church at Killimor, about eight miles from where we crossed the Shannon, we were totally spent. We camped there for the night without incident and rose at dawn the following morning to press on."

"How many days had you been retreating for now," I asked, not realising that my innocent question would touch a very raw nerve.

Donal Cam glared at me, before replying with great deliberation, "We were not retreating. We were marching north to join our allies in order to continue with our rebellion against the English. I would beg you to never use that word in my presence, young sir."

"Sorry, I didn't mean to offend you," I replied, before adding by way of deflection, "it must have been difficult to have had to leave Munster under such circumstances."

"It was that. But I was determined to return and reclaim what was mine. We had spent three nights in Brosna Wood preparing the boats for our river crossing and I vowed that they would not be my last in Munster. And to answer your earlier question, as we set off from Killimor on 10th January 1603, we were entering the eleventh day of our march north. But we had suffered tremendous losses in the previous ten days. We had left Glengariff with one thousand souls. We were now less than three hundred."

"My God," I exclaimed, "that's shocking. Had so many died?"

"Many had, for sure. Killed in the fighting, eventually succumbing to sickness or injury along the way, or, indeed, drowned in the Shannon. But others, I have to admit, simply dropped out when they found the going too hard for them or got lost when they could no longer keep up. Even since crossing the Shannon, we had sustained further losses due to the damned O'Madden's and other pursuers firing on us and we were forced to abandon some men exhausted by the march or weaken by wounds. We even had to leave behind some worn out beasts of burthen which didn't make the onward march any easier for the rest of us. The largest proportion of our losses was from among the civilians, but I had also lost one hundred and twenty of the four hundred soldiers I had left Beara with. So, we advanced from Killimor a much depleted force, with eighty armed men in front, the baggage following immediately after, and two hundred men bringing up the rear. We proceeded with surprisingly little trouble that morning, but just before midday my scouts came back with news that Sir Henry Malby was waiting to intercept us at Aughrim and that he had five companies of men and two troops of horse."

"Oh shit," the words escaped involuntarily from my lips.

"You could say that," responded Donal Cam, "but ………"

"Don't tell me," I interrupted, "I'm going to have to wait until I get to Aughrim to hear what happened?"

"Correct," he said. "Enjoy the rest of your river walk. It's certainly a fine day for it."

And with that, as I was now well used to, Donal Cam gradually disappeared. I was left standing alone on the river bank, in a bit of a daze, trying to take in all that I had just witnessed. I slowly emerged from my dream state to realise that yet another cruiser was passing along the river and that the occupants were waving to me in a friendly fashion. I lifted a hand and returned the wave in a rather distracted manner. Once my mind had caught up with where I was and I had recovered sufficiently from the scenes I had just witnessed, I collected myself and set off once again along the bank of the river. However, I continued to marvel at how O'Sullivan Beare and his followers had continued to triumph over unbelievable adversity, albeit at a terrible cost.

In stark contrast to the terrible images somehow shown to me by Donal Cam from over four hundred years ago, the rest of my riverside journey was filled with nothing but the beauty of nature. One section of the embankment, where the vegetation hadn't been cut for some time, was teaming with different varieties of bees and butterflies. It was like walking through a wonderful corridor of nature, where these colourful creatures buzzed and danced ahead of me and I was transfixed by both their beauty and their plentiful numbers. Sheep and lambs frequently congregated in small groups on the embankment ahead, watching me closely as I approached and then scattering en masse when I got too close for comfort. I passed the grey edifice of the fifteenth century Meelick Church, which a local man resting at a gateway told me was the oldest church still in continuous use in Ireland. Beyond the church, I came upon the spellbinding sight of dozens of large dragonflies flitting and darting around me. I stopped to watch them for ages and tried repeatedly to get a decent photograph of one in flight, but they moved so fast that it was pretty near impossible. Then it was past the churning roar of the mighty Shannon cascading over Meelick Weir and on to the small riverside Meelick Quay, where a few pleasure craft languished in the calm waters well above the weir. By this stage the clouds had parted to reveal blue skies and warm sunshine. I have to admit to feeling a little envious of the people I spotted relaxing on the decks of their boats, with their feet up, enjoying the peace and tranquillity of a gorgeous afternoon. I wondered if any of them had any idea of the horrors that had occurred just downriver from here all those years ago.

Just past Meelick Quay, the route finally veered away from the river and started to head inland, leaving the grassy banks behind for country roads and the occasional field. I had a couple of surreal moments along the way that had me thinking that I had somehow wandered into the middle of a Father Ted episode. The first was when I was crossing a patch of rough grassland, before entering a number of fields, and I encountered a black rabbit, which just kept hopping ahead of me for a time. There was a house nearby and I assumed that it was a pet rabbit on the loose and this was later confirmed. Such was my network of followers on social media that, after I had posted a photo of it, the owner contacted me to say that it was hers and that it was called Benny. I didn't know it then, but I would subsequently stay with the owner's mother. Then, not long after the black rabbit encounter, I was passing through a field of cattle and trying my best to not attract attention to myself. This strategy was working very well. The cattle didn't seem to notice me and appeared quite happy to continue grazing and lazing in the sun. But, just as I was about halfway through the field, my mobile started ringing loudly. My cover was blown! Heads suddenly began to lift from the grass. I reached for my trouser pocket where I normally carried my phone only to discover that it wasn't there. The phone continued ringing and, in the silence of a field full of cows, it seemed louder than ever. Heads suddenly turned in my direction. Then I remembered that my phone had been in the pocket of a jacket that I had taken off earlier and stuffed into the top of my rucksack. It continued to ring; becoming ever more insistent. I now had the full attention of all the cattle. I kept on walking and at the same time struggled out of my rucksack and went fishing for my mobile. I could feel all these big bovine eyes staring at me. I found my phone and answered it to discover that it wasn't Father Ted, but Dorothy Casey from the Central House B&B in Tipperary ringing to see how I was getting on! It was lovely to hear from Dorothy and very kind of her to call, but her timing could certainly have been better. I proceeded to have a long chat with her as I continued to make my way to the exit stile and thankfully the cattle gradually resumed their grazing and lazing, now that the annoying ringing had ceased.

I joined the roads again close to Brackloon Castle, a sixteenth century fortified tower house originally owned by the O'Maddens, the clan that had harassed O'Sullivan Beare's party after they had crossed the River Shannon. The castle is now a rather striking and unusual private residence, although I suspected that the current owners had little use for the castle's 'murder hole', once used to pour boiling water or burning oil on any would be attackers. Although, come to think of it, it could still prove useful for deterring unwanted cold callers. Another couple of kilometres by road brought me to my destination of Clonfert. I arrived early evening and, although the going had been easy, it had been a long day and I was pretty tired. I stopped and sat on a wall opposite Our Lady of Clonfert Church, home to the Clonfert Madonna, a fourteenth century painted wooden statue. From here, I phoned Josephine Lynch, who, at this stage, I believed ran a B&B in Clonfert. I was only half right. Josephine confirmed that she did indeed run a B&B, but also informed me that it wasn't in Clonfert. In fact it was closer to Meelick, which I had of course passed through hours before. I thanked Josephine for the information and said that I would try to find somewhere in Clonfert to stay the night. I hung up and practiced a few of my favourite Anglo-Saxon phrases, before applying myself to solving this unexpected hitch. I was pretty sure that there wasn't any other accommodation in Clonfert and a search on my phone soon confirmed this to be the case. Resigned to another night under canvas, I set off to look around the village to see if there was anywhere suitable to pitch my tent and also somewhere to get food.

I spotted a woman outside her house and I stopped to ask if there were any shops or bars nearby. To my dismay, she told me that there wasn't anything in Clonfert and that I would have to travel quite a distance to the next village to find a shop or bar. However, she told me to wait a minute and she went to get her husband, who she thought might be able to help me. And it was at this point, as had so often happened on my travels, that my fortunes suddenly flipped through 180 degrees! For her husband happened to be Christy Cunniffe, a local archaeologist and great advocate of the Beara-Breifne Way. He was delighted to meet someone who was walking in the footsteps of O'Sullivan Beare and I was delighted to meet someone who was so enthusiastic and knowledgeable about the ancient route. Needless to say, I kept my powder dry in relation to my personal encounters with Donal Cam earlier in the day, even though the subject of the Shannon crossing did, inevitably, come up in conversation. We talked passionately about my walk to date and some of the historical aspects of the places I had passed through and it was some time before my accommodation problem was even mentioned. I then told Christy that I had been planning to stay at Lynch's farmhouse, but had just found out that it was miles away, back towards Meelick. "No problem," he said, "I'll drive you over there. But first, have you seen the cathedral?" I confessed that I hadn't yet and he smiled and said, "Now, you simply can't pass through Clonfert and not visit the cathedral. You phone Josephine and tell her you'll be over later and then I'll show you around the place." I couldn't believe my sudden change in fortune. Seemingly, by random chance, I had met this wonderful man and, at a stroke, not only was my accommodation sorted, but I had a lift and a visit to Clonfert Cathedral added to the bargain. I put the call into Josephine and then Christie drove me the short distance to Clonfert Cathedral. He then proceeded to give me a guided tour of this wonderful twelfth century house of worship, pointing out many of the details that would have been totally lost to me had I visited on my own. The cathedral was entered into via a stunning Romanesque doorway, which was carved with a remarkable array of motifs, many of which were badly worn by time and weather, but others clearly identifiable as human and animal heads. Inside, Christie pointed out more stone carvings on the chancel arch including angels, a mermaid and even a wyfren, which was a new one to me. Apparently, a wyfren is a two-legged dragon, which was commonly depicted in medieval times.

Following my amazing guided tour, Christie drove me all the way to Lynch's Farmhouse B&B, near Meelick. Josephine greeted me with a superb evening meal, which by this stage was much needed and very welcome. Then, after I got cleaned up, Josephine's husband, Kieran, kindly dropped me down to the local bar, simply known as 'The Shop', so I could finish my day in the time honoured fashion. After downing my pint and gratefully collecting some donations from the other customers, I walked the kilometre or so back to my B&B in the dark. Before turning in for the night, I found out that Josephine was the mother of the woman who owned Benny the Bunny. This news seemed to me to cap off a remarkably strange day rather neatly.

****

I had a very comfortable night at Lynch's Farmhouse B&B and Josephine made sure that I didn't leave her home hungry as she served me a very hearty cooked breakfast and made me a packed lunch. Kieran then very kindly drove me back to Clonfert and dropped me close to Christie Cunniffe's house where I had finished up the previous day. Grey skies had returned and they remained for most of the day, but thankfully there was no rain. It was quite warm and humid though, the cloud cover acting like a large, soft duvet, spread out over the sky, and trapping the heat between it and the patchwork quilt of the land below.

I wasn't too far out of Clonfert, before I left the road and entered grassy fields and laneways. These in turn led into thick woodland that bordered a huge 'open cast' peat mine, the land beyond the treeline stripped bare on a massive industrial scale. The route twisted and turned between the trees, over ground that was thick with pine needles and moss, as soft to walk on as the most luxurious carpet. I eventually emerged from the woods and joined a long lane way and it was on this laneway that I had another surreal animal encounter. Yesterday it was a black rabbit, but today a little red squirrel came bounding up the lane towards me. It stopped every so often, stood up on its hind legs to look around it as if it was searching for something, and then continued running towards me. If it was aware of my presence, it didn't appear to show any sign of it. It was literally only a few metres away from me, before it turned around and headed back in the other direction, but continuing to stop and look around every so often, as if still searching. It finally skipped into the verge and that was the last I saw of it. I was a good distance from the woods by this stage and there were no trees nearby, so I thought it a highly unusual place to see a squirrel.

The laneway eventually joined country roads for a further four kilometres, before I crossed over a tributary of the River Suck to follow a grassy track alongside an old canal waterway running towards Ballinasloe. As with my walk along the banks of the

Shannon the day before, the banks of this small waterway were also teaming with colourful butterflies and industrious bees. I stopped here for lunch and enjoyed the wheaten bread and bacon that Josephine had very kindly prepared for me, before I set off once again. The route continued along the abandoned canal in a north-west direction, but well before reaching the town of Ballinasloe, it veered off to the west towards the village of Aughrim. I then followed a torturous route of laneways and roadways for many kilometres and, as I came closer to Aughrim, I began to encounter numerous signs by the roadside pointing out sites associated with the Battle of Aughrim. This was a decisive battle fought between the Jacobite forces of English Catholic King James II and the Williamite forces of Dutch Protestant Prince William of Orange on 12th July 1691. It was one of the bloodiest battles fought on Irish soil, resulting in 5,000 to 7,000 dead, and effectively brought an end to Catholic Jacobite resistance in Ireland and symbolised Irish Protestants' victory. For many years, Aughrim was the focus of Loyalist and Orange Order celebrations in Ireland on 12th July, simply known as 'the Twelfth'. It wasn't until the early nineteenth century, that the focus of commemoration shifted to the less decisive Battle of the Boyne, which had occurred a year before Aughrim on 1st July 1690. The reason for this appears to have been largely down to a 'new style' Gregorian calendar being adopted in Ireland in 1752. This meant that the 'old date' of 1st July now became the 'new date' of 12th July and over time the battles and dates somehow merged.

"*It is at Aughrim of the slaughter where they are to be found, their damp bones lying uncoffined*", was how a contemporary poet wrote of the Irish dead, following the Battle of Aughrim. It was difficult to relate this horror to the green and pleasant fields that surrounded me, as I stood at one of the signs and tried to imagine the dreadful scenes of battle that tore through this land over three hundred years ago.

"It wasn't the first and it wouldn't be the last," a familiar voice beside me announced in a manner laced with a fair slice of world weariness.

"Ah, I've been expecting you, Mr Beare," I said, in my best Blofeld impersonation, which was totally lost on him of course.

"We had our own battle here," Donal Cam continued, ignoring my theatrics, "when we ran into Captain Henry Malby and his troops. Nothing on the scale of this bloodbath in 1691, of course, but certainly the hardest battle we had to fight on our long march. Our previous skirmishes had mainly all come about as a result of us passing through territories where we weren't welcome – almost opportunistic attacks by our foes as we came within range. However, this was the first time that forces loyal to Elizabeth had intentionally set out to intercept us and block our escape. Captain Malby had assembled a large army consisting of five companies of foot, two troops of horse and a swarm of 'Queen's rabble'. I have no doubt that he intended to wipe us off the face of this earth; every last man and woman of us. And, to be honest, for a time, that's exactly what I thought was going to happen."

He paused briefly, before continuing, "As I told you before, when we arrived here on 10th January 1603, the four hundred strong army of fighting men I had set off from Glengarriff with had been reduced to two hundred and eighty. I had deployed eighty ahead of the civilian party and the remaining two hundred, led by myself, took up the rear. However, when my advance party caught sight of Malby's formidable army - the neighing of their horses, the sheen of their brilliant armour, the braying of their trumpets, the sound of their pipes, the beat of their drums, all joyously and proudly anticipating victory - it greatly unnerved the men and they fled in fear. I had to rally my remaining soldiers and I had to do it quickly."

All at once, the landscape around me altered. Signs and roads and farmhouses and hedges suddenly disappeared to be replaced by open fields and bog land. The skies darkened and the air rapidly became much colder and I now found myself peering over the heads of a large mob of men, who were all focussed on one individual standing amongst the group. "Listen to this," whispered Donal Cam in my ear, "this guy is good." Almost immediately, the man who was holding court began speaking in a voice that was loud and clear and obviously well used to addressing crowds and commanding respect. It was of course O'Sullivan Beare.

"Since on this day our desperate circumstances and unhappy fate have left us neither wealth, nor country, nor children, nor wives to fight for, but, as on this instant the struggle with our enemies is for the life that alone remains to us, which of you, I ask in God's

eternal name, will not rather fall fighting gloriously in battle and avenging your blood, than like cattle, which have no sense of honour, perish unavenged in cowardly flight? Surely our ancestors, heroes famed for their high spirits, would never seek by a shameful flight to shun an honourable death even when they could fly. For us it will be proper to follow in their footsteps, especially as flight offers no salvation. See the plain stretching far and wide without hindrance of bog, without thick woods, without any hiding-places to which we could fly for concealment. The neighbouring people are no protection for us. There is none to come to our aid. The enemy block the roads and passes, and we, wearied with our long journey, are unable to run. Whatever chance we have is only in our own courage and strength of our own arms. Up, then, and on them, whom you excel in spirit, courage, achievements past, and holy faith. Let us remember this day that enemies who have everywhere attacked us have heretofore been routed by the Divine mercy. Above all let us believe that the victory is the gift of God. Let us think that Christ our Lord will be with His servants in their utmost need, and that for His name and holy faith we join issue with heretics and their abettors. Fear not the worthless mob of enemies who are not as used to fight as we are, much less as famous. Wherefore, I do hope they will turn tail when they shall see us heartily resist, even as I expect you will show forth your faith and courage."

As O'Sullivan Beare finished his rallying call, a loud cheer of support erupted from the crowd. "I told you he was good," a grinning Donal Cam shouted into my ear, so I could hear him above the uproar. The cheering had barely begun to subside when it was replaced with shouts of "Make ready men" and "Here they come" and other such frantic warnings. I looked around to see the Royalist cavalry thundering towards us, with spears held forward in full attack mode. They were still a distance away, but were obviously intent on running O'Sullivan Beare's men through with their spears and trampling them under their horses' hooves, which would break up his ranks and throw them into confusion. Acting quickly and decisively, O'Sullivan Beare marched his column of two hundred men through an adjacent patch of boggy ground towards a thin copse of trees not far off. His earlier protestations about there being no bog or hiding place, were obviously not entirely true. My companion and I remained in position and had an excellent view of events as they quickly unfolded in front of us. On reaching the boggy area, the Royalist cavalry dismounted, obviously not wishing to risk riding their horses through such treacherous ground. Instead they joined their pike-men in running laboriously through the bog, attempting to make it to the copse and seize it before O'Sullivan Beare's men could reach it and close ranks. At the same time Royalist musketeers took up position and began firing at the rebels as they ran towards the tree line. I heard commands being shouted by O'Sullivan Beare and I saw about forty of his men turn to face the Royalists and let go a volley of musket shot toward Malby's men. It didn't appear to have much effect on the Royalists and a volley of fire was soon being sent back in the opposite direction and I saw about a dozen of O'Sullivan Beare's marksmen fall. The noise of these exchanges was incredible and the smoke from the musket fire hung thick in the air in dense white clouds above the battlefield. O'Sullivan Beare's remaining marksmen fell back and it seemed at that moment that the entire party of rebels was about to be overwhelmed by the greater Royalist forces. But then, O'Sullivan Beare gave a command and his entire division suddenly turned round to face and attack their enemy. It was a bold and unexpected move and it caught the Royalists totally off guard. One moment they had been confidently giving chase to what appeared to be a spent force of ragged rebels and the next they were being attacked by a unified army of brave and angry men with plenty of fight left in them yet.

The unexpected about turn struck terror into the Royalists and some began to fall back in disarray, while others fled the scene entirely. However, other braver souls amongst the Royalists held their ground and prepared to meet the ranks of O'Sullivan Beare's men bearing down on them. O'Sullivan Beare had cleverly posted his marksmen on either side of his front rank and, as the distance between the opposing factions closed, another loud burst of musket fire filled the air and I saw a number of Royalist soldiers fall. Then the ranks of both factions fell upon each other and close and bloody, hand to hand, fighting ensued, with swords swinging wildly and spears jabbing and thrusting with deadly purpose. I watched in horrible fascination as one of O'Sullivan Beare's men, Captain Maurice O'Sullivan, was knocked to the ground by the pike of a Royalist leader, Richard Burke - their names provided to me by Donal Cam as we watched. As Richard Burke was about to thrust his pike again at the fallen captain, another of O'Sullivan

Beare's men brought his sword swiftly down on Burke's arm, taking off his hand at the wrist, so that both hand and pike suddenly fell to the ground. Captain Maurice, who was wearing a coat of chainmail and obviously not seriously injured by Burke's first blow, quickly got to his feet and ran Burke through with his spear. If Burke wasn't finished by this stage, then the final vicious and bloody blow delivered by the sword of a third O'Sullivan Beare man certainly left no doubt.

Both armies were now enmeshed in the most brutal, close quarter combat and it was difficult for me to make out much of what was going on, such was the tangle of limbs and weapons in the general melee. However, due to his fine uniform, I did manage to make out Captain Henry Malby amongst the throng and he was fighting as vigorously as any of his men. I watched as he appeared to turn to call out to his men behind him; perhaps it was a rallying cry to give his men courage. As he turned back to face O'Sullivan Beare's men, I watched as the blade of a sword sliced through the air towards his head. In the fracas it was difficult for me to see who actually brandished the sword. I continued to watch, as the blade of the sword completed the arc of its swing and, at first, I thought Malby had been missed. But then, almost in slow motion it seemed, his head toppled unceremoniously from his shoulders and his body crumpled awkwardly to the ground. One of O'Sullivan Beare's men immediately spiked the fallen head on the point of his spear and held it aloft for all to see. I'm unsure as to whether this man was the same man who had beheaded Malby, but there was no mistaking that the man now holding Malby's head atop his spear was O'Sullivan Beare himself and he was clearly consumed with battle rage.

The royalists, seeing the decapitated head of their leader, quickly lost heart in the fight and I saw a few of the cavalry mount their horses again and ride off. The rest of the Royalists soon followed on foot, leaving a heap of bodies behind as they fled from the onslaught unleashed upon them by O'Sullivan Beare's army. The surviving Royalists retreated towards Aughrim fort, with O'Sullivan Beare's men in hot pursuit, their cries of "Victory" beginning to fill the air. Even those soldiers of the advance party, who had abandoned their posts at the first sight of the enemy, now joined in the chase, emboldened by the others success and perhaps wishing to redress their earlier cowardice in some way. However, perhaps spotting, as I had, the additional companies of Crown forces coming to the rescue of their fleeing comrades, O'Sullivan Beare ordered his men to cease their pursuit and to regroup. They chased off the remaining Royalists and others who had been hounding the civilian contingent of O'Sullivan Beare's party while the battle had been raging. Some of O'Sullivan Beare's men hurried about the scene of carnage and collected any arms and other objects discarded by the enemy. Exhausted by battle, but buoyed by victory, the group hurriedly set off on its long march once again and I watched for a time as the bedraggled but victorious group of refugees continued northwards.

The landscape around me altered once again. The open fields and bog land suddenly transformed and the signs and roads and farmhouses and hedges reappeared before me. The skies lightened, the air became warmer and once again I stood before the Battle of Aughrim 1691 information sign. Donal Cam was still standing beside me.

"Wow, that was something else," was the best I could manage as I tried desperately to readjust to the present. Donal Cam simply nodded at this, as if he was expecting more, and, after a pause, I added, "That speech you gave was unbelievable. I could see how the mood of your men changed as you spoke, from being resigned to a humiliating defeat to believing that they could, at the very least, go out in a blaze of glory. It was inspirational." Donal Cam seemed to like that very much, as a huge smile broke out across his face.

"I have to admit that it sounds better every time I hear it," he chuckled proudly.

"And that sudden switch from running for the woods to a full frontal attack was incredible. It caught Malby's men totally off guard," I continued.

"Ha ha," Donal Cam laughed, "a little trick I learned from Red Hugh O'Donnell. I had used it before to great effect and it certainly proved very effective on this occasion also. Do you know, at the end of our battle, the Royalists had lost one hundred men, including Captain Malby and Burke, while we lost only fourteen."

"It was certainly a resounding victory," I agreed and then, after another pause, I added, "but, my God, it was so bloody and brutal."

"What did you expect, son?" he asked in a condescending tone, "pillows of feathers and sacks full of straw? We were literally fighting for our very lives. It was either kill or be killed. And in such a situation you did whatever you had to do to survive."

"Even lop off heads?" I asked.

"Yes," he replied sternly, "even lop off heads."

"Did you take off Malby's head?" I said, finally coming to the question that I had really been wanting to ask.

"What if I did," he replied evasively, "such practice was common place in my day. If Malby had held the day at Aughrim, it would most likely have been my head hoisted upon a spike for all to see." And then he added, as if it had just occurred to him, "One must always endeavour to get 'a head' in life son; wouldn't you agree?", and this was followed with the heartiest laugh, as if it was the funniest thing he had ever heard.

"Very droll," I responded, finding it difficult to join in with his mirth after witnessing such scenes, "but I have to agree that displaying Malby's severed head in the middle of the fight, did certainly put the fear of God into the Royalists. It was that as much as anything that sent them scarpering."

"It certainly wasn't pretty," he concluded, "but it was effective and, as I said before, in such a situation you did whatever you had to do to survive; even if it meant lopping off heads."

Wishing to move on from the gruesome subject of decapitation, I asked Donal Cam, "Why did your men collect Malby's arms and other things the Royalists had discarded after the battle?"

"I had thought that they might come in useful at some stage," he replied, "but it didn't really work out that way. Anyway, that's another story for another day. I'll see you again near Glinsk. Farewell for now." And with that he was gone again, just as suddenly as he had appeared. I was now becoming so used to these bizarre interludes in my journey that I simply turned and continued on my way. However, although I left the site of the battle behind, it wasn't so easy to leave behind the brutal scenes I had just witnessed. Donal Cam had certainly seemed delighted with the outcome, which was surely justifiable in its own right. But I also wondered if he perhaps viewed the resounding victory against the odds as some sort of redress for the terrible defeat he and his northern allies had suffered at Kinsale, just over one year before on Christmas Eve 1601.

I headed on into Aughrim village and stopped at Finn's Bar to have my usual reward of the black stuff. It was provided 'on the house', and I took it outside to sit on one of the benches in the warm sunshine while having a chat with the bar's owner, Catherine Finn. I had just finished my pint, when a 4x4 vehicle pulled up. It was Tim and Martin, who I had passed on the road earlier and spoken to briefly. They were both ministers associated with one of the more obscure Protestant churches and Martin, who was based in Ballinasloe, had been giving Martin, who was based in Lurgan in the North, a tour of the battlefield sites around Aughrim. They had promised to give me a lift into Ballinasloe if they spotted me in the village on their return. And true to their word, they showed up with perfect timing and drove me all the way to my accommodation on the outskirts of Ballinasloe. During the ride, the fact was not lost on me that here we were, people from two very different religious backgrounds, happily sharing a car journey together from a site, where three centuries before, people from those same two religious backgrounds were just as happy to kill each other with pikes and muskets! The only thing that Tim and Martin were armed with was a selection of religious tracts and I had a few of these thrust into my hand as I stepped out of their vehicle. Not wishing to appear ungrateful, I accepted these and agreed to consider their invitation to a prayer meeting the following morning before waving them on their way. It was a small price to pay for my lift and, to be fair, they were not at all pushy. And, to be honest, I had no intention of attending their prayer meeting.

The house that Tim and Martin had dropped me outside belonged to David and Michelle McPhillips, who were friends of an ex-work colleague of mine, and they had very kindly agreed to put me up for the next two nights. David and their son, ten year old Cillian, were in Dublin watching a rugby match, so Michelle welcomed me in and, while I got freshened up, she cooked me a wonderful dinner of steak and chips, while looking after fourteen month old Liam at the same time.

Chapter Nine: Bridging the Gap
(Days twenty-two to twenty-five - Aughrim to Ballinlough)

The following morning David was back home in Ballinasloe and, after cooking me breakfast, he and the two children, Cillian and Liam, dropped me out to Aughrim village once again. Aughrim comes from the Irish *Eachroim*, meaning 'the ridge of the horse', which possibly has something to do with the shape of the low hill just south of the village. I had just waved David and the children off, when a message popped up on my phone. It was from Michelle to say that I had left without the lunch she had prepared for me. I apologised and told her that it would do me for the following day and then I went in search of a shop to try and replace my missing sandwiches. However, it was a Sunday morning in a small rural Irish village and so my options were extremely limited. Thankfully there was a very small shop open next to a filling station by the main road on the edge of the village. But here I found that the shelves were not exactly groaning with suitable supplies. I could pretty much either buy a loaf of bread or a six pack of Wagon Wheels! I settled for the Wagon Wheels and paid the elderly gentleman behind the counter, who seemed genuinely surprised to have made a sale. I asked him if there was a vending machine or anywhere that I could fill my flask with tea or coffee, but he told me that he sadly didn't even have a kettle or he would have made me up a flask. I thanked him anyway and headed back into the heart of the village, stopping briefly at the Battle of Aughrim Visitor Centre, which was closed, and wandering through an adjoining public park, which was open. I also made a quick visit to the scant ruins of Aughrim Castle, which stood alongside a High Cross monument to all the soldiers who died in the 1691 battle. As I was passing through the village, I spotted a woman stepping through the side door of Valerie's Bar. The pub was obviously not open for business at such an early hour, but the owner, Valerie Seale, and some staff were in tidying up after a late event the night before. Valerie very kindly opened the door to my tentative knock and then led me into the bar, started up the coffee machine and filled my flask with hot coffee. Hospitality continued to follow me wherever I went. With coffee in my flask and Wagon Wheels in my rucksack, it was high time I was rolling out of Aughrim to re-join the trail.

What followed was another day of pleasant weather and mixed terrain. Roads, fields, bog land and forests all featured, but there were no hills and I made fairly good progress as a result. However, some sections along the route were very overgrown with vegetation, which did make the going pretty tough and distinctly unpleasant at times. As I fought my way through these choked paths, I was drenched in sweat, scratched by brambles and, worst of all, absolutely plagued by flies! The flies were particularly annoying today and they seemed intent on buzzing and flying into ears, eyes, nose and mouth at every given opportunity. My 'Buff' neck scarf became my saviour, as I was able to wear it balaclava-like so that only my eyes were exposed. Despite these obstacles, I began to feel my legs getting stronger today and my pace really started to pick up on those occasions when my legs were unhindered by tangled weeds or brambles. Or electric fences, for that matter.

I quite literally had a terrible shock stepping out of a field at one stage. I had just crossed a large field of cut grass and was looking for a stile to take me out onto a laneway. However, there didn't appear to be one and so I had little option other than to step over the electric fence that was bordering the field. Careful now. Hold wire down with handle of walking pole. Left leg over first. Left foot safely down. Steady now. Right leg over next. Almost clear. Almost there. Walking pole moves. Wire slips. Wire contacts inner thigh. Feckin' hell! It nearly floored me! The right hand side of my body was temporarily numb from the painful shock. I'm convinced that the fence must have been powered from the mains as the shock was so intense. I would obviously need to be much more careful in future. Thankfully the wire wasn't higher or my voice might have ended up a few octaves higher also! Anyway, I survived my shocking experience and was able to continue on to reach a very significant milestone on my journey. Because between the village of Aughrim and the townland of Sonnagh, I reached the half-way point on my Ireland Way trek, with five hundred kilometres covered since setting off from Castletownbere. I celebrated in style. Well, to be honest, I celebrated on a stile. I sat on the top step and had a mini celebration with my Wagon Wheels and coffee!

Later, I enjoyed a lovely encounter with a small herd of calves in a field I was passing through. Like their older counterparts, they all made a bee line for me as soon as they spotted me and continued to follow closely behind me as I went. They were very curious and also very sweet. It often seems to be the case that a herd of cattle has one particular character who is considerably bolder than the rest – the leader of the gang – and this group of ten 'youngsters' was no different. When I stopped and turned to face them, a lovely grey and white calf eventually came right up to me and licked my hand a few times. He was very cute and gentle, but his tongue was like the coarsest grade of sandpaper available!

Long lanes and roads twisted and turned through bog land and fields before finally bringing me into the woods of the extensive Clonbrock Estate, just northwest of the village of Ahascragh. I crossed over the Bunowen River, a tributary of the River Suck, and, about half a kilometre beyond the bridge, I arrived at the exit of the Clonbrock Estate and sat down to await the arrival of David, who I had contacted earlier. He soon turned up with Cillian and drove me back to his house in Ballinasloe, where I was to stay a second night. We enjoyed a Chinese takeaway meal for tea and then Michelle's father, Willie Tully, arrived to drive me and David into town. Willie knew everything there was to know about Ballinasloe and obviously relished the opportunity to impart as much knowledge as possible to one as ill-informed as myself. His lesson began in the house before we left and continued pretty well non-stop as a running commentary for the whole drive into the centre of Ballinasloe. Every house and building we passed seemed to have a story attached to it and Willie knew all the detail. It was all very interesting and highly entertaining, but it's fair to say that if there had been a donkey with us, it would have eventually toppled over, as Willie would have talked its hind leg off! Among all the fascinating facts that Willie bombarded me with, there was, however, one that stood out for me head and shoulders above the rest. This was the fact that Ballinasloe was actually twinned with Ballycastle, the end point of the Ireland Way and, of course, my ultimate destination. This twinning arose from the fact that both towns are famous for their horse fairs - the Auld Lammas Fair in Ballycastle, which is held in August each year, and the Ballinasloe Fair, held every October. I idly wondered if anyone in Ballinasloe might like a horse brought up to Ballycastle for the Lammas Fair – I would be happy to take it if it was prepared to carry my rucksack! I also learned that the name Ballinasloe comes from the Irish *Béal Átha na Sluaighe*, meaning 'the mouth of the ford of the crowds'. This reflects the fact that the town originally developed as a ford or crossing point on the River Suck, a tributary of the Shannon, and also that it has been an important meeting place since ancient times. Willie dropped David and I at Ryan's Bar, where Michael Ryan, one of the two brothers who ran the pub, served me a pint of Guinness 'on the house' and posed for a photo with me and my banner behind the bar. The bar was crammed and in high spirits as earlier in the day the Galway hurling team had beaten Clare by one point to qualify for the All-Ireland Final. As I pushed through the crowds of people to take my seat beside David again, it occurred to me that Ballinasloe, 'the mouth of the ford of the crowds', was certainly living up to its name in Ryan's Bar!

****

The following morning, I enjoyed another superb cooked breakfast courtesy of David and Michelle. They also made sure that I was well provided for as regards lunch and Michelle was at pains to make sure that I didn't forget it for a second time! I waved farewell to Michelle and Liam, and David and Cillian then dropped me back to the exit of the Clonbrock Estate, where I picked up the Ireland Way route once again. I once again reflected on how fortunate I was to meet such wonderful people of my journey. David and Michelle had welcomed me, a complete stranger, into their lovely home in Ballinasloe for two nights and looked after my every need. They were such an unbelievably kind, generous and hospitable family.

Today was quite similar to yesterday in many regards, including the terrain and the weather - more fields, bog land and rural roads, although thankfully the climate did feel a little fresher. And although I didn't receive any nasty electric shocks along the way, I did manage to succumb to a much more conventional mishap. As I was approaching a metal stile and was preparing to climb over it, I noticed that there was a gap in the hedge to one side of it. So, rather than wasting energy by climbing over the stile, I decided to nip through the gap instead. Very handy I thought, as I stepped through the opening quite briskly. Unfortunately, I didn't see the strand of barbed wire just above ground level and hidden in the grass and weeds. My left foot caught under it as I went through the gap and suddenly I was pitched forward. As with the previous 'tortoise' incident, once I started to lose my balance, the weight of my rucksack made normal recovery very difficult, if not impossible. So I fell face first into the undergrowth! Thankfully, I managed to put my left hand out in time to break my fall and I escaped with nothing more than a few scrapes and scratches. Between fields of bullocks, electric fences and hidden 'trip wires', I was beginning to wonder if I was going to survive this walk!

Much later, I stopped on a small bridge over the Riven Shiven for a little break. While there, a middle aged couple happened by and as they were the first people I had encountered since being dropped off by David and Cillian hours before, I was only too happy to engage in a little conversation. The woman was from Ballygar and she was with her brother. He was home from Australia to see the family and together they were revisiting some of their childhood memories, including this little bridge.

"It's always so peaceful here," she said, before asking me about my walk. So I filled her in and told her that I was raising funds for cancer research and that my walk was in memory of my wife, Jacqui, who I had lost to ovarian cancer. "Really," she sounded a little surprised, "that's my name also."

"Spelt with a 'q-u-i'?" I asked, always conscious that most spelt it with 'k-i-e'.

"Yes," she confirmed, "short for Jacqueline." She then asked me where I was intending to stay the night.

"The Coffee Drop in Ballygar," I replied.

"Oh," she said, looking a little concerned and glancing at her brother, as if wondering if she should say anything further. I was beginning to think that perhaps there was something wrong with the Coffee Drop, but seeing my anxiety she quickly added, "Oh, don't worry. The Coffee Drop is fine. It's just that I know the owner, Pat Greally, very well. The thing is, he lost his wife, Helena, to ovarian cancer just a couple of months ago."

I was quite shocked to hear this news, but at the same time I was quite astonished. What were the chances of me meeting a woman called Jacqui on a bridge in the middle of nowhere and being told that the man I would be staying with that very night had only just recently lost his wife to ovarian cancer? I thanked Jacqui for the warning and before heading on, I agreed to not say anything to Pat about his loss unless he should raise the subject himself.

I left the bridge over the River Shiven behind and almost immediately the route veered off sharply in a south-easterly direction and followed alongside the river for a time. As I had already discovered on many occasions, the Ireland Way doesn't always take the most direct route between towns and villages. And the very twisty route into Ballygar today was no exception. At one point I estimated that I was only two kilometres away from the village, but the directions on my guide map then brought me on a convoluted five kilometre route that first took me further away from the village before bringing me back. It wasn't as if the longer route was more scenic or that it kept me off busier roads, so the logic of it defied me. However, I decided to stick with the official route on this occasion and I suppose, if there was reward to be had, it lay in me passing by an unusual folly at Killeroran graveyard on the outskirts of the village. This was a fifteen metre high replica Round Tower built in the nineteenth century by a local landlord, Denis Henry Kelly, as a 'leacht' or memorial to honour himself. This bizarre monument to vanity certainly stood out from the surrounding landscape and at least provided a little distraction as I weaved my way to Ballygar. However, when I did finally arrive in Ballygar, it was to a village bustling with crowds, market stalls and live music! I had arrived in the middle of Ballygar Festival Week and there was a tremendous buzz about the place. After hours of isolation and peacefulness, it was strange to suddenly walk into this cacophony of sights and sounds. I weaved my way through the crowds to reach The Coffee Drop, where Pat Greally quickly showed me to my room. He seemed to be in a bit of a rush and, perhaps thankfully, there was little time for conversation before he handed me my key and disappeared off. By the time I had freshened up and attended to my laundry duties, I was too late to get something to eat in the local restaurant, so I made do with a burger and chips from a street van that was doing a roaring trade among the multitude of hungry festival goers.

****

The following morning, I shed a few tears as I left Ballygar in the rain. It had been a while, but sometimes circumstances would just catch me unawares. When I had booked a room in the Coffee Drop B&B a few days before, the owner, Pat Greally, had readily agreed to put me up free of charge when he learned that I was walking to raise funds for cancer research. What I didn't know at the time of booking was that Pat had lost his wife, Helena, to ovarian cancer just a few months beforehand. She had only been 51 years of age; just three years younger than my Jacqui when she had been taken by the same cruel disease. I had learned about Pat's loss from another woman called Jacqui the day before, while en route to Ballygar and had agreed to say nothing to Pat unless he raised the subject. So after studiously avoiding 'the elephant in the room' and chatting about the weather and what I would like for breakfast, it came as a huge relieve to me when Pat suddenly said, "I believe you met a friend of mine on the road yesterday." Pat told me that Jacqui had phoned him to say about our encounter on the bridge as she wanted to avoid any awkwardness. I was so glad that she had, as Pat was then very open and told me about his loss and we had a good chat about our respective experiences. While I was three and a half years down the road of loss and grief, things were still very recent and raw for Pat. He was soldiering on and keeping busy with the coffee shop, the B&B and his love of gardening, but the pain of his loss was very evident and, recalling how devastated I was in the months after Jacqui's death, I really felt for him. We hugged tightly before parting and I vainly hoped that I was able to absorb just some of his pain in that brief moment of contact. I like to think that Pat had found meeting me useful and that he had got something positive out of our encounter. Again I wondered at the nature of fate that had somehow conspired to draw our two lost souls together and at the same time allow the intervention of a mediator called Jacqui to literally 'bridge' the gap between us.

It had been an emotional encounter and the tears I shed as I was leaving Ballygar, weren't only for myself and my Jacqui. They were for my many friends and their partners who had been separated from each other far too soon by cancer. And they were now also for Pat and Helena. I now felt like I was walking in honour of all of them, in the hope that, in the future, others would not have to suffer the consequences of this terrible disease. I knew that my contribution, in the overall scheme of things, was absolutely miniscule, but at least I was doing something and it was that thought that kept me going. My tears were for those who had already fallen, but my steps were for those who still had hope.

Thankfully, the tears did not last long and things did soon brighten up a little. My mood gradually improved and, although the skies remained stubbornly grey, the rain soon stopped to create pleasant and warm walking conditions. Walking is certainly a great mood enhancer - the physical nature of it and the fact that you are outdoors in the fresh air amongst Mother Nature and going somewhere entirely within your own control. And, although it was a very long walk today, it was hugely gratifying. I finally felt that my walking legs had returned again and I made very good progress, covering the thirty-four kilometres in nine hours. Once again it was a twisting path that I followed, which gradually wound its way northwards by degrees, via forest tracks, country roads and open fields. I occasionally stopped to feast on the large, plump, juicy blackberries that were growing in abundance - ripe for the picking and so sweet. However, by the time I reached the village of Creggs, seventeen kilometres from Ballygar, I needed something a little more substantial to sustain me on the rest of my way. Thankfully, I received a better welcome than O'Sullivan Beare's men had when they had called here looking for food centuries before. On 11th January 1603, O'Sullivan Beare's entourage had set up camp at Mount Mary, a couple of kilometres south of Creggs. They had endured an eighty kilometre trek to escape pursuit following their battle at Aughrim. They were tired and hungry and had run into the first snow they had experienced on their journey. Indeed, many of the party died from cold and exhaustion. O'Sullivan Beare had sent a few of his men into Creggs to look for food, but the locals had chased them off by hurling rocks at them. I obviously couldn't hold the present village population responsible for the unsympathetic actions of their ancestors, but I nevertheless kept a careful watch as I proceeded along the main street of this place that seemed to have a strong association with rocks. Even the very name of the village, Creggs, comes from the Irish *Na Creaga*, meaning 'the rocks'. However, I was made very welcome and met only very friendly and helpful people. A lady in a small supermarket made me up a fresh sandwich, which I enjoyed with a mug of tea while sitting outside.

Suitably refreshed and refuelled, I made my way on through the village, pausing briefly to admire the rather austere monument to Charles Stewart Parnell, a popular figure in Irish and British politics during the nineteenth century. The monument had been unveiled by Taoiseach Eamon DeVelera in 1946, on the centenary of Parnell's birth, to recognise the fact that Parnell had given his last speech in this village just two weeks before his death in 1891. Charles Stewart Parnell was also known as 'The Blackbird of Avondale' after his birthplace of Avondale in County Wicklow. Given my fondness for the humble blackbird and its strong association in my mind with Jacqui, I was delighted to learn that Creggs had consequently adopted the blackbird as its official logo. In the absence of any corporeal connection, these little perceived spiritual associations had come to mean so much to me.

I headed on out of the village, past the roofless shell of the nineteenth century Presbyterian church, and continued on quiet rural roads for the next seven or eight kilometres. Friendly horses and donkeys, pleased to have some company, and neat thatched cottages undoubtedly added to the pleasure of my journey. However, what really stood out for me on this section of the Ireland Way was the tremendous impression of 'big skies' over the wide open landscapes of the River Suck valley. By this stage, the dark, grey clouds had receded to leave only billowing, white clouds floating in blue skies that seemed to go on forever. It was a wonderful illusion, probably enhanced by the flat and seeming endless landscapes of the area, so that in whatever direction one looked, the horizon was not hemmed in by hills or mountains, but disappeared into the distance as far as the eye could see. The roads then gave way to lanes and barely discernable tracks through fields, weaving past a number of small loughs, before merging into lanes again and then a track through a wooded area.

This eventually deposited me onto a road right next to the imposing ruins of a seventeenth century fortified house, known as Glinsk Castle. The castle ruins were on an elevated site, atop a small hill, and as I paused to take a few photographs, I sensed a familiar presence beside me. I glanced around and, sure enough, there was the debonair figure of Donal Cam standing beside me, looking up at the castle.

"Ah, Glinsk Castle," he observed, "or what remains of it. Home of MacDavitt Burke, Lord of Clonconway. Mind you, this impressive pile wasn't here in my day. This was built in the mid-seventeenth century on the site of the previous castle – the one I had hoped to call on many years before. Perhaps you weren't aware of that?"

"I wasn't," I admitted.

"Anyway, being a Lord, it was clear where MacDavitt's allegiances lay," he continued, "and I therefore knew that I couldn't expect any assistance from him. But I also knew that he had ample supplies of food and animals. We hadn't eaten or slept for thirty-six hours, since leaving Killimor, and we were desperate for some sustenance. An attempt to raid some food from a village we had passed close to earlier had been unsuccessful."

"Creggs?" I suggested.

"Indeed," he replied, "the place of the rocks. And they had plenty of those and the buggers seemed keener to share their rocks with us than any of their food." Then he continued, "The countryside was now also deep in snow and it was bitterly cold. Hunger and cold had already claimed many of our party and my remaining followers were pretty despairing. I needed to come up with a plan. Do you remember the arms and other items we collected from Malby's dead after the battle at Aughrim?"

"I do indeed," I replied, intrigued by what was to come.

"Well, some of us disguised ourselves as Royalists, wearing the clothing and carrying the flags taken at Aughrim, and marched towards the original castle on this site, to the beat of the drums we had also taken. We had hoped to fool MacDavitt into believing that we were battle weary soldiers loyal to the Crown so that they would welcome us in and feed us and maybe even allow us to rest for a time."

"You really thought that might work?" I asked dubiously.

"You have to remember that in Ireland at that time, by far the largest proportion of men fighting on the side of the Royalists were actually Irish. Elizabeth had been very successful in dividing the clans of Ireland by offering reward and protection to those who sided with her. A band of Royalist Irish soldiers seeking assistance at a castle loyal to the Queen would not have been entirely out of the ordinary. Even if we could just get close enough, before they realised our deception, we might be able to capture some supplies before making our getaway."

"So how did it go?" I enquired in all innocence.

"Bloody awful," he replied. "Unfortunately, MacDavitt had been warned that we were on our way and so his guard was up before we even arrived. He had ordered his people to hide their food, drink and animals before we got anywhere near to the village. And a large crowd of villagers had assembled to welcome us, not with food and drink, but with rocks and any other missiles they could lay their hands on, just like at Creggs. So we were forced to retreat and had to remain hungry for another day."

"Where did you go to from here," I asked.

"We headed for Slieve O'Flynn, a low hill about ten miles north-west of here near Ballinlough, and at nightfall we set up camp in the thick woods there. Since we had fought and won our battle at Aughrim, we had been marching non-stop and covered almost fifty miles. We were exhausted by the time we reached Slieve O'Flynn and, lighting fires, we hoped to at last enjoy some rest and warmth. However, no sooner had we begun to yield our weary limbs to rest when a friendly local came to warn us that MacDavitt's men had followed and that they were planning to surround the camp and attack us at daybreak."

"A friendly local," I said in surprise, "surely that was unusual?"

"It certainly was. It was the first help that had been offered to us since we had left Glengarriff and I was immensely grateful for the timely warning. I felt that my soldiers would be too exhausted to defend our position and so I decided that it would be best for us to leave the woods immediately. Though, I have to tell you that it was no easy task rousing my people from the slumbers that they had so longed for and so badly needed. Nevertheless, we prepared to break camp, building our fires higher before leaving to give the enemy the impression that we were settled there for the night."

"I hope that this ruse was more successful than the previous one at Glinsk," I offered cautiously.

"Fortunately it was. It was daybreak before MacDavitt's men discovered that we had deserted the camp during the night, leaving nothing but fires. Our escape from the woods was long and torturous though. The branches of the trees were so thick and tangled that they totally blocked out any light that might have been provided by the stars, so that we wandered through the woods as if blind. Thankfully we had some Connacht men to lead the way, but the rest of us had to follow, not by sight, but by the sound of familiar voices. And even that was made all the more difficult due to the noise of the wind whistling through the branches of the trees. After four miles, we finally emerged from the woods only then to encounter snow so deep in places that some of us sank in up to the waist, as if we had fallen into pits."

"I'm familiar with the feeling," I said, recalling my experiences on Knocklayde Mountain at the start of the year. "It's a frightening experience and I can only imagine that it's even more so in the dark."

"Getting them out was not an easy task either," Donal Cam continued, "as those trying to drag them out at times seemed more likely to be dragged in themselves. Then the snow turned to rain and it poured on us so heavy that we were scarcely able to bear the weight of our soaked clothing. And the winter wind coming over the mountains coated our mantles, our hair and even our eyelashes with ice. "

"Good Lord," I said, "and here was me thinking that my walk was tough!"

"And there was still more to come. MacDavitt's men hadn't given up the chase yet. When they had found our camp at Slieve O'Flynn deserted at daybreak, they followed our tracks and caught up with us later that morning and then set about attacking us with missiles. We made for the Curlew Mountains with MacDavitt's men giving chase and never letting up. We reached the top of a high hill in the Curlews that evening and some of my men declared that they would rather turn and fight the enemy than quit this spot before they had taken food and sleep. The rest chimed in with the same vow and so I rallied my troops and our small army turned to face our relentless pursuers. By this stage of our journey, my number of soldiers was well depleted and, out of those remaining, not more than sixty were still capable of fighting after our arduous hike through the snow and the rain. But we simply couldn't keep running from MacDavitt's men. In the end, MacDavitt's dogs proved to be all bark and no bite and they were easily driven off after a brief skirmish when we turned and fired on them. At last we could finally rest our weary bones. We butchered two of our remaining horses and those who, unlike myself, didn't object to eating horse flesh, ate their fill and then we collapsed and, out of sheer exhaustion, slept where we fell for a good six hours."

"Surely you must have been tempted to take your share of the horse meat?" I ventured. "You must have been starving by this stage?"

"Well, I would be lying if I didn't admit to being desperately hungry. The roots and berries I had been surviving on were not the most plentiful in the depths of winter and provided little nourishment anyway, but the very smell of the horse flesh sickened me to the stomach. There was no way I could bring myself to touch it, much less eat it. It's the practice of pagans; not of one who holds his Christian values dearly, such as myself."

"So what happened the following morning?" I asked, wishing to move on from the unappetising subjects of both horsemeat and religion.

"Well, just as at *Poll na Copall* on the banks of the Shannon, the hides of the horses we had killed came in useful once again. Of course, not for boats this time, but for boots. Many had worn out their footwear after walking hundreds of miles over rough terrain and so they set about making brogues from the horses' hides. Nothing fancy, mind you; just strips of hide bound around the feet as best they could. But they were certainly better than the tattered remains some left behind and infinitely better than continuing through the snow in bare feet. When we were ready to leave, we trudged down off the slopes of the Curlews and made tracks for a wood in the neighbouring Bricklieve Mountains known as *Diamhbhrach*, meaning 'Solitude'. It turned out to be appropriately named, as many of our party became separated from the main group as we entered the woods. Some were suddenly overtaken by extreme tiredness once again, dropping behind and falling asleep wherever they chanced to settle down. I had pushed on, wishing to go deeper in among trees where we would be more secure, and, by the time I realised that we were losing people along the way, we were down to only twelve in number. I ordered a fire to be lit, which I hoped would act as a beacon to guide the others to us when they awoke. It worked and, before daybreak on day fourteen of our march, all the stragglers had caught up with us again. However, the fire had also attracted the attention of others!"

"Oh no," I said. "Who was it? Surely not the MacDavitt's again?"

"Ah, we've already got ahead of ourselves. We'll leave that for another time," he replied, obviously wishing to keep me on tenterhooks. "You must be getting hungry yourself and you would be best getting along to your comfortable bed for the night."

There was perhaps more than a hint of sarcasm in his tone as he spoke, but, before I could comment, Donal Cam once again faded away, leaving only the dark and empty windows of Glinsk Castle to bear witness to what had just transpired. Once again I marvelled at the hardships that O'Sullivan Beare and his followers had endured all those years ago. I certainly was fortunate to be able to enjoy ample food and the luxury of a warm bed most nights, but perhaps the biggest contrast of all was the support I received from the locals along the way, something that was very rarely offered to O'Sullivan Beare. The relentless pursuit and attack that he and his people faced, often from their fellow countrymen, must have been soul destroying to say the least. The worst I had faced in terms of pursuit and attack had been from the occasional herd of bullocks. The stoicism and endurance of O'Sullivan Beare's party during their ordeal was truly astonishing.

However, although I had faced little on a par with what O'Sullivan Beare had during my Ireland Way walk, I couldn't help but compare it to the long and difficult journey that Jacqui had faced during the final months of her life. O'Sullivan Beare had been constantly under attack from his Royalist enemies. Jacqui had been constantly under attack from a different, but just as persistent, enemy called cancer. Battles would be fought and the enemy would be chased off for a time, only to return again and continue with its relentless pursuit. Like O'Sullivan Beare, Jacqui had kept going, against hopeless odds, hoping to reach a place where she would free of her enemy at last. I didn't yet know how O'Sullivan Beare's journey would end, but unfortunately Jacqui's enemy had proved to be just too powerful in the end. I suspected that O'Sullivan Beare's end might not be too dissimilar. However, despite the daily hardships and the relentless suffering that Jacqui had had to endure, the way in which she had soldiered on throughout it all had also been truly astonishing.

From Glinsk Castle, I only had about a further kilometre to walk to reach the village of Glinsk itself and enjoy yet another warm welcome from the locals. I made my way to the home of Joe Tarley, after receiving directions from a small shop, and Joe then showed me across the road to my accommodation for the night. The two storey farmhouse had been the family home up until a few years before, when they had moved into a modern bungalow. Although it was literally only across a single lane road, it took a bit of time to make the journey from door to door, as Joe was on crutches. He had broken his right ankle only a few weeks beforehand when he had leapt over a low wall and landed awkwardly. Being a farmer, this was more than a minor inconvenience for him, but thankfully family and friends had rallied round to help keep his farm and his livelihood going. I was delighted to be provided with a whole house to myself for the night. Joe told me that he wouldn't usually let it out to just one person, but that when he learned of my walk for charity he was more than happy to make an exception. When I had booked my accommodation, we hadn't really discussed the rate for the night, with Joe simply passing it off with a comment such as, "Don't worry, I'll not be too sore on you." So I thought, before accepting the keys, I had better clarify the issue. When I asked how much, he said, "Forty euros will cover it, but don't give it to me - give it to your cause." It was yet another fantastic gesture by a very generous soul. The kindness shown to strangers had definitely improved immensely since O'Sullivan Beare and his followers had passed through here.

Glinsk is from the Irish *Gleann Uisce*, meaning 'glen of the water', but it wasn't water that I had in mind when I left the farmhouse and walked the short distance back into the village. Here I met my friend and former work colleague, Delia Skan, in the Glencastle Bar and she treated me to my customary beverage and joined me for a photograph with my banner. Delia had very kindly driven all the way from Belfast so that she could walk with me for a bit and put me up in her house near Williamstown for the following two nights.

****

I enjoyed a great rest in Joe Tarley's farmhouse and, after a DIY breakfast from items I had picked up in the small shop in the village the evening before, I set off once again to pick up the trail. The section of the Ireland Way I'd walked from Ballygar to Glinsk and that now continued towards Ballinlough, was known as the Suck Valley Way, as it follows the valley of the River Suck. It was a very pleasant meander over country lanes, fields and bog land, with occasional glimpses of tributaries of the River Suck, but precious few of the river itself. The weather was mostly sunny, with a brisk breeze to keep conditions pretty comfortable for walking. The occasional brief shower did blow in, but they disappeared again almost as quickly as they came. I finally parted way with the Suck Valley Way north of the sleepy village of Ballymoe and from there the rest of the journey was on roads, including some quite busy stretches.

My friend Delia walked out of Ballinlough to join me on the final stretch back into the town, which was my final destination for the day. She joined me for a drink in Campbell's Bar in centre of the village and, after I searched unsuccessfully for somewhere to stamp my Ireland Way passport, she then drove me to her house a few miles away on the road to Williamstown. It was a small bungalow just set in from the main road and, although quite old, it had everything I needed for a comfortable stay. The house had originally belonged to her parents and it was where Delia had been raised with her siblings and spent her formative years before qualifying as a medical doctor and moving to Belfast. Delia unfortunately had to return to Belfast that evening, but before she left she cooked me a delicious meal and then introduced me to her good neighbours, Michael and Margaret Whyte. Delia had been extremely thoughtful and caring to come all the way to County Galway to open up her house to me and get me settled in and Michael and Margaret were going to exceed my expectations over the next couple of days. The chain of kindness I was experiencing on the Ireland Way was showing no signs of breaking any time soon!

Chapter Ten: Flying High

(Days twenty-six to twenty-eight - Ballinlough to Keadue)

I woke just after dawn the following morning to the unmistakable sounds of a herd of cattle. Oh God, they've come to get me. I'm surrounded. Those were my immediate thoughts, as I dragged my confused mind out of the fog of sleep. But I soon discovered that they were grazing in the field beside Delia's little Galway hideaway and thankfully behind a secure fence. As I peered out the window at them, the early morning light was just beginning to bathe the field and the livestock in a soft warm glow and, despite my lingering aversion to cattle, it presented a heavenly scene. After breakfast, Margaret arrived to ferry me back to Ballinlough to begin my day's walk. It would be a long one today and I was keen to get on the road as early as possible. Margaret left me off close to Campbell's bar and I headed out of town towards Lough O'Flynn, the lake that gives Ballinlough its name, which in Irish is *Baile an Locha*, meaning 'town of the lake'. Lough O'Flynn lay about one and a half kilometres north of the town and, when I reached the small marina on its southern shore, I was confronted with the most beautiful and tranquil of scenes. The waters of the main lake were ruffled slightly by a light breeze, but the water's surface within the sheltered marina was mirror smooth and reflected the sky, the trees and the colourful rowing boats perfectly. The route skirted the east side of the lake for its two and a half kilometre length, crossing over a rather narrow River Suck at one stage. I was reminded at this point that Lough O'Flynn is the source of the River Suck and that the River Suck is the main tributary of the River Shannon. I thought that this would be my last sight of the River Suck, but little did I know then that I would soon be seeing more of it than I ever imagined possible! From the northern end of the lake, the route swung northeast and I continued along a minor road for a further seven kilometres. This road was pretty straight and often I was faced with seemingly endless stretches of tarmac ahead of me that narrowed and narrowed to a pinpoint in the far distance, where it finally met the white clouds gathered on the horizon. I eventually reached the village of Loughglynn, named after another lake just to the north. I didn't linger here, as there wasn't much to linger over, but instead stayed on the tedious tarmac for another eleven kilometres to reach the town of Ballaghaderreen. My old 'friend', Tar McAdam, had well and truly returned and, unfortunately, he stayed with me for the whole of today's trek. He was still as hard as before, but at least he had cooled down considerably since I had last spent a lot of time in his company back in County Cork.

Ballaghaderreen was bustling with people and traffic when I arrived, which I took to be its normal state given its location just off the N5 national primary road between Longford and Westport. I purchased some supplies in a small store near the main square and then enjoyed my lunch on a bench on a traffic island under a small oak tree. It might not sound like a very salubrious place for a break, but it was actually quite pleasant and a good spot to watch the world rush by, as I leisurely munched on my sandwich and sipped from my flask of coffee. The small oak tree I was sitting under was the only apparent clue as to the town's name. Ballaghaderreen is from the Irish *Bealagh an Doirín*, meaning 'the way of the little oak wood'. I presumed there were, or at least used to be, more trees somewhere around the town, as one small oak hardly makes a wood; not even a little one. After visiting the local library and availing of their Wi-Fi to make and refine some plans for the days ahead, I heaved on my rucksack once again and set off for the village of Monasteraden, my stopping point for the day. After a few hundred metres, I returned to the library, collected the walking poles that I had left behind and set off for a second time. Jacqui used to say that I would forget my head if it wasn't screwed on! Once back on the route, it took me over hills and past forests, but still stubbornly stuck to tarmac roads that twisted and turned in a convoluted fashion through the countryside. Judging from my map, the direct route from Ballaghaderreen to Monasteraden was less than eight kilometres, but the 'roundabout' route taken by the Ireland Way was nearly twice as long! It was often very tempting to cut corners and take shortcuts, but once again I remained pretty determined to follow the official route as closely as possible. The roads I walked on were mainly very quiet minor roads, but there were also a few stretches of very busy main road, which necessitated frequent sidestepping onto verges to avoid the fast oncoming traffic. Occasional views of the distinctive shape of County Sligo's Benbulbin Mountain in the far distance, a shadowy grey presence often disappearing behind darker grey washes of rain sweeping in from the Atlantic, provided some distraction from the tedium of the road.

Eight and a half hours after departing from Ballinlough that morning, I was relieved to catch my first glimpse of the bell tower of St. Aidan's Church in Monasteraden, peeking up above the trees. The tower was beautifully highlighted in the evening sun and framed against the blue waters of Lough Gara in the background. Naturally, due to their 'aspiring' heights, the towers and spires of churches often provided the first indication that I was nearing the next town or village and, as in this case, it also often provided a welcome sign that the end of my day's journey was within reach. Monasteraden is from the Irish *Mainistir Réadáin*, meaning 'Aidan's monastery' after a monastery was founded here by St. Aidan in the sixth century. Nothing remains of the monastery today, although the more recently constructed church still bears the saint's name. Despite the welcoming sign from the church, when I finally reached the village I instead made straight for Drury's Bar; drawn to the dark side as usual. I stepped into the small pub and joined the four local men inside, who looked very much like they were part of the fixtures and fittings. I ordered my pint of Guinness, had my photograph taken and chatted to the men. They were all friendly enough towards me, but there was one among the group who was downright ignorant and rude to the others and to one man in particular. I began to feel a little uncomfortable and, when he let fly a string of angry curses at the poor man, I tried to defuse the situation by joking and asking if there was another pub in the village where a man might get a drink in peace. "Unfortunately not," said one of the others with a laugh, "but don't mind him. That's the way he always is. It's just banter." But it didn't seem like just banter to me. It seemed to me that there was some history between the two main protagonists and, whatever it was, it wasn't going to be forgotten or forgiven anytime soon. When I glanced at the barman to see how he was reacting, he just rolled his eyes as if to say that this was fairly typical – he had obviously seen it all before and didn't feel the need to intervene. However, it was the first time that I had ever felt uneasy amongst locals on my journey and I decided that it was time to drink up quickly and leave. Thankfully, I had contacted Margaret earlier and I didn't have too long to wait before she pulled up outside and I was able to make my escape. I never felt personally threatened at any stage, but it just wasn't a nice atmosphere to be in and I was very happy to leave it behind. Thankfully, my spirits, not to mention my body, would soon be lifted sky high!

Margaret drove me back to Delia's place near Williamstown where I had a quick shower and something to eat. I was about to settle down and catch up with my social media blog, when Margaret's husband, Michael, phoned with an offer I simply couldn't refuse. All thoughts of blogs were quickly abandoned as I got ready to head out on a totally unexpected adventure. It turned out that, as well as being an engineer and running his own business manufacturing parts for boilers, Michael was also a fully qualified pilot and owned his own light aircraft. He arrived five minutes later and gave me a lift back to his place and we then walked the short distance to a large shed out behind the house. This shed was his 'aircraft hanger' and I watched in wonder as Michael pushed a light aircraft out onto the short grass outside and positioned it facing towards the far end of the field, which actually turned out to be the runway. It was a small, two-seater aircraft and Michael informed me that it had been built from a kit by a friend of his. I have to admit that the cockpit seemed rather flimsy as I climbed into it and took my seat beside Michael. He showed me how close and fasten the wobbly Perspex door and also how to buckle up and adjust the seat harness. He ran through all the necessary safety checks, making sure that there was enough fuel in the tank and that a certain lever adjusted a certain flap as it was meant to. He started the engine and handed me a pair of headphones with a microphone so that we could continue to communicate over the noise of the aircraft, which was considerable. Just ten minutes after boarding, we were hurtling towards the far end of the field, gaining speed rapidly as we approached the boundary fence. Michael pulled back on the joystick and the shuddering of the wheels trundling over the ground suddenly disappeared as we lifted off smoothly and zoomed well clear of the fence line to begin climbing into the sky.

I had of course taken off from runways in commercial aircraft many times, but this was a totally unique experience. For one thing I had the 'pilot's eye view' out the front of the aircraft, but the biggest difference was in terms of scale. It was akin to the difference between riding in a huge luxury coach and driving a small rickety go-kart. Being strapped into such a small aircraft with just a thin sheet of metal between my feet and the air below certainly heightened my sense of vulnerability. But Michael had clocked up hundreds of hours of flying experience as a qualified pilot and I felt secure in his hands and I was able to relax and enjoy the views as we climbed and levelled out at a height of twelve hundred feet. And the views were fabulous as we spent the next half hour on an aerial tour of much of the Suck Valley Way that I had covered on foot over the last couple of days. I actually saw much more of the River Suck in our thirty minutes in the air than I had in previous forty-eight hours on foot. It was also incredible to see many of the landmarks I had encountered on the ground from this unique perspective – the long silver ribbon of the River Suck itself, snaking through the landscape, the empty shell of Glinsk Castle standing defiantly upon its grassy knoll, the stonewall of an unusual circular graveyard on the edge of Monasteraden, the dark waters of Lough O'Flynn and the pretty small marina, as well as a number of familiar towns and villages I had passed through. We even flew over Delia's house at one point and we were flying low enough to be able to pick out much of the detail. Even the individual cattle in the fields were clear to see and I was tempted to ask Michael to dive-bomb the beasts to give them a taste of their own medicine!

Depending on the wind direction, our speed increased to over 100mph at times, while on other occasions it dropped as low as 60mph, but either way, it didn't take us very long to cover the same ground it had taken me days to traverse on foot. There appeared to be two weather fronts closing in on us from opposite directions, but Michael kept a close eye on these and deftly steered us away from any potential trouble. The rainclouds did create some beautiful scenes though, as the sun spilled through the gaps and cascaded crepuscular rays of amber to illuminate the land and water beneath. The waters of the River Suck itself now picked up and reflected the glow of the sunlight, giving some credence to the thought that its name derives from an old Irish word *succín* , meaning 'amber'.

All too soon, the light started to fade and the rain began to make an appearance, dotting the windscreen with sporadic drops. Michael decided it was time to head for home, but for some reason he politely refused my offer to take over the controls! After a very smooth landing, I helped him push his plane back into the shed and we then joined Margaret in the house for a cup of tea and some cake. I could not have imagined a more fabulous way to end the day. It was a truly wonderful experience and one that I would surely never forget.

****

I locked the door of Delia's house behind me for the last time and climbed into the passenger seat of Michael's work van, where Margaret was waiting to give me a lift all the way back to Monasteraden. Fortuitously, it suited Margaret also, as she had a delivery of back boilers to drop off in Limerick for Michael. Margaret dropped me outside Drury's Bar, where, although there were no obvious signs of life, I could almost imagine the regulars still bickering inside, as if trapped in some unending loop of animosity. I waved Margaret off, as she headed on towards Limerick, thinking that I would certainly miss my time with her and Michael. They were yet another couple to be added to the growing list of fantastic people that I had met along the Ireland Way. It occurred to me that, although I may have been walking the route alone, it was by no means a solo effort. Without the help of all these good people, I'm not sure that I would have made it this far. It certainly would have been a lot harder.

After flying high yesterday evening, my feet were firmly back on the ground today. I dragged on my rucksack and, checking my map, chose what I believed to be the right road to leave the village by. I passed an old, rusty, red petrol pump, standing alone and forlorn by the roadside - a relic from the past that still displayed the price of fuel at six shillings and sixpence. It added to the feeling that this village was caught in some sort of time warp and I subconsciously quickened my pace a little to make good my escape from Monasteraden. Just beyond St Aidan's Church, my elusive Pacman made one of his increasingly rare appearances to provide reassurance that I had indeed chosen my road wisely - for a change! Further out the road, I was raucously greeted by a group of four donkeys. When they first spotted me they ambled over from the far side of their field to the roadside fence to see if I had anything for them. Seeing that I hadn't, they protested noisily and didn't let up with their loud braying until I had disappeared from their sight. For some reason, they reminded me of the four guys I had met in Drury's Bar the previous evening!

About four kilometres out of Monasteraden, I came across the ruins of Moygara Castle, set rather commandingly on top of a low hill close to the North West corner of Lough Gara. Both the castle and the lake took their name from the O'Gara family who ruled the area around the lough from the thirteenth century. The castle was built around 1500 and legend had it that it used to have golden gates that were now hidden in the depths of Lough Gara itself. The fairly tedious, although mercifully quiet, country roads continued for the next fifteen kilometres or so, taking me generally in a north-easterly direction, between the Curlew and Bricklieve mountain ranges, and towards the village of Ballinafad on the southern shores of Lough Arrow. However, rather than continuing into Ballinafad, I left the roads about a kilometre outside the village to join a series of farm lanes and then grassy tracks that took me northwards, up into the Bricklieve Mountains, where O'Sullivan Beare's party of refugees had camped on the thirteenth day of their exodus. Although quite challenging in terms of elevation, it was great to finally leave the tarmac behind and exhilarating to be back in the mountains again after so long spent in the 'lowlands'. As I climbed higher into the mountains, guided by rough stone walls, softened somewhat by the long dry grass and dainty blue harebells growing alongside, I was rewarded with some fantastic views over Lough Arrow and the surrounding countryside. Stopping to have a closer look at a pretty harebell bloom, I was reminded that in Jacqui's home county of Antrim, the harebell was once believed to be a fairy plant, also known as the goblin's thimble, and that it was bad luck to pick it. I was content to simply admire its delicate, almost paper like, blue petals and not risk incurring the wrath of any little folk by interfering with such a whisper of a flower.

"I'm glad you've time to stop and pick the daisies," a voice suddenly rang out behind me.

"Feckin' hell!" I shouted out involuntarily. Looking round to see Donal Cam standing nearby, I then added indignantly, "Do you mind? I thought I had warned you before about your sudden loud appearances. And for your information, it's a harebell, not a daisy, and I have no intention of picking it." After taking a moment to compose myself, I then said, "Anyway, now that you're here, I suppose you will want to continue with your story. You left me on a bit of a cliff-hanger last time when you said that others had noticed the fire you had lit in the woods near here."

"Apologies for startling you again," he said in a conciliatory tone. "It's just that I get excited at the chance to speak with someone again - someone who's alive, that is. Anyway, the fire had been lit to guide the stragglers back to our main group, but it also caught the attention of Oliver Lambert, the Governor of Connacht. It would have been disastrous for us if he had sent his men to investigate. And, as dawn broke on our fourteenth day, men did come to investigate why there was a fire lit in such an isolated spot in the mountains. But, thankfully, they were not Lambert's men, but friendly locals. We were now deep into Connacht and there were now more people disposed to our way of thinking in these parts."

"Siding with the rebels, you mean?"

"Exactly," Donal Cam replied. "They brought us a present of food, which was very welcome, particularly by the small number of us who had refused to eat horseflesh. They also reported back to Lambert that the fire in the hills had been lit by labourers who were in the mountains looking for stone. Sometimes the English could be so gullible. They accepted the story as the truth, believing that the Irish were mad enough to engage in such an activity in the middle of winter. Anyway, they left us alone, which was a blessing. We had sufficient problems without being faced with another attack. Some of our party had grown seriously foot-sore from the hard weather and the long march, including my great friend The O'Connor Kerry, who was suffering intensely. I would really have preferred to have got moving again, but I had to take account of the poor condition of these men also. Thankfully the locals covering for us had bought us some valuable time and so I decided that we should continue to rest in the woods until nightfall. However, even after resting all day, O'Connor was still in a bad way. But we could not risk staying in the one place any longer. A night march was now necessary for all. O'Connor, who was about the same age as my uncle Dermot and just as tough, decided he had to take drastic action regarding his feet." Before continuing with his account, Donal Cam looked at me with a smirk on his face and asked, "How strong is your stomach?"

"Pretty robust," I replied, before asking, "why?"

"You'll find out soon enough," he replied and then continued, "O'Connor, lying stretched on the ground, addressed his feet in the following manner, *"Have you not gone through the most difficult trials these last three nights? Why do you now shrink from the toils of one night? Are not my head and the safety of my whole body more precious to you, my most delicate feet? What doth it avail to have fled so far if through your sloth we now fall into the hands of the enemy? I will assuredly make you shake off this sluggishness."* Then, with the utmost effort and weight of his armour, he struck his feet against the ground and squeezed out all the pus and blood."

"Oh man," I protested, "that is gross! I'm glad you didn't show me that."

"There were battle hardened warriors among us who witnessed it and almost doubled over with nausea at the sight. As I said, he was a tough old bugger and once he was finished, he promptly got up and began to march with the rest of us, although it was plain to see that he was in great discomfort. We knew we had to avoid the more direct highways and paths to O'Rourke's stronghold between Lough Key and Lough Arrow, as they would almost certainly have been blocked by our enemies. But none among us were familiar with these mountains. We desperately needed a guide who knew his way around these parts. It was then that a miraculous event occurred. A man clad in linen garments, in his bare feet and with a white wreath around his head, suddenly appeared before us. He carried a long wand, tipped with an iron point, and overall he presented an appearance calculated to inspire awe." Donal Cam must have noted the puzzled look on my face, for he asked, "What? You don't believe me?"

"Hey, I'm currently talking to a four hundred year old ghost who is acting as my guide, so I'm hardly in a position to cast doubt on what you saw, am I? No, it was just the thought of someone walking over these mountains in his bare feet – it reminded me of someone." I was of course thinking of Stephen Bell, aka Wildfoot, the barefoot adventurer who had completed the Ireland Way before me. "So what did this vision with a wand say to you?"

"He said that he knew that we were fleeing from the tyranny of heretics; that we had routed the loyalist forces at Aughrim and that we were now on our way to O'Rourke's castle and needed a guide. He then said, *"Therefore a desire has seized me to conduct you thither."* I wasn't sure at first if we could place our trust in this man. It may have been a trick to lead us into the path of the enemy. But what choice did we have? Left to our own devices we would never find our way to O'Rourke. I ordered that two hundred gold pieces be given to him and hoped that that this would ensure his loyalty, but he said, *"I accept this gift, not as a reward, but as a token of my good will towards you, as I have resolved of my own good will to do you this service."* Nevertheless, the darkness of night, the unknown country and the strange guide, all served to multiply our fears as we groped along after this mysterious figure. We slipped over loose stones, waded through snow heaped up by the wind, fought against exhaustion and swollen feet as we pushed on through the bitterly cold night. O'Connor suffered more than anyone. His feet and legs were inflamed and his blisters became ulcerated, but he kept going, such was his determination. A lesser man would have given up long before."

My own 'injuries' never felt more trivial, as I listened to Donal Cam relate the tale of almost superhuman endurance by his elderly friend.

Donal Cam continued, "Our guide led us on a route using little used narrow passes and valleys through the Bricklieve Mountains, which took us on a long loop around the top of Lough Arrow and then south. In the dead of night, we reached the little village of Knockvicar and here we were welcomed into the houses of the locals to warm ourselves at their fires and to refresh ourselves and purchase food. When we decided to move on the following morning, O'Connor, whose ulcers had been crustated by the heat from the fire, was not able to stand, much less walk. Four of his comrades carried him on their shoulders until they found a stray horse, lank and blind with age, and they placed him on its sharp, skeletal back without bridle or saddle. Some led the blind beast, while others whacked it along from behind as we crossed the plain towards Leitrim. After daybreak, the guide showed us O'Rourke's castle in the distance. He assured us that all danger was now past and then he bade us farewell and disappeared back into the wintery landscape, like a ghost."

"It's hard to imagine that," I said with a smile.

"Ha!" he mused, "I never thought that four hundred years later, I would be doing the same thing. I must also bid you farewell at this point, young sir." And with that he disappeared back into the summer landscape, although, before he completely faded away, I'm sure I heard him say, "I'll see you again in Leitrim."

Looking at my maps, I could easily appreciate the long detour O'Sullivan Beare's party had had to make to avoid running into the enemy on their way to Knockvicar. The most direct route, between Lough Key and Lough Arrow, was only a distance of about twelve kilometres. However, the route on which O'Sullivan Beare's guide led the refugees, and hence the route I would be following, was a distance of approximately thirty-eight kilometres. A significant extra distance for sure. How much easier it would have been for me to take a shortcut between the loughs. I didn't have to worry about any enemies blocking my way, after all. But no; if an old man, as crippled as O'Connor was, could manage the longer route to Knockvicar, then surely I could. And if this walk was truly in Jacqui's honour, then I could surely 'go the extra mile', or however many extra miles it was, to properly honour her memory. So I set off once again over the Bricklieve Mountains, determined to continue following in the footsteps of O'Sullivan Beare.

The top of the mountain was divided by a deep and wide valley or pass that ran north to south. It provided my legs with a good workout, as I crossed from one side to the other and tackled a steep descent, followed closely by an equally steep ascent. I picked up a dirt track, which cut through the thick purple heather covering the far side of the mountain, and followed this and the subsequent grassy pathways and laneways towards a striking feature situated on a headland before me. This was the prominent white dome shape of one of the Carrowkeel Neolithic Tombs sitting atop the northerly Carrowkeel hill of the Bricklieve Mountains. The ancient passage tomb was shining white, highlighted by the late afternoon sun. The tomb I could now see before me was only one of twenty-one passage tombs in the area. The name Bricklieve comes from the Irish *An Bricshliabh*, which means 'the speckled mountains'. It's possible the name is simply a reference to the mountains being 'speckled' with cairns, but it has also been suggested that the cairns themselves used to sparkle in the sun when their exteriors were speckled with quartz rock in the past. My crossing of the mountains had certainly been speckled with delights and, as I made my way down and around the lower slopes, I encountered yet another one. For the Ireland Way route brought me right through the Sathya Sai Donkey Sanctuary.

Like The Donkey Sanctuary outside Liscarroll that I had visited weeks beforehand, this site was given over to the care of abandoned, neglected and abused donkeys. It was a pleasure to wander through the rolling hills where these gentle creatures now enjoyed the company of others and the freedom to graze, laze or roll in the dirt as they pleased. There were donkeys of all ages, shades and sizes on show and it was all quite idyllic looking as they relaxed in the early evening sunshine, against a patchwork quilt of fields in the background that stretched away into the distance until it met a long line of Sligo mountains on the horizon. The pathways led me further down off the hillside until I joined a minor road and from here it was only just over another kilometre into the village of Castlebaldwin. It had been a long day; I had covered over thirty kilometres and I was really looking forward to resting my weary feet.

I had hoped to find both accommodation and food in the Clevery Mill Guesthouse on the edge of the village, but I arrived to find it all closed up. So, with plan A not working out, I headed on and called into McDermott's Bar and Restaurant in the centre of Castlebaldwin to at least satisfy my thirst while I worked on a plan B. As I sat with my pint of Guinness and guidebook, a man on the barstool next to me started chatting with me in a very friendly manner. It transpired that he lived in the village and, when he learned that I was looking for somewhere to stay, he offered me a spare bed in his house. Not yet having anywhere else sorted, I thought why not and accepted his kind offer. He had a pint in front of him, but was quite sober at this stage and he seemed like a decent chap. He gave me his address and directions and said I could call whenever I was ready. So that was plan B sorted. I ordered some food and continued to chat with my new found friend, as he continued to order one drink after another. To be fair he always offered to get me one also, but I told him that I needed to stay reasonably sober for my challenge. By the time I was finished my meal, he was quite drunk and I had decided that I now needed a plan C. I headed to the Gents and while away from the bar searched on my phone for accommodation in the area and found a B&B about two kilometres out of Castlebaldwin. I phoned the Tower Hill B&B and thankfully there was a room available and, even more thankfully, the landlady kindly agreed to collect me from McDermott's Bar in her car, saving my feet from any additional torture. After delaying for a little while, I returned to the bar and paid for my food. I then thanked my drunken friend for his kindness and told him that I had decided to walk on for another bit while the weather was favourable. He seemed quite surprised and a little annoyed at my change of heart, but, before he could collect his thoughts and say anything intelligible, I grabbed my rucksack and headed for the door. Once outside, I was very pleased to find my getaway car waiting for me with the engine running and Muriel Gardiner in the driving seat. It was the second day in a row that I had had to beat a hasty retreat from my chosen watering hole. I hoped that normal convivial service would soon be restored.

****

I had a restful night at the Tower Hill B&B and Muriel set me up with a great breakfast the following morning. She also very kindly offered me a much reduced rate, which I was very happy to accept. The only downside to my choice of accommodation was the fact that it was about two kilometres off route. Unfortunately, Muriel had other guests to attend to and so was unable to give me a lift back into Castlebaldwin. So, I set off on foot down the very long drive, hoping to hitch a lift when I reached the main road. It was a beautiful morning and the Tower Hill B&B was set in the heart of the countryside with gorgeous views across to Lough Arrow. A proud mare and her long-legged foal were prancing around in the field just below the house and it presented an idyllic rural scene. An air of absolute tranquillity followed me as I progressed down the drive. It abruptly disappeared though once I reached the very busy main Dublin road, where vehicle after vehicle thundered past. However, despite the volume of traffic going in my direction, and me wearing my most pleading of faces, no one was prepared to slow down, never mind stop, in response to my outstretched thumb. Mind you, the cars were probably occupied by people rushing to get to work and probably the last thing they needed at that time of the morning was to have to interrupt their journey to pick up a rucksack carrying stranger with a weird look on his face! After having completed half the journey to Castlebaldwin on foot, I gave up trying to hitch a lift and simply resigned myself to doing the extra distance. Thirty minutes after leaving my B&B, I arrived back in the small village and called into a roadside store to replenish my food supplies for the day's journey ahead. I then re-joined the Ireland Way trail and began a long trek around the northern end of Lough Arrow, first heading generally east and then southwards! My route over the Bricklieve Mountains the previous day had followed part of the Miner's Way, which was made up of paths used by miners who once worked in the Arigna coal mines, and today I continued in the footsteps of those miners of old. Arigna is a village just a few kilometres north-east of Keadue - my destination for today - and was the centre of the mining industry that thrived for over four hundred years until the mines closed in 1990. The Ireland Way actually follows the path of many different 'Ways', from the Beara Way in the south to the Ulster Way in the north, and the Miner's Way was simply another example of this symbiotic relationship.

Although it had been a beautiful morning to start with, it wasn't long before grey skies started to close in, bringing a few brief showers with them that were sufficiently heavy to encourage me to struggle into my wet gear. About a kilometre out of Castlebaldwin, I left the tarmac and climbed over an old stone stile into the first of many fields that I would encounter today. I passed through one field that had a large herd of cattle in it, but they took no interest in me at all and just continued grazing as if I wasn't there. I thought that I had perhaps finally lost my 'animal attraction' until I climbed over a metal stile a little later and entered another field, where another large herd of cows and calves were happily grazing. On this occasion, however, they all immediately stopped grazing as soon as I appeared and headed straight towards me. I decided not to risk venturing through this overly inquisitive herd and instead climbed back out over the stile again and managed to find a way around the field and continue with my journey, being closely tracked by the herd on the other side of the hedge all the while! It would be great if farmers ran their electric fences about a metre out from the hedges to provide a safe corridor for walkers. It would also discourage walkers from taking shortcuts or diversions into areas where they probably shouldn't be. And whilst on the subject of discouraging walkers, I also came across a gate into a field with a 'BEWARE OF THE BULL' sign displayed on it. This certainly had a discouraging effect. However, I couldn't see an alternative way around this field and, as I also couldn't see any bull from where I was standing, I decided to take my chances, although I kept pretty close to the hedges, just in case a quick dive through them might become necessary. Thankfully, it didn't.

It had stopped raining by this stage, but the skies were covered with a thick, impenetrable layer of grey cloud and the outlook remained dull. The route gradually took me higher into the low-lying hills to the north of Lough Arrow and, despite the gloomy weather, I paused frequently to take in the views over the grey waters of the lake and towards the dark shadows of the Bricklieve Mountains that I had crossed the day before. There was nothing as challenging as the Bricklieve Mountains to contend with today, but the low level hills still presented some steep climbs along the way that continued to test my calf muscles. Fortunately, my support sock, together with the exercises that Noel Rice, my Belfast physio, had urged me do twice a day, seemed to be holding things together just fine.

Beyond the sadly abandoned sprawling complex of Cromleach Lodge, a grassy path took me right past a huge thick slab of rock that was balanced precariously on a number of smaller upright stones. It almost appeared as if the weight of the massive slab had, over time, slowly driven the upright stones partially into the ground. It was a rather bizarre sight and there were no signs or notices anywhere around that could shed some light on this rather unnatural structure. I later discovered that this was actually Ireland's second largest portal tomb or dolmen. It is known as the Labby Rock and is believed to be some five thousand years old, having been built during the Neolithic period. The huge slab, or capstone, is estimated to weigh seventy tons and how people that long ago managed to position it on top of the supporting stones is still a mystery. The rock takes its name from the Irish word for bed, 'leaba', and, according to Celtic folklore, it is the place where two young lovers, Diarmuid and Grainne, slept when fleeing the wrath of an older man who had been promised Grainne's hand in marriage by her father, the High King. Local tradition also claims that if an engaged couple should lie on top of the Labby Rock before they are married they are sure to have many children. I remembered encountering a similar 'stone bed' in north-west Spain while on my Camino two years previously that was reputed to have similar fertility powers. There, a bishop had destroyed the stone to put an end to any 'love on the rocks', but the Labby Rock still appeared to be open for business!

From the Labby Rock, the grassy path continued for a time before the route took off through rough, upland fields that were populated with little more than stone walls, clumps of thistle and hardy looking sheep. When I reached the small, elevated village of Highwood, I found a convenient garden bench behind the local church and rested here for a while and had my packed lunch. It was a supremely relaxing spot and I watched the swallows swooping and turning in the air as they hunted insects to bring back to their young nesting in the 'mud huts' beneath the church eaves; each approaching parent being met with a cacophony of squeaks from hungry mouths anticipating their next meal. As I was getting ready to move on, a group of six people arrived and we got chatting. A couple of the group lived locally and they were showing their relatives from America, who were visiting Ireland for the first time, around the local sights of interest. My rucksack and attire also piqued their interest in my walk and, when I did eventually get on the road again, it was with a few extra Euro notes in my pocket.

Beyond Highwood, the route headed eastwards along country roads and lanes and through increasingly persistent rain, until I reached the village of Ballyfarnon in the late afternoon. Here a busy main road took me through the village and on for about a kilometre, before I branched off and stepped through the modest entrance gates to Kilronan Castle and started up the long drive towards the castle itself, which was constructed in the 1800's and now operated as a luxury hotel. The room rates undoubtedly would have been well in excess of my budget, so, before reaching the castle, I followed the way marker that directed me off the drive, over a wooden stile and into the castle estate's extensive woodland. Here, utterly delightful forest trails led me through the ancient woods, the thick forest canopy providing me with some shelter from the rain, and then along the northern shore of Lough Meelagh, 'the lake of the marsh'. Tall firs mixed with more indigenous species, such as oak and ash, and the trails twisted and turned around giant trees that soared into the skies above, their trunks often encased in wonderfully textured bark. One tree in particular looked as if strips of bark had been woven around its trunk like strands of thick interlaced rope in a complex but uniform pattern, as if it was wearing some sort of arboreal Aran sweater.

The path continued close to the shores of Lough Meelagh and gaps through the trees afforded frequent views of its dark foreboding waters, rendered cold and grey by the ominous sky above. The forest path abruptly ended when it met a narrow roadway, which I soon realised was the main drive up to Kilronan Castle - the previous drive probably being the 'staff' entrance to the hotel. I continued to eschew the comforts undoubtedly on offer at the castle and instead followed the drive in the opposite direction towards the castle's main entrance. And here, just inside a unique triple-arched stone gateway, I came upon an even more unique and most bizarre stone gatehouse. It was built around the same time as the castle and, although it was now unoccupied and pretty dilapidated and covered in weeds, the walls were very much intact and sound. A nearby sign informed me that the building had been constructed from "*what is termed 'river-worn' stone ... carefully chosen by the masons to maximise the illusion of the decayed nature of the building .... to make the building appear to grow out of the landscape.*" The resulting asymmetrical structure, with its roughly pointed arched openings and almost haphazardly placed stonework, conjured up images from a dark fairy-tale in my mind. It was as if the gatehouse had been designed by Antoni Gaudi in collaboration with Hans Christian Anderson and was perhaps not abandoned at all, but still home to a goblin or two!

I pushed on for the final kilometre or so to the town of Keadue. Thankfully the path continued along the edge of the lough and, for the most part, kept me off the main road. I passed St Laisair's Holy Well and Kilronan Abbey graveyard, where a carved stone above the entrance announced that the body of 'Carolan, the last of the Irish bards', who died in 1758, lay interred within. This was Turlough O'Carolan, to give him his full name, and he had been one of the best music composers and harpists of Ireland, which was pretty remarkable given the fact that he was blinded by smallpox when he was about eighteen years of age. The town I was on my way to, Keadue, holds an annual O'Carolan Harp Festival to celebrate the bard's life and music. The path reached a small car park at the east end of Lough Meelagh and at this point I had to divert away from the way-marked trail and follow the road for the final stretch towards my accommodation for the night.

A sign on the way into Keadue proudly proclaimed the residents pride in their town, announcing a string of Tidy Town Awards stretching back to the year 2000 and right up to 2017. And upon arriving in the small, picturesque town, I wouldn't have been surprised to learn that they were in line for the 2018 award also. Given my sweaty and dishevelled appearance after being on the road for nine hours, I almost felt like I should turn around and leave before I was 'tidied away' by some eager citizens for lowering the town's pristine standards. However, I needn't have feared and, when I arrived at the Harp and Shamrock Bar and B&B, I was given a very warm welcome by Mary Roddy, who ran the establishment along with her mother-in-law, Ann. It was after seven by the time I got settled into my room and cleaned up and I was now more than ready for something to eat. It was then that I discovered one of the key advantages that this small town had over its rivals when it came to maintaining its 'tidy town' status. For there was absolutely nowhere in the town to eat out. Never mind a restaurant or a bar offering pub grub, there wasn't even a chip shop or burger bar! So while other towns and villages had to battle against the scourge of fast food packaging littering their streets, Keadue had a head start because there was nowhere to generate the rubbish in the first place. But while it helped make for a tidy town, it did nothing for my empty stomach. Thankfully, there was a very small shop just off the bar and I was able to buy sufficient supplies to see me through to breakfast the next morning, although a sliced loaf, a tin of sardines and a couple of tomatoes didn't add up to the most appetising of meals. But never mind – there was always a pint of Guinness in the bar to help wash it all down.

One wall of the bar was almost completely taken up with a display cabinet that contained an impressive collection of over one hundred and twenty model cars and trains. They had been collected over many years by the landlady, Ann Roddy. They were all still in their original packaging and I joked with Ann that they must be worth a small fortune. But she wasn't interested in parting with them for any money. "The grandchildren would love to get their hands on them though," she said, "although that would be just to play with them. I've told them that they can have them all, but not until I'm dead and gone. Of course," she added with a laugh, "I hope they might be far too old for playing with toys by the time that happens."

Chapter Eleven: Finding Leitrim
(Days twenty-nine and thirty - Keadue to Ballinagleragh)

My breakfast in the Harp and Shamrock B&B more than made up for my meagre meal the previous evening and, to improve things even further, Mary Roddy give me a great discount on the room rate. I stepped out onto the immaculate streets of Keadue and was soon reminded again of the town's close association with the celebrated harpist, Turlough O'Carolan, as I encountered a stone monument in a small park, a colourful mural covering the gable end of a building and even a beautiful bog oak sculpture all dedicated to the musician.

I retraced my steps back to the small car park where I had left the trail yesterday. The weather had improved considerably and the views across Lough Meelagh were quite stunning as the still waters reflected beautifully the blue sky and white clouds above, along with the dark green trees and paler green reeds that surrounded the lake. I noticed a small island in the lake, nestled among the reeds, and learned that this was not a natural feature, but rather a man-made island or *'crannóg'* constructed from soil, rock and timber during the seventeenth century for defence or habitation. I left the car park and re-joined the way-marked trail, which led me through the tall trees of Knockranny Wood and past the overgrown remains of a megalithic court tomb. As I worked my way round the southern shores of Lough Meelagh, I was rewarded with distant but fairly clear views of the magnificent edifice of Kilronan Castle amongst the trees on the opposite bank of the lake and the reflective quality of the lake's surface continued to delight. I emerged from the trees into a clearing by the shore line and spotted a small drove of five donkeys in the distance that appeared to be wandering freely. As soon as they spotted me, they ambled over to meet me and jostled for position to get the most attention and pats. They were very friendly and such gentle creatures and I enjoyed their company, but I had to keep moving. However, when I did set off again, they followed me along the shoreline path in single file for some distance, as if I was an over optimistic gold prospector on the Oregon Trail. In fact, it wasn't until I entered the next wooded area that they finally gave up on playing 'follow the leader'.

These woods had a real ancient feel to them and thick moss smothered the floor and even crawled up the tree trunks in places, as if the very ground was trying to hold the trees back from reaching for the sky above. One tree had fallen across the path in a tangle of branches. To my overactive imagination, it looked like an Ent from Tolkien's *Lord of the Rings* on its hands and knees, struggling to get up again, fighting against being dragged down into final submission. Large mushrooms and toadstools dotted the forest floor and my vision was filled with various lacklustre hues of green and brown, apart from the occasional splash of colour offered by the bright red berries adorning the stems of wild arum plants. These plants, which resemble red hot pokers sticking up out of the ground, are also known by a bewildering array of common names, such as lords-and-ladies, devils and angels, cows and bulls, cuckoo-pint, soldiers diddies, priest's pintle, Adam and Eve, bobbins, naked girls, naked boys, starch-root, wake robin, friar's cowl, jack in the pulpit and cheese and toast. Whatever you choose to call them, the most important thing to remember about the plant is that the berries are extremely poisonous.

I escaped the dark and slightly eerie woods and tramped over an area of open ground, at the same time gradually moving further away from 'the lake of the marsh'. Soon I was back on the tarmac again, as I joined a series of minor roads that took me westwards and then turned south towards the small village of Crossna, about four kilometres away. I came to a fork in the road and the way marker directed me to the left, even though the road to Crossna was on the right. I could see from my map that after a short way along the left fork, I was then meant to cut across fields to join the right fork. It didn't seem particularly logical, but I decided to follow the directions anyway. So off I went down the left fork, past Regan's Bogside Inn, until I came to a way marker directing me over a stile and into a field on the left hand side. The route then simply ran down the field right alongside the roadside hedge until it met another stile that led out onto the same road again. Again, it just didn't make any sense and I was beginning to feel a little bit irritated as I started to climb over this second stile. As I descended the other side of the stile, my foot snagged on a bramble and I stumbled out onto the roadside. I managed to keep my balance, but not my decorum. "For f#ck sake," I shouted out in annoyance. Only then did I look up to see an elderly farmer standing on the road with his bicycle. "Sorry," I said, but he just laughed and told me that perhaps I shouldn't be drinking so early in the day. His name was John James Reagan and, in addition to being a farmer, he also owned the bar I had passed by only minutes earlier. We had a great talk about all sorts of things and he showed me the path to take across the fields to connect with the right fork of the road. I shared with John James my view that these diversions through the fields just didn't make any sense, but he said, "Well, sometimes there's a bit of money to be made if farmers can encourage the route through their land." He didn't say that he himself was a beneficiary, nor did I ask, but the fields in question were right next to his bar and home. He offered me a cup of tea back up at his bar, but it was a bit early in the day for stopping and so I decided to push on. More roads and many more rough fields followed before I reached Clancy's Bar near Crossna and by the time I got there I was definitely ready to stop for a break. The bar was open, and I was able to collect another stamp in my Ireland Way passport. However, I preferred to sit outside at a little picnic table, so I could throw off my boots and cool off in the shade for a bit, as I had my simple lunch of ham and cheese and beer. It was only a small beer, but I reckoned that I may as well have a proper excuse should I trip and stumble again.

The road sign opposite the bar said I was now only two kilometres from Knockvicar, which, as the main road goes or 'as the crow flies', was certainly the case. From there, it should only have been another ten kilometres to Leitrim Village, today's final destination. However, immediately after leaving Clancy's bar, my map steered me off the main road and instead directed me along a minor road that went on for what seemed like forever in the wrong direction, before finally looping back in towards the village of Knockvicar.

This village was where O'Sullivan Beare and his remaining followers had rested for the last time before reaching O'Rourke's castle and the end of their epic march. However, when I arrived in Knockvicar, I decided to push on rather than resting again. My often elusive mate, Pacman, made a 'welcome' reappearance in the village and guided me over a bridge spanning the Boyle River and further south and then west into a parklands. I knew instinctively that I was heading away from my intended destination, but, given the strange and convoluted route often taken by the Ireland Way this was not particularly unusual. So, it was some time before I fully accepted that something was badly wrong. I had been relying on my route maps and the way markers up to this point, but now I dug out my guidebook from my rucksack and consulted the appropriate section. It was then time for another flurry of curses, much worse than John James Regan had witnessed, as it suddenly dawned on me that the Miner's Way and the Ireland Way had actually parted company at Crossna. I had unwittingly continued to follow the Miner's Way, which was now on a return loop back to Ballinafad and the Bricklieve Mountains. And that little traitorous turncoat, Pacman, had now decided to ditch the Ireland Way in favour of the Miner's Way. Looking at my guidebook, I could now also see that I should have taken the direct route from Crossna to Knockvicar rather than looping round the countryside as I had. If my legs hadn't been so tired, I would have kicked myself for being so stupid. But there was nothing else for it. I wearily made an about turn and trudged all the way back to Knockvicar, continuing to curse under my breath as I went.

I eventually made it back to Knockvicar and this time I stopped for a rest, just as O'Sullivan Beare's party had done all those years ago. It was very warm now and I was getting quite tired and I still had ten kilometres to go before reaching Leitrim Village – or so I thought! I crossed over the Boyle River again to stand and stare at Pacman on the way marker post to make sure that I hadn't somehow misinterpreted his direction the first time. But, no - I had read him right and he was pointing in completely the wrong direction for the Ireland Way. I called him a few choice names and then turned my back on him and walked out of Knockvicar, hopefully for the last time. At this point, I never wanted to set foot in the village of Knockvicar ever again! From my guidebook map it looked like it was a straight road from here to Leitrim Village, via another smaller village called Cootehill about three kilometres away. The white clouds had thinned considerably during the course of the day and the afternoon sun was now beating down on me relentlessly. I stopped in Cootehill and called into M J Henry's Bar for a glass of iced water and to replenish my warm water carrier with a fresh and cold supply. I envied the locals and the holiday makers relaxing and enjoying the craic inside the bar out of the heat of the sun, but I mopped my brow with a damp cloth and headed out once again to face the long road to Leitrim. It's just a pity that I took the long road to Carrick-on-Shannon instead!

While I could blame the maps and Pacman for my earlier detours, I only had myself to blame for the next one. In my defence, I was very hot and tired and ever so slightly demoralised by this stage and my attention levels had consequently taken a serious dip in the late afternoon. Tar McAdam was up to his old tricks again! It wasn't until I was two kilometres out of Cootehill that I realised my error. The road I was blindly following had started off in the right direction, but then it had begun to turn towards a large body of water, which I hadn't been expecting. I checked the maps app on my phone and discovered that the large body of water was Lough Drumharlow and that I was, indeed, way off course. Worse still was the fact that there was no shortcut to get me back on track, which meant my only realistic option was to return to Cootehill and pick up the correct road to Leitrim Village. I was on the verge of meltdown at this point. I was either going to explode with anger or sit down on the verge and sob my eyes out in hopelessness. Thankfully, just before my slow brain could make up its mind on which meltdown option to take, a car approached heading in the Cootehill direction. It was practically the only car I had encountered on the two kilometre stretch of the road I had already covered. I immediately stuck out my thumb and prayed to whoever might be listening. The small car flew on past me and a few choice Anglo-Saxon words followed in its wake! But then a remarkable thing happened. The brake lights of the car lit up and the car pulled in about fifty metres up the road. I ran to catch up with it before the driver had time to change his mind. It was being driven by a young guy called Padraig and after I quickly explained what had happened, he agreed to give me a lift back into Cootehill. He jumped out to open the boot of his car, which was filled with musical instruments, which he quickly rearranged to make room for my rucksack. Padraig played with a local band and was on his way to a gig in Sligo. "I almost didn't stop for you," he confided as we headed off, "I'm already running late, but you looked pretty desperate when I passed you." I filled him in on the lowlights of my day and he said, "Gee, you've had a rough old day for sure. It's a pity I'm running late, or I would have quite happily taken you on to Leitrim." I have to admit that, had he been able to drive me to Leitrim, I would have been severely tempted to avail of the offer. I had probably already walked the equivalent distance anyway. As it was, however, he had to drop me at a crossroads on the edge of Cootehill. He pointed out the correct road to take, wished me luck and then he took off towards Sligo.

The next seven kilometres to Leitrim Village thankfully passed without further incident or diversion, but it was very slow going and at times I began to wonder if I was ever going to reach my destination. In fact, at times, I began to doubt if Leitrim Village even existed, because I didn't see a single road sign for the village until I was practically in the place! It almost seemed to me, after the day I had had, that Leitrim Village didn't really want to be found! But when I crossed the River Shannon yet again, I knew I was close. When I finally arrived I was exhausted. Between all my wrong turns, I estimated that I had clocked up an extra twelve unnecessary kilometres on top of the twenty kilometres I had actually needed to walk from Keadue.

When I reached the centre of this large village, I checked into the Leitrim Lodge and had a very welcome pint of Guinness at the bar. An older man on the bar stool beside me noticed my rucksack, etc. and asked me what I was up to. I explained that I was raising funds for cancer research by walking the Ireland Way and he grumbled into his pint, "What? Those useless beggars?" I was really taken aback and I could immediately feel my hackles rise. I'm normally a very non-confrontational sort of chap, but, after the day I had just had, I wasn't going to let a totally uncalled for comment such as that go unchallenged. "What do you mean?" I snapped, "they do great work. Save lots of lives. I hope you never get cancer and need their help." He seemed to be equally surprised by my outburst as I had been by his and said, "Sorry, what did you say you're doing again?" "Walking the Ireland Way for Cancer Research," I repeated slowly and clearly. "Oh my God," he said, looking horrified, "sorry, mate, my hearing isn't the best. I thought you said it had something to do with carrying out research for Ireland Today. They're useless beggars, they are. But no, oh God no, cancer research, I'm all for that. No offence intended. Good for you. Here, let me get you a drink. Marie, Marie, here, get this man another pint." I told him that there was no need and that it was clearly just a misunderstanding, perhaps compounded by my Northern accent, but he wouldn't be satisfied until he had bought me a pint. Our conversation improved considerably from there on and I told him about the awful day I had had with all my wrong turns. We raised our glasses and he said, "Apologies once again for my stupid mistake. My name is Vincent Moran, by the way, but you can call me 'moron' if you like." "After the stupid mistakes I've made today," I replied, "I don't think you're the only moron in the bar." "To all the morons," we both toasted together, laughing as we chinked our glasses.

Two pints was more than enough for me and so when I finished my second, I bade farewell to Vincent and headed to my room to get cleaned up. However, I returned to the bar later, not to resume drinking, but to meet Breifne Earley for dinner. Breifne had walked the Beara-Breifne Way in January 2016 and he had consequently taken an interest in my journey, as I had his. It was Eileen O'Roirdan in Millstreet who had first brought my attention to Breifne and since then we had both been keen to meet up and compare notes. Having been christened Breifne and having lived most of his life in Leitrim Village, it was perhaps inevitable that he would be drawn to being an 'early' pioneer of the Beara-Breifne Way, which ends here in Leitrim Village, in what was the Kingdom of Breifne in Gaelic Ireland. And Breifne was certainly no stranger when it came to challenges. Among his long list of achievements, his greatest was probably winning the World Cycle Race in 2014, which saw him cycling thirty thousand kilometres around the globe - an incredible accomplishment, the story of which had been captured in his book 'Pedal the Planet'. It was all the more remarkable, given that, just a few years earlier, he had been severely overweight and on the brink of suicide. I found Breifne to be a very humble and generous man and, of course, he was very knowledgeable about O'Sullivan Beare's march. After insisting on paying for my meal, Breifne showed me to what remained of O'Rourke's Castle, which was where Donal Cam O'Sullivan Beare and his remaining thirty-five followers finally found the sanctuary they had sought, after their epic journey.

After all the extensive and well preserved castle ruins I had encountered on my trek to date, I'm afraid the ruins of O'Rourke's Castle were somewhat disappointing. All that now remained of this stronghold that was built in 1540 was an ivy strewn, ten by forty foot stone wall at the edge of a harbour car park. It pretty much blended into the background and might have passed unnoticed if it hadn't been for Breifne directing me to it and showing me the memorial plaque erected next to the wall. O'Rourke's or Leitrim Castle was built by Brian O'Rourke and it provided refuge for many Irish Chieftains during the 'Nine Years' War'. It was one of the last of the Irish castles to fall to Queen Elizabeth in the early 1600s and O'Rourke was the last Irish Chieftain to succumb to the imposition of British rule. One side of the memorial plaque bore the O'Sullivan coat of arms and was inscribed with the words,

> *"HERE ON JANUARY 14TH 1603 BRIAN OG O'ROURKE WELCOMED DONAL O'SULLIVAN BEARE AND HIS FOLLOWERS AFTER THEIR EPIC MARCH FROM GLENGARRIFF IN 14 DAYS. THOUGH ONE THOUSAND STARTED WITH HIM ONLY 35 THEN REMAINED. 16 ARMED MEN. 18 NON COMBATANTS AND ONE WOMAN, THE WIFE OF THE CHIEF'S UNCLE DERMOT O'SULLIVAN."*

My own epic march was by no means over, but this was certainly a significant landmark along the way. I was now standing at the very spot where O'Sullivan Beare and his small band of remaining followers finally ended their incredible fourteen day march in the middle of winter all those years ago. Ignoring injury time, it had taken me twice as long to walk the same distance and that was in the middle of summer with all my modern walking gear and with all the help and support I had received. O'Sullivan Beare's party was almost constantly under attack and often cold, starving and exhausted. It was, by any stretch of the imagination, a truly incredible feat of endurance and perseverance. It was really quite humbling and certainly put my modest achievement to date into some perspective.

I thanked Breifne for showing me to the ruins of the castle. I think I would have had some trouble finding them on my own. For heaven's sake, look at the trouble I had finding Leitrim Village itself! It was getting late and time for us to go our separate ways, but before leaving for home, Breifne was able to advise me on the best route to take out of Leitrim towards Drumshanbo. So hopefully my next day's journey would be less peppered with detours than today's. It would certainly need to be!

****

It had taken me ages to reach Leitrim Village and the following morning it took me ages to leave, but thankfully not due to any wrong turns this time. I was up early as usual, but unfortunately I had to wait around for a bike hire shop opposite my accommodation in the Leitrim Lodge to open up. Not because I had decided to hire a bicycle for the rest of my journey, tempting though that was. No, it was because the bike hire shop, 'Electric Bike Trails Ltd', was where I could get my Ireland Way passport stamped with the official stamp for Leitrim. This being a significant stop on the Ireland Way and the final stop on the Beara-Breifne Way, I was determined not to miss out on collecting this key stamp. I called at the shop at 8am and saw from the sign on the door that it wouldn't be opening until 9am. The Leitrim Lodge didn't serve breakfast, so I decided to call into the plusher Marina Hotel and have a leisurely breakfast there while waiting for the bike hire shop to open. However, when I returned at 9am it still wasn't open. I phoned the number on the sign and spoke to Eileen, one of the owners of the shop. She informed me that she was currently out giving a bike tour, but that her son would be opening the shop at 10am. Still determined not to leave Leitrim without my stamp, I explored the village a little more and was eventually drawn back to O'Rourke's Castle. It didn't exactly come as a huge surprise when I heard a familiar voice beside me say, "It's not much to look at now, but I can tell you, back in the winter of 1603 it was the most wonderful sight to behold."

"I was wondering when you were going to make an appearance," I said to Donal Cam.

"Well, I saw you here yesterday evening, but you had company and I thought it best to remain hidden," he replied.

"Yes, that was probably wise," I agreed. "So, what was it like finally getting to O'Rourke's castle after more than fourteen days of marching?"

"It was unbelievable. We reached Leitrim fort at around eleven o'clock on the fifteenth day of our journey, on 14th January 1603. We were totally exhausted, but so joyous to have reached this place of sanctuary. Brian Og O'Rourke received us with great hospitality and gave directions for our sick to be attended to and for all our other needs to be met. But our joy was greatly overshadowed with sadness at the huge number of our party who did not make it. Out of the one thousand who had followed me out of Beara on New Year's Eve, only thirty-five arrived at O'Rourke's alongside me that cold January morning." Gesturing towards the memorial plaque, he added, "That's mostly accurate. The thirty-five were made up of sixteen armed men, eighteen non-combatants, or sutlers, and one woman. But she was not the wife of my uncle Dermot as stated here. Dermot's wife had stayed behind in Beara along with my own wife and children to await safe transportation to Spain, where they would be safe until we were somehow reunited at a later date. The woman that arrived here with us was in fact the wife of one of the sutlers and she had proved herself to have strength and determination equal to any of the battle-hardened men in our group of survivors. Dermot and O'Connor had also shown tremendous courage and resilience, given their advanced years. It was remarkable that they had been able to endure the extreme hardships of a march that many others half their age could not. And although the plaque correctly states that only thirty-five arrived with me on 14th January, it fails to acknowledge that some other bedraggled and exhausted survivors, who had become separated from the main group and had fallen behind, did finally make it to O'Rourke's castle over the following few days. However, it pains me greatly to admit that, out of the one thousand who had followed me out of Beara, only about fifty of us made it to Leitrim."

"The rest didn't all die though? Some deserted?" I asked hopefully.

"True. Some civilians did choose to leave the march at various stages along the way, though I would hesitate to call them deserters. What I had asked of them was almost impossible and I can understand why some felt it was beyond them and decided to settle with some of the more welcoming communities along the route, though they were few and far between. Some civilians were also forced to leave when we came under attack by our enemies and people were scattered in the melee and literally had to run for their lives and never found us again. And many of my soldiers were paid mercenaries and some, particularly the Connacht men, chose to return home once we came close to their own territories. However, I have to accept that the greater proportion of our one thousand, particularly among the six hundred civilians, did actually die on the march; either shot or stabbed during the fighting, drowned at the Shannon, or succumbing to illness or the extremes of cold and hunger we faced along the way. That any of us survived to reach Leitrim at all was nothing short of miraculous."

"Having walked the route myself during fine weather and with the luxuries of time and hospitality at my disposal, I would have to agree," I said, before echoing his words, "nothing short of miraculous. So, now you had reached the safety of Leitrim, was that it – the end of your journey?"

"No, not at all. Reaching Leitrim was incredibly important, but it only a staging post for me. My ultimate goal was to reach the camp of Hugh O'Neill at Slieve Gallion in Glenconkeyne, north-west of Lough Neagh. Here I hoped to regroup with O'Neill's army and continue with the fight against the English."

"Good Lord! You don't give up easily, do you?" I said.

"I simply couldn't," Donal Cam replied. "If I was to stand any chance of remaining in Ireland, there was nothing else I could do. To the English, I was now a rebel through and through. I had nailed my colours to the mast. I had burnt my bridges. It was either fight or flight and I wasn't ready to abandon Ireland yet! After recovering sufficiently in Leitrim for a few days, I gathered my few remaining soldiers and joined forces with Hugh Maguire, a Fermanagh rebel who had also taken refuge in O'Rourke's castle, and my previous commander, Richard Tyrell, who had brought a force of Connacht men to Leitrim to meet us. We set off, with three hundred armed men and several sutlers and other unarmed people, to undertake another difficult journey yet further northwards in order to treat with O'Neill as to renewing the war."

"So, like me, your journey northwards didn't end here?" I asked.

"That's right," Donal Cam replied and then added, "so, it looks like you'll be enjoying my company for another while yet."

"That's good," I said, "I'm keen to hear how your story continues."

"Oh, believe me, there's plenty more to tell. O'Neill was more than one hundred miles away and we had to cross three flooded rivers flowing into Lough Erne, which could not be forded during winter. And to add to our woes, the whole of the lough and its islands and the country around it were held by a Royalist garrison under Conor Roe Maguire. He was kin to Hugh Maguire, but he had sided with the English and was known as 'the Queen's Maguire'. He had brought over many Irish, especially mercenaries, to the English side and he presented a considerable obstacle to our passage north. But, once again, I'm getting ahead of myself. The rest will have to wait for another day. You will probably be in Ulster when we next meet. Good luck until then."

"Thank you," I replied, as I once again watched Donal Cam's image dissolve before my eyes. I think it was the first time he had wished me luck. I was delighted to discover that he had journeyed on into the North from Leitrim. All the material I had read about his march had concentrated on the route from Glengarriff to Leitrim, the Beara-Breifne Way, and so I had naturally assumed that this would bring O'Sullivan Beare's story to a close. I was delighted to hear that there was another chapter or two to be told. Although it appeared that it would be no less harrowing than what had gone before, I was pleased that I had yet more encounters with Donal Cam to look forward to. In addition to admiring his leadership and determination in the face of adversity, I had also grown to like the man as a person - if indeed one can regard a ghost as a person?

I left the castle ruins and wandered back to the bike hire shop. It was now finally open and I entered to collect my coveted stamp – blue, as opposed to all the previous red stamps, to signify the end of the Beara-Breifne Way. I was now, at last, free to go. I headed back out of Leitrim the way I had come in the day before to pick up the trail again about a kilometre outside the village. I now joined the Leitrim Way that stretched from here to the village of Dowra, twenty-seven kilometres to the north. It started with a delightful path that ran alongside a canal for most of its ten kilometres to Drumshanbo. The skies were grey, but, after all the roads I had endured in the heat the day before, it was a pleasure to stroll along these peaceful river banks, with little to disturb the tranquillity other than the odd duck, canoeist, stand-up-paddle boarder or occasional boat sailing past. I waved my flag at a small blond haired boy and his mother cruising past on one and the skipper called out of the cabin window to me as he glided past, "Fair play to you mate!" I have to admit that it added a little spring to my step. It seemed to me like the Irish equivalent of "*Buen Camino*" that locals had called out to me when I was walking the Camino de Santiago in Spain two years before.

About a kilometre before Drumshanbo, the path reached Lough Acre, but rather than diverting around the lake, it led directly onto a floating concrete pontoon that took me on a magical walk out over the surface of the lake. It was quite a strange feeling, as the individual sections of the pontoon dipped and rose again with each step as I moved further out into the dark body of water. It was the closest thing to walking on water that I had ever experienced and it certainly provided a unique perspective on the ducks, reeds and water lilies that populated the edges of the lough. Under the grey sky, the calm surface of the water had a silver quality to it and it was enchanting to see the ducks almost perfectly reflected in its mirrored surface. The pontoon led to a small jetty and I stopped there for a coffee break and to enjoy the tranquillity of the lough. It didn't last though, as I was soon joined by a middle aged couple with two young boys, who were very curious about my walk and bombarded me with one question after the other. I didn't mind though. It was great to see them taking an interest and I happily answered their questions about how far I walked each day, where I had started, where I would finish, when I would finish, etc., etc. After a while though, their parents took pity on me and dragged them away so my air of tranquillity could be restored once again.

There was a Visitors Centre at the end of the walkway and, after my break, I headed round to it to have a quick look and also to use the toilet facilities. I left my rucksack with a lady, called Marrie, at the reception desk. When I returned from the rest rooms, Marrie was talking to another woman, who turned to me and said, "So you're the guy walking the Ireland Way then". It was Eileen from the bike hire shop in Leitrim Village who I had spoken to on the phone earlier. After a brief chat with her, I had a quick look in the display area of the Visitors Centre and there I met a man called Donal. Not Donal Cam though. This Donal was a reporter with a Cork newspaper and was currently working on an article about 'slow travel'. "Well, you won't get much slower than me," I told him. He took a few notes about my walk and said he might include me in his piece. I bumped into Donal, his wife, Rachel, and Eileen a little later as they were about to set off on their bicycles. It turned out that Donal and Rachel were Eileen's bike tour clients for the day. Eileen was able to point me in the right direction for Drumshanbo, which was where they were heading also. They headed off on their bicycles and I followed on foot, quickly losing sight of them as they disappeared round the first bend.

Drumshanbo was only a kilometre away, so it wasn't long before I was stepping up a set of stone steps onto the 'high street' of this pretty town. Marrie in the Lough Acres Visitor's Centre had told me to look out for this unique High Street, which is actually higher than the Main Street running right alongside it. Drumshanbo takes its name from the Irish *Drum Sean Bhoth*, meaning 'the ridge of the old huts', which possibly had something to do with its origins as an iron and coal mining town. It had certainly cleaned itself up since then and was now a very prosperous looking and charming little town. I waved to Donal, Rachel and Eileen and the young family I had met at the jetty, who were all enjoying lunch outside a small café on High Street. Rachel came running over and invited me to join them. I would have loved to, but unfortunately I had just eaten and really needed to push on after my late departure from Leitrim Village.

Drumshanbo is situated at the southern end of Lough Allen, a seventeen kilometre long lake on the River Shannon, and the rest of my day's walk essentially took me the length of the lough, to the small village of Ballinagleragh at the lough's northern end. Quiet country roads, lanes and pathways, with numerous stiles to cross, carried me further up the eastern side of the lough, along a route sandwiched between the lough's silver waters to my left and the russet hills of Iron Mountain to my right. About five kilometres out of Drumshanbo, I passed a small house and exchanged greetings with two woman and two men who were very busy clearing out an overgrown garden. I was about fifty metres beyond the house when one of the women called me back and offered me a cup of tea. I initially declined, but then she mentioned cake and I was hooked. She was Margaret and the other woman was Aimee. They were both retired nurses and had recently moved from England and were now busy tidying up the property they had acquired. The two men were neighbours who were helping out with the heavy work in the garden. Aimee was English, but Margaret was originally from these parts and it had always been her dream to return home when she retired. "It's a bit of a nightmare at the minute though, trying to get this place sorted," she said, rolling her eyes, "but we'll get there. People have been very kind to us and those two out in the garden are just great." Margaret sat me down at the kitchen table and made me a cup of tea and a sandwich, while explaining that she had worked with cancer patients as a nurse and, when she spotted my banner, she couldn't let me go past without offering me something. I was very grateful for the hospitality; even more so when the promised cake appeared. As I watched the two men toil outside, it almost seemed to me that the kindness being shown to Margaret and Aimee by their neighbours was being paid forward in some small way and that I was the fortunate recipient. After indulging in their hospitality, I left their little dream house with a huge smile on my face.

The sky remained covered in a blanket of low lying grey cloud that, like a huge eiderdown pulled over the earth, trapped the heat underneath and made the going rather warm and sticky at times. But, for the most part, it was quite a pleasant ramble along the narrow roads and lanes between hedges adorned with glossy red rose hips and succulent blackberries, the latter providing the occasional juicy snack. Sheep paused and lifted their heads briefly from grazing to watch me pass by and swallows balanced on overhead wires and looked down on me as I walked beneath. I came across the odd abandoned stone cottage, resting forlornly by the roadside or standing incongruously in the middle of a field. They always held a strange fascination for me. There was something about their determination to remain part of the landscape in spite of the blows that time had dealt them that I could somehow relate to; on some sort of elementary level. Once full of live, but now just being. Still there, still standing, despite the fact that their once thick thatch had long disappeared from their roofs to be replaced by rusting sheets of corrugated tin. Their windows now just blank, dark, staring holes, while their weathered, paint-stripped doors still attempted to keep the elements out. There was something noble in the way they appeared to remain resolute in the face of adversity. Whether my affinity for these abandoned dwellings arose out of any subconscious awareness of certain parallels with my own feelings of abandonment was certainly open to question.

It wasn't until I was about three kilometres from Ballinagleragh that I got some relief from Tar McAdam again. A way marker directed me off the road and into picnic area close to St Hugh's Well. I took advantage of the picnic benches and sat down to enjoy a short rest and a cup of coffee from my flask. I then followed a lovely grassy path that brought me to the well, which was dedicated to the patron saint of the village I was destined for. The water in the well was crystal clear as I passed, but apparently it sometimes turns bright orange. However, it isn't due to some mystical or spiritual phenomenon associated with the patron saint, but rather a perfectly natural occurrence due to the water running off the iron ore rich Iron Mountain above. The grassy path was a delight to walk along and at one stage I passed through a long, magical tunnel of green, as the branches of the trees wrapped up and over the pathway, completely enclosing it in a canopy of leaves. However, it wasn't too long before I joined a minor road once again and this then dropped me down to meet the busier main road between Drumshanbo and Ballinagleragh.

I was less than a kilometre out of Ballinagleragh, when the Ireland Way threw me another googly. I was so close to my destination that I could almost taste the Guinness! But then, there he was. Standing at a junction, bold as you like, was my erstwhile friend Pacman and he directed me down a side road. I checked my guidebook and unfortunately Pacman was right this time. Not only did the route then double back on itself, but it also started to climb steeply. However, it did get me off the busy main road and it didn't take me too far off course. In reality, it probably only added about ten to fifteen minutes onto my journey, but I was absolutely sweltered by the time I finally reached the small village of Ballinagleragh, or *Baile na gCléireach* in Irish, meaning 'town of the clergy'. And the first building I spotted on my approach was indeed a church, but I continued on past it and made my way to another place of devotion called Rynn's Bar, where I ordered the most clerical of pints, which came served all in black except for its white collar. "Bless me Father, for I have sinned," I intoned as I lifted the cool pint of Guinness to my lips and relished the initial impact of its refreshing taste. Rynn's Bar was one of those typically Irish pubs that had both a small food store and bar under the one roof. It only had a handful of customers when I arrived, but it was full of life and I had a great chat with the locals while I awaited the arrival of John McGrorty. John ran the Gables Restaurant and B&B about four kilometres back, on the shores of Lough Allen, and he had agreed to collect me from Ballinagleragh when I arrived. During my conversation with the landlady of the bar, Kay Rynn, we were both greatly surprised to learn that we were both born in the same town-land of Tattyreagh, outside Omagh in County Tyrone. It also turned out that Kay knew my father and had gone to school with an aunt of mine! She had met and married a local man, John Rynn, when she was much younger and had subsequently moved to Ballinagleragh, where they had run the bar together for many happy years. Unfortunately, John had died suddenly of a heart attack one morning about ten years ago while behind the bar and Kay now ran the establishment alone. It was really nice to meet her and the other very friendly locals in the bar and, when John McGrorty arrived to collect me, I left the bar in good spirits and also with some generous donations.

John drove me to his B&B, where I was the only guest for the night. He used to run a restaurant on the premises also and I was disappointed to learn he had had to close it the previous year due to 'problems with temperamental and unreliable chefs'. I had actually been banking on having dinner in the restaurant and unfortunately there were no eating places nearby. Thankfully, John very kindly drove back to Ballinagleragh to pick up some supplies and then prepared an excellent dinner for me. My accommodation for the night was located in a beautiful location on the eastern shore of Lough Allen and, after dinner, I took a stroll down to the jetty to watch a large flock of wild geese forage in the field above the shoreline and a heron take off laboriously from the shallows, eventually settling into graceful flight as it gained height and momentum. The sky was still a sombre grey and the waters of the lough dark and gloomy, but, despite this, it was still an idyllic and peaceful spot to rest up before the next day's push for the border.

Chapter Twelve: Invisible Borders

(Days thirty-one to thirty-five - Ballinagleragh to Drumlegagh)

After breakfast, John dropped me back into Ballinagleragh, where I picked up the trail again under a dreary, cloud laden sky. I had a pleasant start, following country lanes hemmed in by leafy hedgerows, but unfortunately, after about two kilometres, I left these rural pathways behind to join the main road again. Another two kilometres brought me into the village of Dowra, which is notable for being the first village on the River Shannon. On entering Dowra, a sign painted on the gable wall of a building caught my eye and appealed to my sense of humour. It simply read *"The Olde Village Shop, open 'til we close"* and it said a lot about the relaxed, laid back attitude of many people in Ireland. This was P.S. Loughlin's shop and I called in and met Christina Loughlin, who very kindly provided me with another stamp for my passport as well as a freshly prepared sandwich for my journey. My guidebook cautioned, *"When leaving Dowra, don't get confused with the Miner's Way trail, which goes back south as it is a looped walk."* As if I ever would do such a stupid thing!

A series of quiet country roads took me further north, by turns diverting away from and then coming back close to the now much narrower Shannon, even crossing it a couple of times, but all the while being reminded that I was drawing closer to its source. And that source lay somewhere in the distinctive, elongated shape of Cuilcagh Mountain, which had now become a regular and familiar feature on the horizon before me. Cuilcagh Mountain, which I had traversed while walking the Ulster Way three years earlier on my first '1000K4J', was now only a few kilometres away. Although I wouldn't be crossing Cuilcagh on this occasion, its presence acted as a constant reminder of just how close I also now was to the border with Northern Ireland. The ridge of Cuilcagh Mountain actually delineates part of the border between Northern Ireland, which is part of the United Kingdom, and the Republic of Ireland, which is not, having parted company in 1921 following the Irish War of Independence.

About midway between Dowra and where I would eventually cross the border at Blacklion, I gratefully left the roads and followed a lane to a small car park and then a pathway to the Shannon Pot, a deep pool once believed to be the source of the River Shannon. It was actually a slight diversion off the official route to visit the Pot, but the River Shannon had been such a significant presence during my journey that I felt that I couldn't simply pass it by, even though it was, in actual fact, not the true source of the longest river in the British Isles. At sixteen metres across and at least fourteen metres deep, the Shannon Pot is essentially a spring, but quite a large and spectacular one. Standing at the edge of the almost circular pool of deep, dark, mysterious water, it was easy to appreciate how it was for centuries believed to be the source of the mighty Shannon. And, as you would perhaps expect in Ireland, it was surrounded by myth and legend. Legend has it that Síonnan, a granddaughter of the Celtic God of the Sea, Manannán Mac Lir, followed Druids to this secret place, which they regarded as the Well of Knowledge and which they visited to practice their magic. When the Druids left, Síonnan was filled with curiosity and went to look into the well to see what was so special about it. Suddenly the well erupted and streamed down the hillside, slicing through the countryside and dividing the land in two. Her lifeless body was carried along with it, transforming her into a goddess and queen of all the rivers in Ireland. There are variations to this legend, with some referring to Síonnan disturbing the Salmon of Wisdom and others to her eating forbidden fruit from the Tree of Knowledge, but they all end with her drowning and lending her name to the Pot and the River Shannon itself. It makes little difference as to which version of the legend you are drawn towards, as there is, unsurprisingly, a more mundane scientific explanation behind the Shannon. Its true source is actually up on the slopes of Cuilcagh Mountain, where a number of small streams disappear into sinkholes in the sedimentary rock of the mountain and flow underground to eventually re-emerge in the Shannon Pot. I turned to head back to the small car park and stepped back over the little footbridge that spanned the trickle of water flowing from the Shannon Pot. It was incredible to think that this little trickle would grow and grow to become the wide expanse of water that I had first crossed at Portumna twelve days previously and that O'Sullivan Beare and his followers had struggled across over four hundred years before.

When I got back to the car park, I joined a largely off road route that presented a challenging hike over fairly mixed terrain, including a few steep hills through rugged farmland, segregated by roughly built stone walls and suitable only for the hardy sheep grazing there. At the top of one particularly long hill, I stepped through an opening in a high stone wall and entered the mossy and tranquil woodland of Burren Forest. It was quite incredible stepping into this totally green world. I was surrounded by green - the floor of the forest, the canopy of the forest and even the very trucks of the trees themselves – everything was a rich shade of green! A short walk through the forest, with its very welcome raised wooden walkways, brought me out onto the far side of the area known as the Cavan Burren. Not nearly as famous or as extensive as its County Clare namesake, this smaller Burren in County Cavan is similar in that it's an area strewn with limestone rocks deposited randomly across the land during the ice age. The name Burren comes from the Irish *Boireann*, meaning 'great rock' or 'stony place' and the area I passed through was certainly littered with cragged rocks. Together with the occasional twisted and gnarled bush, they gave the landscape a pretty bleak and barren appearance, although the sheep seemed to be in their element. I began a gradual descent over the stone littered fields towards the border village of Blacklion, being rewarded with panoramic, although rather gloomy, views of both MacNean loughs, Upper and Lower. Their grey waters stretched out from either side of the causeway of land on which Blacklion and its cross-border neighbour, Belcoo, rested. At an old abandoned farm house, I picked up a rough lane that descended further to join a narrow country road, which finally brought me into Blacklion.

I called into Barney's Public House and, rather than ordering my usual pint of Guinness, I decided to do something a little bit different to acknowledge the fact that I had now reached another significant point on my Ireland Way journey. I was now only a few steps away from the border between the Republic of Ireland and Northern Ireland that had been in existence for almost one hundred years. The village of Blacklion is on the Republic side of the border and the village of Belcoo is on the Northern side. The villages are only separated, in physical terms anyway, by a short road bridge that spans the Belcoo River flowing between the upper and lower loughs of Lough MacNean. So I had a half pint of Guinness in Blacklion and had my photo taken alongside a sign displaying the village's name and then I walked over the bridge to Belcoo, a distance of roughly half a kilometre, and ordered a second half pint of Guinness in the Customs House Inn and then had my photo taken against a sign for Belcoo. I was fortunate to find a willing volunteer in each pub who was prepared to accompany me along the streets in each village, half pint in hand, to find a suitable sign to take my photograph. My movement across the border was totally unimpeded and seamless. There were no stops and no checks. In fact the roadside speed signs at either end of the bridge provided the only obvious visible clue that I was actually moving from one country to another. Signs cautioned drivers entering the 'South' that speed limits were now in kilometres per hour, while signs for drivers entering the 'North' advised that speed limits were now in miles per hour. At the time of my walk there was still tremendous confusion over the implications of the UK's decision to leave the European Union and, in particular, its possible negative effect on the border between the Republic and the North. I could only hope that travel between the two would continue to remain as easy as I found it as I walked across from Blacklion to Belcoo.

I was soon to discover that the 'invisible' border also offered absolutely no barrier or impediment to the wonderful hospitality I had been receiving on my Ireland Way journey. After checking into the Bella Vista B&B and getting freshened up, I called back to the Customs House Inn for something to eat. It seemed that word had reached Katy, the manager, about my challenge and I was subsequently treated to a superb three course dinner 'on the house'!

So, that was the southern stretch of my Ireland Way now complete, which was essentially the Beara-Breifne Way plus the much shorter Leitrim and Cavan Ways. I had now covered almost eight hundred kilometres from Castletownbere to Blacklion.

Tomorrow I would begin the three hundred plus kilometre Ulster Way section of the Ireland Way, which stretches from Belcoo to Ballycastle, via Belleek and Pettigo, up through the Sperrins to Downhill and finally across the North Coast to finish. This was a part of the route that I was more familiar with, having walked the complete Ulster Way in 2015, as my first '1000K4J' trek. In some ways that familiarity was comforting and reassuring, in that I would no longer be dealing with pathways and landscapes that were totally unknown to me. However, on the other hand, that familiarity brought with it concerns, for I had memories of certain punishing stretches that I had hoped to never have to revisit again!

****

I enjoyed a very relaxing stay at the Bella Vista B&B, run by Fran Doherty, which was located in a superb setting on the edge of Lower Lough MacNean. After completing my regular morning exercises to keep my calf muscle in good condition, I was served a great breakfast by Fran in a dining room overlooking the lough, where I was able to watch a swan and its three cygnets glide effortlessly through the silver waters as I ate my first 'Ulster Fry' of the journey. Before leaving, Fran gave me a nice discount on my room rate as well as a generous donation, keeping the long chain of hospitality and generosity unbroken. I headed round to the Customs House Inn again to see the owner, Clara, to thank her personally for the lovely meal the night before. It turned out that Clara's sister had been following my journey on social media and had tipped her off that I was in town and she in turn had spoken to Katy, the manager. It wasn't the first time that Clara had helped me out. She had put me up free of charge for a night in the Customs House Inn three years previously when I had been walking the Ulster Way. She would have done the same again this time only for the fact that they were fully booked due to it being a festival weekend in the village. Clara and I were delighted to see each other again and it was great to have some time for a brief chat and a catch up before I set off to begin the Northern section of my Ireland Way trek.

It was all fairly familiar territory, as I headed out the Lattone Road past the old train station, then turning off at St Patrick's Well to start a long climb up the Ballintempo Road, passing St Patrick's Church on the way. As I climbed higher, I was rewarded with fine views back over Upper Lough MacNean and Cuilcagh Mountain in the far distance. About four kilometres out of Belcoo, I left the road and turned into Ballintempo Forest and followed seemingly endless paths through the evergreens. It was a blessed relief to reach Lough Formal, in the heart of Ballintempo Forest, and here I took a short but rather steep detour off the route to climb up the rough grassy slopes of a small hill called Formal Beg to its viewing point. Here, I braced myself against the strong winds to take in the views of the surrounding countryside. Most of the rest of the day was spent trekking over gravel and stone laneways through a series of repetitive forests, linked by short sections of road. After Ballintempo, came Big Dog and then Conagher Forests. It was pretty tedious going with little of interest along the way to break up the sheer monotony of walking through these commercial forests.

However, there was the odd encounter with wandering livestock to bring some distraction. I followed a brown cow up a lane for some distance. It kept looking back over its shoulder at me, as if to say, "For goodness sake, are you still there?" It eventually ambled through a gap in the hedge and into a field to escape its persistent pursuer. I also followed behind a small flock of five rams on another lane. They were less comfortable with me following behind and they eventually broke into a run and trotted up the hill ahead of me and then scattered into the surrounding rugged moorland. However, before leaving the lane, two of the rams squared up to each other for an almighty head butt, which left one of them in such a daze that, for a moment, I swore it was going to collapse in a heap. But it soon recovered its 'senses' and followed its companions into the long grass. As the paths climbed higher, I frequently looked back to see the unmistakably long and flat-topped, blue-grey profile of Cuilcagh Mountain, dominating the horizon once again and not at all dissimilar to the much more famous Table Mountain that overlooks the city of Cape Town in South Africa.

Along the way, I managed to make contact with the Tir Navar Holiday Village in the village of Derrygonnelly and I booked a room for the night. Derrygonnelly was about seven kilometres off the route, but it was the only viable option other than wild camping, which I didn't fancy at all. When I was booking my room, Liam Jones of Tir Navar agreed to pick me up from the exit of Conagher Forest, where it meets the main road between Belleek and Derrygonnelly, and said to phone him when I got there. However, when I reached the agreed rendezvous point, I discovered that I had absolutely no phone signal. I pranced around, waving my phone in the air, but all to no avail. So I headed up the main road in the direction of Derrygonnelly, hoping to either pick up a phone signal at some stage or pick up a lift along the way. Unfortunately, I got neither. Eventually I came to a row of small houses set in from the road and I knocked on doors until, on the third try, I found someone in.

A middle aged man opened the door and peered out through the gap very warily to see what I wanted. Once I explained my situation, the man opened the door more widely and invited me in so I could use his landline. He must have noticed my hesitation in stepping over the threshold and then he looked down at himself, as if only suddenly remembering the state he was in. The entire front of his body was covered in a white powder and, now that the door was more widely open, I could see that the hallway inside was covered in the same white dust. I idly wondered if I had stumbled upon an incompetent drugs supplier, who had panicked while trying to get rid of his supply when a stranger unexpectedly knocked on his door. He looked up again, through glasses that also had a fine dusting of white, and laughed before saying in an Liverpudlian accent, "Sorry about the mess. It's not what it looks like. I dropped a bag of flour in the hall and it exploded everywhere. I was trying to clean it up just as you called, but I think I've just made it worse. My name's Bill by the way," he added, wiping his hand on his trousers before holding it out for me to shake. "Come on in. I know Liam well. You can phone him from my living room." What Bill had been doing with a bag of flour in his hall, I really don't know and I didn't ask. However, feeling a little more reassured now that the house may simply belong to a clumsy Scouser as opposed to an incompetent drugs supplier, I followed him into his living room. I phoned Liam Jones at the Tir Navar and explained what had happened and where I now was. Liam said that he couldn't come himself, but that he would "send Sean the butcher to get me". I replaced the handset and sat down, wondering again as to just what sort of a parallel universe I had inadvertently stumbled into in these remote hills. First I had disturbed 'Bill the drug supplier' and now 'Liam the boss' was going to send 'Sean the butcher' to sort me out. Of course, I needn't have worried. Bill was really a very hospitable and friendly chap and gave me a can of cold beer while I was waiting. He was originally from Liverpool and had worked at the docks there. But one night he had been set upon by a gang of youths and badly beaten for no apparent reason – I hoped it wasn't drugs related! This had resulted in terrible physical and mental trauma and he had moved to this little quite spot in County Fermanagh a few years ago to try to rebuild his life. And he had found both the natural environment and the locals very much to his liking. I also liked Bill very much and enjoyed his company for the twenty minutes or so that we chatted, before my executioner, sorry my driver, Sean the butcher arrived.

Sean very kindly drove me to Derrygonnelly and dropped me at the Tir Navar Holiday Village before returning to his butcher's shop. Liam's wife, Aimee, arrived a few minutes later to welcome me. I paid Aimee in advance and she then showed me to my room for the night. The holiday village was on the site of an old creamery and had a total of eighteen en suite bedrooms that were each behind their own front doors that opened out onto a central courtyard. There was also a restaurant on site, but unfortunately this had closed by the time I arrived. So, after ditching my rucksack in my room, I took the short walk into the heart of the village and took up residence for a few hours in a little fish and chip shop, where I had my tea and undertook some necessary planning for the days ahead. I tended to only make fixed plans for three to four days ahead as, although I had a rough schedule, I was never exactly sure where I might be on any given day. But I needed to keep 'putting the feelers out' among my social media following to explore possible accommodation options as I moved along. It had worked very well to date and I hoped that it would continue to do so. I really didn't care if the tent, sleeping bag and sleeping mat, which I continued to carry in my rucksack, never had to be used again.

****

I had a great sleep in a large room at the Tir Navar Holiday Village that would have comfortably slept four. I wasn't quite awake when I heard the annoying sound of a text message pinging into my mobile. I tried to ignore it, but, as usual, it pinged for a second time. Now curiosity got the better of me and I reached out for my phone and squinted at the small screen with bleary eyes. My eyes soon widened as I read the message. It was from Liam Jones, the co-owner of the Tir Navar, to say that he and his wife, Aimee, had been talking about my challenge and that they had decided not to charge me anything for my stay. He had left the money I had already paid to Aimee in an envelope beside the till in the restaurant for me to collect and went on to say that breakfast was also on the house and that Teresa, the cook, would give me a lift when breakfasts were finished. I really didn't mind being woken up to such wonderful news. I had a fairly short walk ahead of me today, so I took my time getting up and eventually sauntered over to the restaurant for yet another cooked breakfast. Healthy eating would have to wait until my walk was complete. For now I needed all the protein and carbohydrates that I could get. I met Teresa in the large, airy restaurant and she handed me my envelope and took my breakfast order. There were only a few other guests in for breakfast, but I got talking to an elderly gentleman and his son, who was about my own age, who were sitting at the table next to mine. They lived in Birmingham, but the father was originally from Derrygonnelly and they were on holiday and exploring the area where he grew up for the first time in many years. "Things haven't changed much," was the elderly gentleman's overall opinion of what he had so far discovered, "It's still as unspoilt and beautiful as I remember it. Apart from the traffic, that is," he added as an afterthought, "the number of cars on the road nowadays is unbelievable." I nodded in tacit agreement, but at the same time I was wondering where they had all been yesterday when I had been trying to hitch a ride into the village. The elderly gentleman very kindly gave me a donation before he and his son left. After my breakfast, I returned to my room to pull my gear together and then went back to await my lift. Teresa soon had everything sorted in the kitchen and she was then free to give me a lift back to my starting point for the day's walk to Belleek.

It was fairly dry when I stepped out of Teresa's car and waved her off, but it wasn't too long before I had to struggle into my wet gear. It turned out to be the wettest day so far on my Ireland Way trek. The last time I walked this part of the Ulster Way, I arrived into Belleek absolutely drenched. However, while I experienced a few very heavy showers on this occasion, there was also quite a bit of sunshine on offer between the downpours. In fact, there was more sunshine than rain - a metaphor for something perhaps? How the balance between my smiles and my tears had also shifted in the intervening years. There was little to distract along today's route, which was all along boring roads, with only the silent Tar McAdam for company. So I therefore had plenty of opportunity to reflect on how things had progressed since I had last walked this way, back in the summer of 2015. Back then, it had only been a matter of months since I had lost Jacqui and I was still in pieces; never believing that things could ever feel in any way normal again. But now, three years later, I could certainly appreciate how far I had come. Not just in terms of the miles I had chosen to travel, but in terms of the emotional adjustment I had been forced to make - learning to live without the love of my life and discovering how to travel on through life without her by my side. Of course, I still missed her terribly and not a single day went by without me wishing she was still here; not just words on some folded sheets of paper I carried with me. But it was clear that the brutally raw emotions of three years ago had now largely been replaced with a calm and stoic acceptance. I realised that this painfully slow transition had only been possible with the support of friends, old and new, including those who I had only met for the first time on my walks. As I tramped along the wet roads towards Belleek, I composed the following words:

You have to admire the resilience of a heart
That keeps on beating after being torn apart
Over time, the muscle knits together again
Encapsulating the loss, the hurt and the pain

Sealing all the sorrow and the sadness away
Only letting them out on the occasional day
Birthdays, death days, wedding anniversaries
When they escape to taunt like old adversaries

But alongside the healing, a chamber is formed
Inside this heart that's permanently deformed
A special new chamber that allows one to cope
As friends gradually fill it with love and with hope

I arrived into the village of Belleek at around lunchtime, thankful for having had a short day's walk for a change – only three and a half hours. Belleek is another border village, with most of it located in County Fermanagh in the 'North', but a small part of it spilling into County Donegal in the 'South'. It also straddles the River

Erne, which flows out from Lower Lough Erne on its journey west towards the Atlantic Ocean. I crossed over the bridge and had a leisurely lunch in the Belleek Pottery Visitor Centre overlooking the river. I then checked into the Fiddlestone Inn, where I met my old friend Raymond behind the bar, who was very happy to pour me a pint of the black stuff and take my photo as I posed with one of the locals and my banner.

****

I woke to the sound of heavy rain drops drumming on the Velux window in my room at the top of the Fiddlestone Inn. I dragged myself out of bed and peered out through the glass. It looked pretty miserable and I wasn't looking forward to venturing out. Just then, my phone pinged and for the second morning in a row I picked up a message that cheered me up considerably. This one was from Andy Hall, the singer-songwriter I had met in Kealkill in County Cork on the third day of my journey. Since then, Andy had been working on a special composition and he had just completed it and sent it through to me. He had recorded himself singing and playing guitar and had sent me a video of his performance. I clicked on the play button and watched and listened and I was completely blown away. It was a reworking of an old standard and retitled, '*It's A Long Way From Tipperary*'. Tipperary was of course where I had restarted my Ireland Way, after my leg injury had put me out of action for almost four weeks, and the lyrics of the song had been modified to reflect the very personal reason for my pilgrimage to Ballycastle.

It's a long way from Tipperary,
It's a long way to go.
It's a long way from Tipperary,
For the greatest cause I know.
Off to Ballycastle,
On the Ireland Way.
It's a long, long way from Tipperary,
One thousand K for J.

It's a long way from Tipperary,
It's a long way for you.
It's a long way from Tipperary,
For the sweetest girl I knew.

Off to Ballycastle,
See you at the fair.
It's a long, long way from Tipperary,
But my love lies there.

At first the words brought tears to my eyes, but after listening to the song a few times, I was smiling broadly. It was a wonderful, thoughtful gesture by Andy and it set me up for the day ahead, regardless of the dismal weather awaiting me outside. But first, I needed breakfast and it was Louise who kindly did the honours this morning. She also prepared me a tasty lunch to take with me and gave me a very generous reduction on the cost of my stay.

It was now time to leave the dry warmth of the Fiddlestone Inn and get on the road for today's walk to Pettigo. And it was a case of "*water, water, everywhere*", just as in '*The Rime of the Ancient Mariner*'. It was raining when I left Belleek at 9am. It was still raining when I arrived in Pettigo at 5pm. And it rained continuously for the whole eight hours in between! I left the River Erne behind, passed Keenaghan Lough, Lough Scolban, Lough Vearty and even a Lough Breen! I passed many rivers and streams. I even walked along roads that had become like streams in the heavy rain. And I stepped around and through countless puddles. Also countless was the number of times I asked myself, "What the feck am I doing out walking in this?" But, of course, the answer was always the same. I was doing it to encourage people to donate money to support cancer research. It was never going to be an easy challenge. It was meant to be tough. And it was. So as the rain inevitably seeped its way through my 'waterproof' layers, I just put my head down and splashed onwards.

I was very fortunate to come across an open hayshed close to Lough Vearty, around the mid-point of the day's journey. I was able to shelter from the rain here and have a bite of lunch. It was quite comfortable sitting on a bale of hay having my tea and sandwiches, listening to the steady beat of the rain on the corrugated sheets of tin on the roof of the barn. Unfortunately, the rain became even heavier after lunch and a strong cross wind also developed, making the conditions even less pleasant to walk in. My 'weather angels', who had accompanied me on my previous walks, had seemingly abandoned me to the elements! With my hood up, my view was continually restricted. I felt like I was some sort of pack animal that had been blinkered to keep it focussed on the road directly ahead, as I continued to carry my heavy rucksack on my back. I couldn't help laughing when "Beast of Burden" by the Rolling Stones came up on the playlist on my phone.

The route continually cut in and out over the border, although this was often only apparent from the maps I was using, as opposed to any tell-tale features on the ground – one country road, lake or hill looked very much like the other, regardless of which side of the border it was on. However, one notable exception did occur when I happened upon a small corrugated tin hut by the roadside that bore a sign stating that it was the '*Tully Customs and Excise Patrol Station*'. This was a well preserved relic of a bygone era when it would have been used by customs officers to monitor and collect duties on goods being brought into and out of the Irish Republic across the border with Northern Ireland. I wondered was it being kept well preserved for a reason, just in case it might need to be brought back into service at some stage in the future, post Brexit! Hopefully this patrol station would remain a relic of the past!

I trudged on through the miserable rain and eventually arrived in Pettigo like the proverbial drowned rat. Unfortunately, my accommodation was about a kilometre on the other side of the village, so I called into Potter's Bar for my usual imbibement before heading out into the rain again for the final stretch to the Avondale Farmhouse B&B. Here Mary Leonard welcomed me in and helped get me dried out. Later on I enjoyed a free taxi ride into and out of the village and a free meal in the lively Pettigo Inn.

****

Mary Leonard, the wonderful proprietor of the Avondale Farmhouse B&B, was rushed off her feet at breakfast. In addition to coping with my straightforward order of an Ulster Fry with tea, she had to deal with the varied demands of four teenage girls who were sitting with their mother at the table next to mine. They certainly kept Mary on her toes and I thought that they were never going to stop requesting food. During a conversation with their mother over breakfast, she explained that they had come from Dublin the day before and were on their way to Lough Derg. The girls' voracious appetites suddenly made sense. Lough Derg is a lake in County Donegal, about seven kilometres north of where we were having breakfast, and it is best known for St Patrick's Purgatory, a site of pilgrimage on the lake's Station Island. Upon arrival on the island, participants remove footwear and socks before commencing prayers, while walking around the island barefoot. During the traditional three-day pilgrimage, the participants are only allowed one meagre meal each day, which consists of black tea/coffee, dry toast, oat cakes and water. So I wasn't at all surprised that the young girls were binge eating for all they were worth, filling their stomachs before enduring 'voluntary' torture for the sake of their souls. I asked the girls if they were looking forward to the experience and they replied with varying degrees of enthusiasm that might have been quite different had their mother not been sitting beside them. I wasn't sure, but I could have sworn that I saw one of them furtively stashing a scone into her pocket while her mother wasn't looking. I wished them all the best, feeling a little sorry for the girls, and went to gather up my belongings for another long day on the road. And, as it turned out, it was much longer than expected, but at least I was able to keep my socks and boots on. And the only praying I did was for a phone signal!

I waved goodbye to Mary and the family of pilgrims and set off on my own pilgrimage under grey skies back in towards the village centre. It had still been pouring out of the heavens before breakfast, but thankfully the rain had since stopped and it even showed signs that it might be starting to brighten up. Just before reaching the centre of Pettigo, I turned left onto the bridge over the Termon River, where I stopped to look over the stone wall to be mesmerised, and almost deafened, by the river's churning, dark waters surging downstream, as if they were in a desperate hurry to reach Lough Erne. As I leaned against the wall of the bridge, I idly wondered if perhaps this was one of the three flooded rivers that O'Sullivan Beare had had to cross, as he and Hugh Maguire made their way north to Slieve Gallion.

And then, as if reading my mind (which he probably was), a voice beside me said, "We took a route much further south of here, crossing the River Erne near Belturbet."

It was, of course, Donal Cam and he was leaning on the wall of the bridge, just to my left. "Nice to see you again," I said, genuinely meaning it, and then adding, "I was thinking that my route mightn't be the most direct to Slieve Gallion, now that I know it's near Moneyneany, which I will be passing through at some stage."

"Yes, our trails parted way when you left Leitrim and headed north to cross the Erne north of the lower lough, while we headed more in a north-easterly direction and crossed the Erne south of the upper lough."

"Flippin' heck!" I said. "That's a bit of a tongue twister! But I think I followed you."

"But you didn't follow me!" he said. "Isn't that just what I've been saying!"

"No, I meant......." I started to say. But then thought better of it and simply said, "Oh, never mind. Please go on."

Donal Cam just looked at me like I was simple and then continued, "The River Erne was pretty flooded and much wider than this little stream," he said, nodding down towards the fast flowing waters of the River Termon below. "However, unlike the Shannon crossing, where we had had to build our own boats, we managed to get our hands on pontoons and cross the Erne with relative ease."

"What about the Queen's Maguire?" I asked, remembering that Donal Cam had told me that Hugh Maguire's kinsman, Conor Roe Maguire, had sided with the English and essentially controlled the areas around the loughs.

"The Queen's Maguire had wrongly assumed that we would try to cross the Erne at a ford where the river entered the upper lough and he led five hundred armed men from their encampment and sailed over the lough in boats and ships to block the ford. However, having already crossed the Erne, we camped that night further up river, about six miles away from the ford. On the following day, when we learned that the enemy were waiting in vain to ambush us at the ford, we attacked and captured their camp. We stayed there that day and night, securing a large flock of sheep and a great herd of cattle and hanging fifty men who had been left to defend the camp." Donal Cam must have noticed me wincing at this, for he stopped and simply demanded, "What?"

"Oh nothing," I said. "Just the way you casually mention that you hung fifty men."

"Well shooting them might have alerted the rest of our enemies," he said, matter of factly.

"Sorry," I said, somewhat exasperated, "I wasn't questioning how you had killed them. It was the fact that you had killed them at all - fifty of them! It just seems that one side was as merciless as the other."

"It was either kill or be killed," he explained once again, as if to a slow learning child. "It was as simple as that. It we had let them go, they would certainly have re-joined the Queen's Maguire and attacked us at some later stage. Better and easier to get rid of them when they had been captured and disarmed. And we certainly had no time to be caring for prisoners." I simply nodded in response, understanding but not condoning, and he continued. "On the next day, Hugh Maguire, thinking it a good opportunity whilst the enemy were at the ford miles away, left the camp with two hundred armed soldiers to raid the friends and abettors of the English. That left me with only one hundred armed men and, fearing that in Maguire's absence I might be attacked by enemy forces, I dismantled the camp, burnt the tents, and took my men and our spoils into a dense wood. As expected, the Queen's Maguire soon heard of the destruction of his camp and the killing of his men. His army of five hundred returned in their ships and boats and disembarked close to the ruined camp. Unfortunately, they managed to track down our whereabouts in the wood and we watched in trepidation as their force of five hundred took up a battle formation, with the obvious intent of taking revenge. My force of one hundred soldiers would not stand a chance if they attacked. I had to give the Queen's Maguire the impression that we were a larger force than we actually were. So, I placed my armed men in front and put the sutlers at the rear. Then I got the women and children to hold long staves, as if they were spears, and placed them as if in reserve, so as to frighten our enemy by a show of numbers. Of course our enemy didn't know that Hugh Maguire and his two hundred men were absent at the time and my deception caused them a great deal of doubt as to whether they ought to attack. It bought us sufficient time. It wasn't until Hugh Maguire and his two hundred men arrived back from their successful raids that the enemy realised their great error. The deceived Royalists, cursing the fact that they had let victory slip from their hands, retreated back towards their ships."

"Ha ha," I laughed, "very well played once again. You are certainly a master of deception, Donal Cam."

This obviously pleased him and he smiled broadly in response. "Sometimes it worked well. Other times, like at Glinsk, it failed miserably. But when you are up against it, it is often necessary to live by one's wits. Anyway, the intention of the enemy now was to merely preserve the garrisons which they had on the islands in the lough, until larger forces were sent to their assistance. However, they didn't have time to make it back to their ships before darkness fell and instead they took shelter in an old deserted stone fortress. Our scouts saw the Royalists enter this fort at night and reported this back to me and Hugh Maguire. The following dawn, when the enemy started out for their ships again, we followed silently and at a distance. They reached the place where their ships and boats were waiting about four hours after sunrise and, after the first party of men had been ferried over to the islands, we launched our attack. Suddenly, the enemy was overwhelmed by our forces and all hell broke loose."

And suddenly, I was no longer leaning against the wall of the bridge over the River Termon, but found myself standing on the cold shoreline of a lough with a dreadful barrage of noise exploding all around me. The sound of muskets being fired peppered the more constant sound of men shouting in panic and screaming in pain, as they rushed towards the boats resting in the shallows of the dark waters, trying desperately to escape their attackers. The enemy of Royalists had obviously been caught totally unaware by the sudden and unexpected attack by O'Sullivan Beare and Maguire's men and were panic stricken as a result. They certainly didn't look like an army in control as they dashed and splashed into the water in an attempt to board the boats. Donal Cam stood beside me and observed what was going on, seemingly with an air of almost cool detachment. The musket fire was coming from the trees that lined the shore a few metres back from the water's edge and at this stage I couldn't see any of the attackers; only the plumes of gunpowder smoke that trailed behind the lethal musket balls as they erupted from the woods. Many of the Royalists fell before they reached the boats, splashing unceremoniously face first into the water as they were thrown forward by the force of one or more red-hot musket balls of lead thumping into their backs. Those who made it to the boats clambered on board as quickly as they could, but such was the haste and confusion that some boats were tipped over and quickly sunk as a result. Other Royalists, with no boats within reach, simply waded into the lough and attempted to swim out to the ships in the deeper waters. However, many of them appeared to flounder due to the weight of their armour and I watched as they were quickly drawn down below the surface of the lough to their watery graves. The barrage continued unabated as if the attackers would not be satisfied until all the Royalists had been annihilated. The cold air over the lough filled with smoke from the muskets as if a mist had suddenly descended over the waters. The sound was deafening and the scale and barbarity of the slaughter sickening. Even those who managed to reach the ships were not safe. I watched as one of the ships was almost capsized as it was overwhelmed by the sheer numbers of Royalists trying to climb on board. Already filled to overcapacity, one side of the ship was pulled low in the water by those hanging from the thowels and trying to climb into it. This ship was still tied to the bank of the lough with a rope and the poor unfortunates hanging from its side made easy targets for the muskets on shore. Countless bodies fell away from the side of the ship as it was deluged with a shower of musket balls. Someone on board managed to cut the rope and the ship was finally freed. Those still hanging on who had survived the musket fire were offered no help by their comrades on board. Still fearing that they might risk capsizing their only means of escape, the men on the ship pierced their comrades with spears and sent them falling back into the lough to drown. With all oars now deployed, the ship set off for the nearest island garrison with the occasional musket ball following. The firing gradually ceased as the few surviving boats and ships were rowed out of range and the smoke filled scene was joined by an eerie silence, occasionally interrupted by the groan of a survivor lying on shore or in the shallows. Such sounds were quickly snuffed out as O'Sullivan Beare and Maguire's men walked among the fallen and efficiently and brutally dispatched the wounded with their pikes; presumable not wishing to waste any further ammunition or gunpowder; although perhaps it was simply quicker to stab the life out of these poor unfortunates rather than having to continually reload their muskets. What I had just witnessed was truly shocking, brutal and merciless.

I looked at Donal Cam and, clearly seeing the look of shock on my face, he simply repeated, "It was either kill or be killed." Before I could reply, the scene around me suddenly transformed once again. I was still beside Donal Cam and still in the past, but now I was standing in a large clearing, filled with soldiers and surrounded by woods, and there appeared to be a bit of a commotion among the men. "Where are we?" I asked Donal Cam, unable to keep the anxiety from my voice, "and what's happening?"

"We're on one of the island garrisons in the lough belonging to the Queen's Maguire. It's the seventh such island garrison we sailed to after attacking the Royalists as they fled in their ships. Unfortunately the Queen's Maguire had escaped our clutches, but my comrade Hugh Maguire still had vengeance on his mind and was determined to take back control of his land and that included the islands."

The commotion among the soldiers grew louder and it was only then that I noticed that there was actually a group within a group. There were about twenty men in the central group and they looked terrified as they gazed into the faces of the jeering mob of more than one hundred men surrounding them.

"The Queen's Maguire had deployed a small force of his men to defend each of his island garrisons," explained Donal Cam. "The men you see cowering at the centre of that crowd are the surviving defenders who surrendered when we stormed their island."

As we watched, the Royalists were herded towards the trees at the edge of the clearing and I saw now that they all had their hands bound behind their backs. Some were clearly resisting being pushed forward and others were loudly begging for mercy as the realisation of their fate became clear to them. I watched in morbid fascination as one Royalist was dragged out of the group and had a noose pushed roughly over his head and pulled taught around his neck. The other end of the rope was thrown over the sturdy branch of an Ash tree and caught by a party of five soldiers who took up the slack in the rope. Without further delay or ceremony, they pulled on the rope in overhand fashion and the captured man was jerkily hoisted off the ground with his head awkwardly forced to one side by the knot of the noose and his legs kicking about widely in a futile attempt to find purchase somewhere; anywhere. The lynch mob cheered and the remaining condemned men shrunk back in horror. It seemed like several minutes went by before the man dangling by his neck finally stopped kicking. Rather than lowering the now dead body gently back to the ground, the five men at the other end of the rope simply let go and the body crumpled to the ground with a sickening thud that was clearly audible over the continued bloodlust of the mob. The noose was removed from the dead man's neck and a second prisoner was dragged forward for the grotesque spectacle to be repeated. The mob clearly intended to hang all twenty prisoners in this fashion, one by one. Perhaps the first to be hung had been the lucky one; he hadn't had to witness the grisly details of what fate had in store for him. Not wishing to witness any more of this horror myself, I turned to Donal Cam and simply said, "I think I've seen enough."

I was back at the bridge over the Termon River. "Bloody hell! These flashbacks to your past are just too real," I said, trying hard to settle my heart rate. I looked at Donal Cam and thought I detected a deep sadness in his eyes. "It was either kill or be killed," he repeated yet again. "But that doesn't mean that I am not filled with sorrow at the terrible loss of life suffered throughout our land, as brother was pitched against brother by the cruel and calculated bribes offered by the English. Most of those Royalists you just witnessed dying at the upper lough were actually Irish, but they had aligned with the Queen and unfortunately paid the price in a brutal struggle for power." After a pause, he continued, "But we had sent the Queen's Maguire packing and Hugh Maguire was almost completely restored as the leader of the Maguire clan. Our campaign was enjoying great success and we were in buoyant mood as we continued our march northwards to join with Hugh O'Neill's forces. Yet again, it seemed like we had a fighting chance of ridding this country of the English invaders. Unfortunately, it wasn't to be the case."

"I'm not even going to ask you what happened," I said with a wry smile, "because I know you'll only tell me that I have to wait until we next meet."

"You know me too well," he said, returning my smile, although a trace of sadness remained. "I'll fill you in on the unhappy details when you are closer to Slieve Gallion. Goodbye for now."

"See you later," I replied as Donal Cam took his leave. I watched the dark, tumbling flow of the Termon River for a little longer, reflecting on the fact that these turbulent waters would eventually mellow and become much calmer as they continued downstream. A metaphor for this violent country and the passage of time perhaps, I thought. I finally decided to move on and I pushed myself off the wall off the bridge and set off once again.

The path of the Termon River delineates the border for much of its length and, as I had found yesterday, my route continued to weave in and out of the neighbouring jurisdictions as it generally followed the river's course for the next ten kilometres. The western sections of the Ulster Way weren't particularly well sign posted with either road signs or way markers, but I had quite detailed maps with me and I had, of course, walked the route once before. So there wasn't really a good excuse as to why I ended up adding another eight kilometres, and roughly one and a half hours, onto my journey today. I'm afraid it was almost completely down to inattention on my part - that, and my inability to multitask or, to be more specific, my inability to read and reply to messages on my phone and follow directions on a map at the same time. Unfortunately, there were two fairly identical forks in the road out of Pettigo. They were less than a kilometre apart, but the first required a left turn and the second a right turn. I managed to pass through the first fork without noticing it, my eyes focussed on my phone's screen instead of the road. Then when I reached the second fork, I wrongly assumed that it was the first fork and, following my map based on this false assumption, I turned left instead of right and started to head way off course. After a couple of kilometres I began to suspect that I may have taken a wrong turn as things did not seem as familiar as I had expected them to. Somewhat contrarily, the mobile device that I liked to blame for my inattention had now lost its signal and so I was unable to check my actual whereabouts on my maps app. I flagged down a passing car that had just pulled out from a nearby house and checked with the driver if I was on the right road for the Ulster Way. He confirmed that I was and I wanted to believe him even though my own instincts said otherwise. But he then uttered the words that left me with little doubt that he knew what he was talking about, "There's actually an Ulster Way sign further along this road." So, now happier that I was almost certainly still on the right road, I marched on. About another kilometre further on I came to the very sign he must have been talking about. But it didn't say "Ulster Way". It said "Causeway Hill Way". Oh no! The doubt immediately resurfaced again. Fortunately, it was around here that I was able to pick up a mobile signal again and, on checking my position on my maps app, I was able to see that I was indeed well off course. From here, it took me over an hour to find my way back on to the right road! A lesson learned the hard way – don't attempt to deal with texts and messages while continuing to walk blind.

I stopped for a quick bite of lunch outside a 'tumbledown' cottage near to where the route crossed the Termon River for a final time. A short distance from where I was sitting, just across the road, was a farm gate. Here two large sheep had noticed my arrival and they stood at the gate looking over, bleating loudly at me as I ate my lunch. After I had finished, I couldn't ignore them any longer and headed over to the gate, fully expecting them to dash away as soon as I got near. But they had obviously been hand reared, because they stood their ground and then started to jostle for position to be the first to be petted when I reached in. They were very friendly and one of them in particular just couldn't get his head rubbed for long enough. They were very sweet, but I eventually had to say goodbye to them and continue with my journey, even though they continued to bleat pitifully after me as I headed up the road.

Apart from my earlier wrong turn, it was actually a fine day's walk. My 'weather angels' had returned and it had stayed dry and cool, with a refreshing breeze, although the sky remained stubbornly dull. The route was quite varied and challenging in places and even my unplanned detour was not without its rewards in terms of pleasant scenery to admire. There had been a lot of quiet country road walking to begin with, followed by endless grey access roads between the green walls of Lough Bradan Forest, but the terrain changed dramatically, as I knew it would, when I reached the slopes of Bolaght Mountain. Here, I left behind the hard-core tracks through Lough Hill and Lough Lee wind farms to stagger and stumble my way over the very boggy sides of Bolaght Mountain, gradually climbing higher as I went. I stopped to catch my breath for a bit when I eventually reached the ancient Ulster Way sign near the top of this 345m high mountain. Unfortunately, the views were less than spectacular given the dreary skies and so I didn't stop for long and I soon began a long and torturous descent down the northern slopes. After fighting my way over the rough, heather-covered bog land, I picked up an old 'turbary' track and followed it down to meet initially quiet and then very busy roads that finally brought me into the village of Drumlegagh, my finishing point for the day. At forty-three kilometres, it was the longest distance I had covered in one day since I had started the Ireland Way. It had, of course, been added to considerably once again by my careless navigation, but my legs felt strong and the soles of my feet had coped much better than before. And I was very fortunate to make it into Drumlegagh when I did, as it started raining heavily just after I arrived. My sister, Teresa, was waiting for me here – in fact she had been waiting for well over an hour as both she and I had been expecting my arrival much sooner! Nonetheless, Teresa welcomed me with open arms and then drove me back to her place near Dromore in County Tyrone, where her husband, Brian, had a cold pint of Guinness sitting on the kitchen table awaiting my arrival. Perfect!

Chapter Thirteen: Sperrins Fog
(Days thirty-six to thirty-nine - Drumlegagh to Cam Forest)

Brendan McManus SJ was waiting for me when I arrived in Drumlegagh again the next morning with my sister Teresa. He had driven down from Belfast to walk with me for a while and provide me with a bit of moral support. We waved Teresa off and then Brendan and I set off out of Drumlegagh and towards Bessy Bell Mountain. Apart from the time my friend Delia had walked a short distance into Ballinlough with me, it was the first time that I had someone join me on a section of the Ireland Way and it was great to have his company. I had first met Brendan when I was thinking of walking the Camino del Norte in 2016. Another friend had loaned me a book called 'Redemption Road', which had been written by a Jesuit Priest who had walked the route in 2011 to help him come to terms with his brother's suicide a few years earlier. The book was essentially about searching for healing and reading it as I did, so soon after losing Jacqui to cancer, had a profound effect on me and confirmed and strengthened my desire to walk the Northern route of the Camino de Santiago. That Jesuit Priest and author was Brendan McManus SJ and it subsequently turned out that he had been in the same class at school as one of Jacqui's best friends. And it was through Jacqui's friend, Sandra, that I was eventually introduced to Brendan and subsequently got to meet him. I remembered bringing a freshly purchased copy of 'Redemption Road' along with me to our first meeting so he could sign it for me, which he very kindly did, and then he very patiently answered all the questions about the Camino del Norte that I could think of to throw at him. We had remained friends ever since and he continued to help me out - it was actually Brendan's tent that I had been carrying in my rucksack for most of my journey, although I had left it and other heavy items behind at Teresa and Brian's for the day.

Brendan joining me for a part of the Ireland Way was greatly appreciated and certainly helped make the start of my journey pass by much easier than I imagine it would have otherwise. It was another damp and gloomy morning and, consequently, any views that might have existed were mostly hidden behind veils of low cloud and mist. However, we did stop occasionally to admire the delicate and intricate patterns created by the dew covered spider webs that decorated the hedges and brambles so abundantly. Brendan and I shared an interest in photography and we both had an eye for nature's detail. The route took us over minor roads into the southern reaches of the Baronscourt Estate, past the pretty Baronscourt Church and through the forested areas of Tamnagh, Crockfad and Upper Cloonty Woods. It became mistier as we progressed and the woods began to take on an almost sinister appearance. I was pleased to have Brendan's company all the more when a strange man appeared out of the fog carrying a billhook. Thoughts of banjos, hillbillies and the movie 'Deliverance' immediately entered my mind. Of course, he turned out to be harmless and informed us that he worked for the Baronscourt Estate. He was checking the woods to make sure that everything was as it should be for the hunting season, which had just started. He presumably needed the billhook to help cut his way through the undergrowth in the woods when necessary. After a brief chat, Brendan and I pushed on along the forest track and through several junctions before coming into yet another wood. Unfortunately Brendan had to turn back at this point as he had a family commitment he had to attend to. We hugged and I thanked him for his good company and then Brendan McManus headed back the way we had come and was slowly consumed by the fog. It wasn't until he had gone that I realised that the wood we had separated in was actually called Manus Wood.

I headed on through the trees and, after a short length of road, joined another forest track leading into Cashty Wood. Here the fog became even thicker and in this spooky world my imagination went into overdrive. The tall pine trees began to appear like row upon row of menacing ghostly shadows, lurking in the mist as if they were watching my progress through their realm. The dead trunk and branches of what might have once been an oak tree, appeared to reach up into the fog, like a giant emaciated hand clawing at the air, waiting to grab and drag anything it caught down into its lair beneath the ground. There was no sign of Donal Cam though!

I soon came to a crossroads in the wood and I took the right turn to begin a long climb up a steep access road to the 450m summit of Bessy Bell. I passed more ghostly shapes on the way - towering windmills this time; their blades disappearing into the fog as they rotated. It was with some relief that I reached the summit of Bessy Bell and leaned against the triangulation pillar for a bit of a breather. The long climb up Bessy Bell had been tough, but, in hindsight, it was a walk in the park compared to the torturous route down the eastern slopes, which meandered through the fog and rough fields of long grass. I often had to guess at the best direction to take, as way markers and tracks were either non-existent or hidden by the fog. To add to my woes, the long grass was extremely wet and the legs of my trousers were soaking before I even had a chance to think about pulling on my waterproof leggings. By the time I reached the laneway at the base of the mountain, not only were the legs of my trousers drenched, but my boots and socks also. However, on the plus side, I had at last descended out of the fog. I squelched for the next three kilometres or so down lanes and along minor roads until I reached a main road running alongside the River Strule. The Mellon Country Inn was only a hundred metres up the main road, so I continued to squelch for a little longer as I made my way there.

The staff at the Mellon Country Inn were very welcoming and would have been quite happy for me to sit inside, but I opted instead to take a seat at one of their tables outside. Here I was able to remove my boots and socks, wring the excess water out of my socks, and then drape them over the back of a chair in the hope that they might dry a little while I had my lunch. With both my liner socks and outer socks hung up, I attempted to dry my feet also by stretching them out in front of me and wiggling my toes in the air. It was only then that I noticed some of the guests in the restaurant gazing out the window at me. This probably wasn't the view they had in mind when they had booked their table by the window. I waved to them and smiled ruefully, but I think they were unimpressed, so, instead, I made myself busy by tucking into the packed lunch that Teresa had kindly prepared for me.

After lunch I pulled on my still damp socks once again and slid my feet into my still damp boots. I usually carried a spare pair of socks with me, but in my eagerness to lighten my load before leaving my sister's house that morning, I had inadvertently left them behind. I headed back along the main road and crossed the River Strule via a footbridge and then followed a series of country roads for about seven kilometres before facing another long, steep climb up Tirmuty Hill and into the Gortin Glens Forest Park. The descent was much more pleasant than what I had experienced on the wet slopes of Bessy Bell. Here I followed winding forest tracks that ran alongside a fast flowing stream for much of its way until the track finally entered the visitors' car parking area. As progress had been very slow coming over Bessy Bell, I had felt that I needed to speed things up a little and so, rather than walking down the forest paths, I jogged down them, deploying the 'Comanche run' technique I had learned from my Dutch friend Ron on the Camino del Norte in Spain. It essentially involved letting the lower legs do all the work and it was a technique that I would use more in the coming days. It seemed to serve me well, but I would later come to regret the extra strain it must have put on my lower limbs.

I left the car park and crossed a main road to climb through another part of the forest, this time skirting round the lower slopes of Curraghchosaly Mountain. After trekking through forests for around eight kilometres, I finally emerged from the trees to take a circuitous but scenic road route into the village of Gortin, via the heather covered hills of the Boorin National Nature Reserve with its beautifully placid lakes, perfectly mirroring the splendour of the surrounding countryside. In Gortin, I made my way to the Foothills Bar & Restaurant, where I had called three years before, but, unfortunately, it was under new management and was now a fancy wine bar. Seeking out an establishment more in keeping with my unkempt appearance, I backtracked down the main street and headed for 'The Gort Inn' instead. I noticed from the signage on the front of the pub that the proprietor, Mr McGuigan, also offered funeral services. I remembered seeing a similar arrangement in Galbally in County Limerick, whereby the business of supplying customers with the means of an early death, together with the necessary after care package, was all neatly provided for under one roof – a one stop shop if you like. I had avoided the bar in Galbally because I didn't like the idea of the barman sizing me up for a box as he poured my pint. But now I was very tired and thirsty after ten and a half hours on the road, so I threw caution to the wind and stepped into The Gort Inn for my dark pint.

It's amazing the different reactions I received on entering public houses, dressed in my hiking garb, with my rucksack on my back, walking poles in hand and my Ireland Way banner draped around some part of me or my rucksack. Some patrons would look up from their drinks, look me up and down and then go back to their drinking. Some would ignore me completely, as if pretending I was invisible – which, given the state of me at the end of a day's walking, was quite a feat of pretence for anyone. And then there were some who would be immediately intrigued and start asking me all sorts of questions about what I was doing. It was this last category that I much preferred as it was lovely to chat to folk after being in the wilderness all day. I have to admit to preferring it also because it often led to donations being made. Fortunately, the patrons of The Gort-Inn fell firmly into that this last category. A group of young folk at the bar in particular were immediately interested and somewhat impressed by my challenge and they subsequently donated some cash to the cause. I chatted with them while waiting for my Guinness to be poured and didn't mind answering all the usual questions that came my way – Where did you start? How far do you walk each day? Are you always on your own? Do you not get lonely? Are you wise in the head? When my drink was ready, I moved outside again, as I was really quite hot and sweaty after the exertions of the day, and sat on the window sill of the pub to enjoy my cold pint in the balmy evening air. My sister, Ann, arrived mid-pint and waited patiently for me to finish my ritual before driving me back into Omagh to visit my spritely ninety-four year old dad, Artie. After dinner, Ann then left me back out to Teresa and Brian's where I spent a second night. It had been a very long, hard day of walking and after I had showered it wasn't long before I was out for the count.

****

The following morning, I decided to leave my camping gear behind me for good to lighten my load from this point on. Taking a sleeping bag, roll up mat and tent out of my pack certainly made quite a difference. I was fairly certain that that they wouldn't be required for the remainder of my journey. Brian then drove me back to Gortin and dropped me at the top of the village. I waved him off and then headed out the main road towards Plumbridge, but once I crossed the Owenkillew River, I swung right and followed a minor road that climbed up the lower slopes of Slievemore Mountain. Thankfully it didn't climb too far before the route turned right once again and began to traverse the hillsides overlooking the Owenkillew Valley. The weather was pretty gloomy once more, which limited the views across the valley. Nevertheless, everywhere was a lush green that was somehow enhanced by the mist and dampness in the air. The hedgerows were adorned with cobwebs that were wonderfully highlighted by thousands of tiny dew drops, decorating their multiple strands and creating beautiful beaded hammocks and delicate necklaces of silver and crystal. Narrow roads and lanes carried me along the side of the Owenkillew Valley for about five kilometres until I passed through Barnes Gap to enter the much longer Glenelly Valley, which must be one of the longest glacial valleys in Ireland. It's certainly the longest valley in the Sperrin Mountains, the magnificent mountain range that I was now very much in the heart of. I had first encountered the Sperrins when I had scaled Bessy Bell and I would essentially now be more or less following this mountain range until I reached Binevenagh Mountain on the North Coast, which was still around seventy kilometres away.

The Glenelly Valley lies within the Sperrin Area of Outstanding Natural Beauty and, despite the poor visibility I experienced as I walked along a fair bit of its length, I could still get a sense of the splendour that lay behind the mist. The name of the valley comes from the Irish *Gleann Eallaigh*, meaning 'the valley of the cattle', and I did see quite a number of the beasts, including a large herd of striking Belted Galloway cattle, looking like a cross between cows and pandas! Thankfully, all the cattle I spotted were securely behind fences and I had no further 'close encounters of the herd kind'. I did meet a pretty little white goat that was wandering loose on the road, but, although it was quite friendly and curious, it preferred to keep out of my reach, perhaps enjoying its freedom too much and fearing that it might be caught and incarcerated once again. About four kilometres beyond Barnes Gap I came across a little shed by the roadside and I noticed that the doors were not locked; the clasp being simply held shut with the blade of a screwdriver dropped through the hole. It had been raining lightly for a time and I was feeling a bit peckish and had been on the lookout for somewhere sheltered where I could enjoy my packed lunch. So I looked around furtively to check that I wasn't being watched, like I imagined a professional crook would do before breaking and entering, and then I withdrew the screwdriver from the clasp and gingerly opened the doors to peer inside. It was empty, apart from a couple of wooden pallets and an old cushion, which I instantly recognised as a makeshift table and chair. It looked like the shed was perhaps used to house a tractor or the like, but whatever it housed it was no longer there, and so I slipped inside and made myself at home. It wasn't quite as comfortable as the hayshed on my way to Pettigo, but it was okay – worth two stars at least! After I had eaten, I put the pallets and cushion back to where they had been and slipped out and secured the doors again. Without the help of a forensic team, no one would ever know I had been there.

About two kilometres later I crossed the Glenelly River near a village called Cranagh, thereby moving from one side of the valley to the other, but it made little difference as I was still following the same seemingly endless valley in the same direction. And that direction gradually brought me closer to my biggest challenge of the day. Crockbrack Mountain slowly came into view, looming out of the mist and not looking in the least inviting. Just before reaching the stone track that would take me off road and up the side of the mountain, I was delighted when a mother and her daughter pulled up alongside me in their car for a brief chat and to hand me a donation. It was very rare for me to be stopped on the road like this and it gave me a little boost as I prepared to face the climb ahead. Then it was onwards and upwards into the low cloud hanging over Crockbrack. Once the stone track petered out, the terrain became very wet, rough, steep and boggy and visibility gradually reduced to about twenty metres. Thankfully there was a fence line to follow all the way to the summit, but I was still very relieved to see the wooden stile at the top begin to take shape before me as it slowly appeared through the thick fog. Once over the stile I was able to follow another fence line across more ankle-twisting, boggy ground to reach the neighbouring summit of

Crockmore. Here, I very gratefully joined a long turbary track cut through the bog land, which gradually became a laneway and then roadway, all the time leading me down off the mountains again and towards the village of Moneyneany.

Danielle Sheridan, who works for Cancer Research UK, met me on the road and walked into the village with me, where I met her dad, Patsy, and her husband Barry, who took me to the local Hogan Stand Bar for my usual P&P – Pint and Photo. Later, Barry drove me to his house near Desertmartin, where he and Danielle, and their very cute baby daughter, Cliodhna, welcomed me in and looked after me for the night. That night, as I snuggled up in my cosy bed and just before falling asleep, it suddenly occurred to me that I was bedding down at the foot of Slieve Gallion, where O'Sullivan Beare and Hugh Maguire had marched to from Leitrim in order to join forces with Hugh O'Neill.

So, it didn't come as a complete surprise to me when I woke up in the middle of the night to see the strangely luminescent figure of Donal Cam sitting on the chair beside my bed. "Hello," I said, somewhat groggily, "I thought you might visit me here. What time is it anyway?"

"I've no idea," he replied, "time isn't a concept I bother with much these days, to be honest. It's still dark though. Anyway, here we are at the foot of Slieve Gallion. Do you want to hear about how the planned rendezvous with Hugh O'Neill went?"

"I certainly do," I replied, adjusting my pillows to sit up in bed and give him my full attention. It was such a different reaction to that which I had experienced during my first encounter with Donal Cam in Ballingeary weeks before; now that I had become accustomed to his appearances.

"Well," he started, "after Hugh Maguire and I defeated the Queen's Maguire at Upper Lough Erne, it took us three days to march our combined forces the fifty miles to O'Neill's camp, just south of Slieve Gallion. But it turned out to be all in vain."

"Seriously?" I said. "After all that!"

"I'm afraid so. When we arrived, we found out that O'Neill had already left for Mellifont Abbey near Drogheda only a few days earlier. There he would present himself on bended knee before Mountjoy, the Lord Deputy of Ireland, and agree terms of peace. Unfortunately, O'Neill had been unaware that Maguire and I were on our way to join him. Many of his northern allies had already surrendered and he believed that the rebellion was finished."

"My God!" I said. "It seems that the rebellion was let down by poor communications once again – just like at Kinsale!"

"Well the circumstances were quite different, but, yes, lack of communication was a huge factor. But unfortunately, back in our time, we didn't have the likes of your little magic silver plate that I've seen you talking into and poking with your finger to keep in touch with others."

I smiled at his rudimentary description of my mobile phone.

"Anyway," he continued, "O'Neill signed the Treaty of Mellifont on 30th March 1603. It wasn't until after it was signed, that O'Neill found out that Queen Elizabeth had died six days earlier on 24th March. Lord Mountjoy had of course been informed of the Queen's demise, but he chose not to share this knowledge with O'Neill. Certainly if O'Neill had been aware that England had lost its Queen and that Maguire and I had marched north to join him, things might have turned out very differently. But the treaty effectively brought an end to the Nine Years' War in Ireland; bar a few final battles in Breifne, where O'Rourke continued to resist the English."

"What happened to O'Neill and the rest of the rebels?" I asked, "I'm guessing that they were arrested and locked up."

"I have to admit," started Donal Cam, "that the terms of the treaty were uncharacteristically generous towards the Irish. O'Neill and Rory O'Donnell, Red Hugh's brother and successor, and many other surviving Ulster chiefs were granted full pardons and the return of their estates on the condition that they abandoned their Irish titles and their private armies and swore loyalty only to the Crown of England. Even men who had fought alongside me such as Hugh Maguire, O'Connor Kerry, Richard Tyrrell and William

Burke were granted pardon and reward. The truth is, King James I, who had replaced Elizabeth, was keen to end the money draining war in Ireland. It had brought England close to bankruptcy and had resulted in the death of at least thirty thousand English soldiers."

"So how did you fair under the generous terms of this treaty?" I asked, hesitantly.

"Not very well, I'm afraid to say," Donal Cam replied with a sigh. "Despite appealing to the new king, I could not by any means get pardon or restitution of my lands. I believe that the English considered it unwise to stir things up again in Beara. My cursed cousin, Owen O'Sullivan, had proved himself to be a loyal lapdog to the Crown and they saw no good reason to upset the situation in Munster now that it was stable."

"That seems rather unfair," I said cautiously, "but I suppose I can see their point."

"Well, I certainly didn't at the time," he retorted quickly. But then he added, "Although, I have had plenty of time to consider it since and I would now have to agree. Things were settled in Munster and they had a trustworthy servant in Beara. Why reintroduce someone like me who had proved himself not only disloyal, but also a considerable thorn in their sides."

"So, what did you do?" I asked.

"Well, what else could I do?" he laughed, "I continued to be a thorn. I returned to join Brian Og O'Rourke in Breifne. O'Rourke had been successfully holding off sustained attacks by the English, who were now concentrating their forces on Breifne, the only remaining corner of Ireland that had not yet surrendered. Like me, Brian O'Rourke had failed to secure any concessions from the treaty, as his half-brother Tadhg O'Rourke had fought with the English during the war and was granted lordship of West Breifne in return. Following a twelve-day siege, a force of three thousand men led by Oliver Lambert, Governor of Connacht, and aided by Tadhg O'Rourke and Rory O'Donnell eventually brought the area, and thus all of Ireland, under English control on 25th April 1603. I finally realised that there was no place left in Ireland for me. I managed to arrange safe passage to Spain, where I lived in exile for the rest of my days. I would never be able to see or set foot in Ireland again."

"What about your saviour, Brian O'Rourke," I asked.

"Poor Brian fled into hiding in Galway," Donal Cam replied, with great sadness, "but, unfortunately, he caught a bad fever and died there in January 1604, just a year after he had so kindly taken me and my thirty-five followers under his wing after our long march. He was a brave and protecting man; kind to his friends and fierce to his foes."

"So that was the last of rebels gone?" I offered.

"Sort of," he replied vaguely. "Ireland was almost entirely laid to waste and destroyed. My nephew and historian, Philip O'Sullivan, later wrote, *"A terrible want and famine oppressed all, so that many were forced to eat dogs and whelps: many not having even these, died. And not only men but even beasts were hungry. The wolves, coming out of the woods and mountains, attacked and tore to pieces men weak from want. The dogs rooted from the graves rotten carcases partly decomposed."*

"Good God!" I exclaimed. "Was it really that bad?"

"Philip had a tendency to embellish at times," Donal Cam admitted, "but on this occasion he wasn't far off the mark. It was dire and it was obviously not a situation that allowed order and trust to be easily restored. Although O'Neill and his allies received good terms at the end of the war, they were never trusted by the English authorities and the distrust was mutual. O'Neill, O'Donnell and the other Gaelic lords from Ulster left Ireland only a few years later, in 1607."

"The Flight of the Earls?" I suggested.

"I believe that is how it is now known," Donal Cam confirmed my scant knowledge of Irish history to be correct, before continuing. "They intended to organise an expedition from a Catholic power in Europe, preferably Spain, to restart the war but they were unable to find any military backers. Spain had signed the Treaty of

London in August 1604 with England, under King James, and they certainly did not wish to reopen hostilities. In 1608, the absent earls' lands were confiscated as punishment for trying to start another war, and those lands were soon colonised by the English and Scottish in the Plantation of Ulster."

I thought about this for a moment. "Don't take this the wrong way," I ventured, "but, I'm kind of glad that happened."

"What?" he cried out in surprise, "and you a good Catholic from Tyrone! O'Neill's very own land!"

"Well, a lapsed Catholic who left Tyrone nearly forty years ago," I replied. "But if the Plantation of Ulster had never happened, my wife's Scottish ancestors would never have arrived in County Antrim and I would probably never have met my Protestant wife."

"Ah, I see," he replied more calmly. "Well, I'm glad some good came out of it." And then after considering this for a moment, he said, "It's good that things have moved on since my day. It's certainly much better to love than to fight."

"If you don't mind me saying so," I replied, "that sounds just a little bit hypocritical after what you've told me and shown me over the last few weeks."

"Sometimes, unfortunately," he said in a reflective mood, "you have little choice. And, anyway, I would argue that I was fighting for love; for the love of my country, for the love of my people and for the love of freedom. Unfortunately, in the end, I lost practically everything I had fought for. But at least I escaped with my life to Spain, where I was reunited with my wife."

Lucky you, I thought, but instead I said, "Will you come back sometime and tell me about how you got on in Spain? I'm afraid I'm just too tired to talk any more at the minute. I need my beauty sleep."

"I can see that," he said smiling and then he added, "of course we'll meet again. There's one more important thing I have to share with you. I'll tell you when you reach the Sea of Moyle."

"That's where I'm headed," I replied, "I'll see you there." I knew that the Sea of Moyle was the stretch of water off Ballycastle, where legend had it that the Children of Lir had spent three hundred years in exile. Perhaps 'exile' was the common thread connecting us all I thought wearily, as Donal Cam faded and my eyes became heavier. However, before my mind submitted itself fully to sleep, the words I had written a few months previously came back to me:

Refugee Heart

There's a place I can never return to
I'm banished for the rest of my days
A place that was full of hope and love
Which I still miss in so many ways

And each time I yearn to go back there
My heart crumbles a little bit more
For the place that I seek is lost to me
I will never again walk on its shore

My beaten heart feels like a refugee
It's impossible for me to get back home
So I have to forge out a new life
And seek asylum wherever I roam

But I can't be nomadic for ever
I have to settle in this strange land
And accept that what I once had
Was like a heart drawn in the sand

****

The following morning, Barry cooked me breakfast while Danielle prepared me sandwiches for the road. Just like three years earlier, when I had passed this way on my Ulster Way walk, they were the perfect hosts and looked after me so well. From the kitchen window, I could make out the dark trees of Iniscarn Forrest, rising up the eastern slopes of Slieve Gallion, although the top of the mountain was hidden in a shroud of mist. It reminded me of my night-time visitor, but, of course, I made no mention of my ghostly guide to my hosts. After breakfast, I said farewell to Barry and

Cliodhna, and Danielle then drove me back into Moneyneany and parked outside the Hogan Stand Bar. Danielle had decided to walk with me for a bit this morning and so we both set off on foot out of the village towards Moydamlaght Forest. We talked about her work as we went and the challenges she faced in her new role as Fundraising Manager for Cancer Research UK. It was great to have her lending me her support in such a practical way and I was immensely grateful to both her and her husband.

When we reached the entrance to Moydamlaght Forest, about two kilometres from our starting point, Danielle had to turn back for work. However, before she went, we nabbed a man who had just returned from walking his dog in the forest and got him to take a few photos of Danielle and I for publicity purposes. Danielle then started walking back to her car while I began the steep climb up through the trees towards Eagle Rock. As I gained height, I was rewarded with some nice views back towards the mountains I had crossed the day before, albeit rather limited due to the ceiling of grey cloud suspended low over the entire countryside. I was mildly surprised to come across a small bevy of young pheasants, speckled brown in their still tatty juvenile plumage. They continued scratching and pecking in the dirt and only seemed slightly curious at my passing. I was more surprised when a small flock of sheep came rushing down the track towards me, only veering off at the last moment to enter the forest and then leap and bound through the trees in spectacular fashion. Soon after, the reason for their hurry was revealed when a man walking two Rottweiler dogs appeared, coming down the track also.

As I worked my way higher through the forest I gradually entered into low cloud cover once again and, by the time I reached the base of Eagle Rock, the rocky cliff face appeared only as a dark foreboding shadow looming high above me. The eerie calling of crows, invisible in the mist somewhere on the rocks above, added to my sense of anxiety and dread at what might lie ahead. I traversed the steep, grassy ground to make my way up and around the cliff face and eventually onto the top of Eagle Rock itself. I now had a kilometre stretch of bog land to cross to reach Glenshane Forest. However, the fog had now become so thick that visibility had reduced to about thirty metres at best. I couldn't see any way markers, if indeed any existed in this bleak landscape, but I had my map and I set off in what I was confident was the right direction. However, when I came to the edge of a deep ravine, I was even more confident that I was going in the wrong direction! I was pretty sure that the route to the forest didn't involve falling into any deep ravines. Not to worry. My maps app would help me out. But it was with great dismay that I then discovered that there was absolutely no phone signal. Okay, still no need to worry. I would just have to go back to basics. I had my map and I had my compass and I had a very good idea of my location, thanks to the obvious feature I had just stopped short of falling into. I just needed to bear North-East. My compass would keep me right. Damn it! The needle in my compass was stuck in the one position. I shook it and tapped it a few times, but it made no difference. I thumped it and bashed it a few more times, but all to no avail. The needle remained firmly stuck. Okay, so now it was time to worry.

I tried my best to work my way toward the forest based on the shape and orientation of the ravine and told myself that all I had to do was keep heading in the one direction. However, this was much easier said than done when traversing over very rough and uneven ground, with no reference points visible. I quickly became totally disorientated and literally hadn't the 'foggiest' notion where I was. I finally stumbled upon a fence line and followed it until I came to a junction, where the fence line split in two different directions. I set out from there in what I thought might be the correct direction and after wandering blindly in the wilderness for about half an hour I came upon another fence. I followed this and came to a junction. Then I realised that it was the same junction I had set out from half an hour before! I had been going around in circles. I was totally lost, but I needed to stay calm. Again, this was easier said than done. It reminded me of the time I was stuck in the snow on Knocklayde Mountain near Ballycastle back in January. Again, I wondered if this was how it was going to end for me, stumbling around a mountain in the fog until I finally collapsed or stepped off the edge of a cliff; whichever came first. And would I not welcome it anyway, putting an end to my long suffering grief. Such thoughts still rushed in to ambush me when my defences were lowered. The demons always seemed to be waiting in the wings; waiting for a chink to appear in my armour and for an opportunity to pounce. But there is something about the human spirit that forces you to fight on; to survive. I had faced this many times before and had become well used to deflecting these assaults. I had become more resilient and more adept at chasing the demons away. I needed to rally my own defences and spur myself into action. "Feck off, you buggers. I am here to stay," I shouted into the fog. It seemed to do the trick and I once again focussed on surviving.

I decided to follow the fence line back in the opposite direction and after some time I came to a gate and a vague track that looked like it was used by farm vehicles. I mentally flipped a coin and followed the track to the right and then had a stroke of luck. A weak signal was now registering on my phone. I didn't think it would be of sufficient strength, but thankfully I was at last able to access my location on my maps app. And using the 'satellite' view on the app I was amazingly able to make out a faint impression of the farm track I was following and where it was in relation to the Glenshane Forest. I was finally able to make my way towards the forest, the little blue dot on my phone's screen, which represented my position, drawing closer and closer to the dark green of the virtual woods. I almost cried with relief when the ghostly shapes of the actual trees came into view in the real world before me. But my trial wasn't over yet.

I reached the tree line and searched for the stile that provided the entry point to the track that would lead through the forest. But, search as I might, I simply could not find it. I knew it was there, as I had used it three years ago. However, I remembered that the wooden stile even then had been pretty flimsy and damaged, so perhaps in the intervening years it had disintegrated and disappeared into the undergrowth. Thankfully, the maps app on my phone came to the rescue again. I took a firebreak down through the forest instead, which I could see from the app would eventually meet up with a pathway and get me back onto the proper route again. The firebreak looked like a nice and clear way through the forest on my satellite view, but in reality it was an incredibly wet, boggy and overgrown obstacle course that proved quite a challenge to negotiate. I got snagged up in the branches of fallen trees more than once. When I eventually reached the pathway, I was exhausted and, once again, my boots and socks were soaking. I looked at my watch. What should have been a one hour crossing of the high bog land between Eagle Rock and the forest had turned out to be a three hour endurance test that almost broke me. I decided to stop here for lunch and a much needed rest. I sat down by the side of the track and wrung out my soaking socks and changed into a dry pair - at least I was better prepared this time. And at least I had made it safely down out of the fog again.

After refuelling, recharging the batteries and resetting my resolve, I gathered up my gear and set off again. I followed the gravel track alongside a small stream, possibly the beginnings of the River Roe, which ran down through the forest for a few kilometres until it reached the Glenshane Bridge. I looked back to the hill I had crossed earlier in the fog and grumbled "Fecking typical", as I saw that the low cloud had lifted and that the top of the hill was now bathed in bright sunshine! It served to remind me that conditions in the mountains could change quite dramatically in a relatively short space of time, either for the better or for the worse. That's why it was important to always have the correct equipment with you to deal with any eventuality – preferably equipment that worked! I would need to replace my compass at the first opportunity and perhaps pay a little bit more than I had for the first one.

After the bridge, the route then turned off the forest pathway to follow narrow grassy tracks through a series of fields, and flocks of sheep, around the lower slopes of Corick Mountain. The cloud cover continued to break up and I was soon sweating under a warm sun and shedding layers as I went. The grassy tracks eventually morphed into farm lanes and then a series of roads that generally followed the flow of the River Roe through Benady Glen and finally into the large village of Dungiven. I called into a store here and sat outside for a short time to decide on what to do next while demolishing a chocolate bar in record time. I had expected to be in Dungiven at least two hours earlier, but getting lost in the fog over Eagle Rock and battling through a cluttered firebreak had put paid to that. However, my more immediate concern was the fact that during the last hour of my journey, the front of my lower left leg, just above my ankle, had started to ache. This was not turning out to be a good day.

The accommodation I was booked into for the night, the Grey Gables, was only about four kilometres on the other side of Dungiven, but the biggest problem was that the formidable mountain of Benbradagh stood in my path. I could see it from where I was sitting; both magnificent and imposing. I remembered speculating, when I had first climbed its 465m height three years before, that its Irish name *Binn Bhradach*, which translates as 'Thief's Peak', was perhaps due to the fact that the strenuous climb could literally steal your breath away. There was no doubting that it was a tough climb at the best of times. I estimated that it would probably take me at least another two hours to reach my accommodation for the night – and that was only if the ache in my leg didn't get any worse. Of course, I could simply have phoned for a taxi and have been putting my feet up in the Grey Gables in fifteen or twenty minutes. That would certainly have been the sensible approach. I was now only days away from my ultimate final destination in Ballycastle. It would be foolish to jeopardise that by risking another injury. The ache in my left leg felt like the beginnings of shin splints, which I had some previous experience of. I knew that the best treatment for shin splints was, once again, RICE – Rest, Ice, Compression and Elevation. Well, the first three would have to wait, although I'm pretty sure that 'Elevation' didn't mean climbing a mountain. But I could be both stubborn and impatient when I put my mind to it and I was still determined to knock off this mountain – today! Leaving it to the following day would only make for a harder day tomorrow. To hell with the pain. It was time to crack on.

And so began the very long and steep climb up the roadway to the top of Benbradagh Mountain. Several times I stopped and almost changed my mind. On one occasion, I even looked up local taxi companies on my phone. But even though the pain in my leg was becoming more troubling, each time I stopped, my stubbornness won out and I pushed on relentlessly once again. I finally reached the stile at the top of the road and laboriously climbed over it. I was now at the point of no return, as no vehicle, taxi or otherwise, would be able to access the area I was now entering. Even though I knew the views from the peak of Benbradagh to be magnificent, I opted not to make the additional trek out to the summit – I'm not totally stupid! Instead, I followed what was known as the 'American Road' down the gentle south-eastern slope of the mountain, passing the site of an old US Navy transmitter site on the way. Unfortunately, the ache in my left leg became more acute on the way down and I was walking with a very pronounced limp by the time I reached my accommodation at the Grey Gables.

Bronagh and Dermot Rafferty had very kindly agreed to provide me with a bed, dinner, breakfast and packed lunch, all out of the goodness of their hearts. Dermot's sister had been following my journey on social media and she had got in touch with the couple to set it all up for me. It was absolute luxury and Dermot and Bronagh were so friendly and accommodating. Bronagh provided me with an ice pack, which I applied to my sore shin with my leg propped up on a chair, as I enjoyed a superb dinner. Meanwhile, Dermot filled me in on some of the history of the transmitter site on Benbradagh – apparently it was a highly secretive site during its time of operation, when it was used by the US Navy as a communications base during the Cold War. Dermot also offered me a can of Guinness. I had totally forgotten about my usual ritual, but, to be honest, I was so exhausted after my eleven hour hike that a Guinness would probably have knocked me out on the spot. However, I noticed that there was a nice little painting of a pint of Guinness hanging on the wall. Dermot had been presented with it by work colleagues a few years back and he didn't mind taking it down from the wall for me to use as a prop for my end of day photo of me with my pint and my banner. It worked out perfectly and was a nice variation on the theme. Later I had a surprise visit by Ann and Annmarie, chair and vice-chair respectively of the Dungiven Committee of Cancer Research UK, who called to wish me all the best for the remainder of my journey. After such an eventful day, I was off to bed as soon as Ann and Annmarie departed. I just hoped that my shin would have settled down a little by morning. The thought of having to interrupt my journey again due to injury was just too much for me to contemplate.

****

After an otherwise blissful sleep at the Grey Gables, I woke with my lower left leg feeling stiff and sore. I was now pretty sure that I was suffering from shin splints, which is a swelling or inflammation of the tissue around the shin bone caused by repetitive weight bearing on the legs. I knew this only too well, as I had suffered from the painful condition only a few days into my Ulster Way walk three years before. The condition is normally associated with running, as opposed to walking, and I assumed that my recent practice of jogging down slopes had led to this latest occurrence. During my Ulster Way walk, I had little option but to rest up and postpone the rest of my walk for two weeks. But what to do now? I had already lost four weeks due to my calf muscle injury back in Tipperary. I was now only five days away from Ballycastle and the completion of my Ireland Way pilgrimage. And my latest injury couldn't have happened at a worse time. Today was the day I was due to face my 'arch nemesis', Donald's Hill, the 399m high mountain that tries to pass itself of as a mere hill. I had been dreading it; both Donald's Hill and the long stretch of bog land between it and the neighbouring Rigged Hill. This had been, without question, the most exhausting and challenging section of my entire Ulster Way hike three years before. And it was one of the reasons why I had been so determined to scale Benbradagh the day before - so that I could tackle the next nightmarish section relatively fresh. After weighing up the pros and cons, I decided to push on. It would almost certainly further aggravate my shin splints, but I was prepared to endure the discomfort for a few more days. I thought of how the O'Connor Kerry had marched on with his ruined feet towards the end of O'Sullivan Beare's epic journey and it persuaded me further. However, I also decided that it would be prudent to stay off the hills today if I could. I examined my maps and saw that I could simply keep to the roads and circle round the hills to my intended stopping point in Cam Forest. It would add on a few kilometres to my journey, but it would certainly be a lot easier than going over the mountains. So that was my strategy for the day ahead sorted. But, I have to admit that I wasn't exactly brimming with confidence, as I hobbled towards the dining area for breakfast.

Not only did Bronagh cook me a lovely breakfast, but she also very kindly prepared me a fabulous lunch to take with me. The rooms at the Grey Gables are normally let as self-catering apartments, but Bronagh and Dermot had gone all out and treated me as their personal guest. After breakfast, I set off from the Grey Gables, admiring the distinctive wedge shape of Benbradagh looming in the background, and started limping up the Legavannon Road. I was back in tortoise mode. My left leg couldn't quite bear my full weight and was sore to walk on, but bearable. I gritted my teeth and hobbled on slowly. After a couple of kilometres, I veered off the main road and followed the route down a long laneway, which passed the Legavannon Pot, a deep plunge pool formed by retreating glacial melt water at the end of the last ice age. The laneway eventually joined a minor road, where I turned left towards Donald's Hill. This road would pass by the foot of Donald's Hill and then continue on around it and it was still my intention to stick to this low level road route. However, when I reached the sign pointing off road and towards the route up the slopes of Donald's Hill, I took my sensible head off, stuffed it in my rucksack and replaced it with my stubborn one. Damn if I was going to cower away from this hill. It was part of the Ireland Way and I had set out to walk the entire Ireland Way. Not parts of it, but all of it. So, before I knew it I was heading for the steep, heather covered slopes of the Donald's Hill. It was a tough climb and the slopes were just as steep and treacherous as I had remembered. In places, it felt like it would just take one slip and I would quickly tumble to the bottom again. Surprisingly, however, my sore leg actually seemed to respond slightly better to going uphill. When I finally made it to the top, I paused to capture my breath and also to take in the breath-taking views of the rest of the Sperrins, Lough Foyle and Donegal. From this angle, the shape of Benbradagh, 'Thief's Peak', actually looked as if a giant's hand had reached down from the clouds and attempted to steal a bit of the landscape, only to have it slip away from its fingers at the last minute, leaving a piece of land 'pinched up' as a result.

I was of course pleased to have made it to the top of Donald's Hill, but now began the section that I had been really dreading ever since I learned that the Ireland Way would cause me to revisit the bog land between here and Rigged Hill. I remembered how I had imagined lying down and dying here three years previously, wishing to be consumed by the very earth. However, the first stretch, over to the roadway splitting the bog land, turned out to be not as bad as I had previously experienced, mainly because I was able to locate a dry, raised pathway through the bog via the satellite view on my mobile phone. I wished that I'd had a decent mobile when I had first walked the Ulster Way. Once again, the satellite view on my phone's maps app proved to be invaluable. It had got me out of the woods near Galbally weeks ago and out of the fog only yesterday. And today it would have been near impossible to locate the raised pathway without the aid of my phone. From an eyelevel view, everything in this wild landscape tended to merge into itself and once again there was a distinct lack of way markers. The second stretch from the roadway to the windmills on Rigged Hill was a different story. It turned out to be worse than I remembered! The ground was so rough and boggy that I stumbled and fell countless times. The crossing seemed to take forever and it was not kind to my sore leg at all.

I sat down for a rest and breathed a long sigh of relief when I finally reached the hard track roadway of the windmill farm. From this point on it was a relatively easy, if rather slow, limp through the wind farm and down through Cam Forest to my final destination for the day. I had only travelled eighteen kilometres today and had only been out for six hours, but I was very happy to call it a day at that, particularly given my gammy left leg. So I waved my flag joyously above my head when I caught sight of my friend Howard Robinson and his little blond daughter, Cali, waiting for me on the track. Howard owned Island Rock Campers and he had planned from way back to put me up in his camper van when I reached this very remote corner of the world in the middle of Cam Forest. He and Cali walked me in for the final hundred metres, Cali now delighted to be carrying my flag. When we reached the van, I discovered that Howard's mother, Margaret, was waiting there to welcome me with a much needed cup of tea. It was my first experience of using a camper van and it turned out to be compact and very well designed. Howard had also stocked the cupboards and fridge with supplies, including a few cans of Guinness – my fondness for the black stuff was becoming very well known. He was a true gentleman. Yet another one on the long list of wonderful people that I was indebted to for the kindness and support they had shown me since I started out on my remarkable journey. After Howard had shown me all the basics regarding the van, he and Cali then headed off with Margaret in her car and left me to enjoy my spot of rural solitude. I sat on a camp chair outside the van, opened a can of Guinness to drink from and strapped two of the other cans to my propped up sore and swollen leg – it wasn't ice, but the cold cans were certainly better than nothing at all.

Chapter Fourteen: Causeway Coast
(Days forty to forty-three – Cam Forest to Ballycastle)

I was woken early by the pitter-patter sound of raindrops on the roof of the camper van on the edge of Cam Forest. It reminded me of waking in a caravan at my friend's home near Lisnaskea three years earlier. Then the rain drumming on the roof had brought to mind a funeral march and had triggered a bout of depression. It was another sign of progress that the sound on the roof of the camper van now simply provoked a more normal response, which was to mutter, "Aw feck! It's raining again." It was still raining when Howard, together with his mum and daughter, called a few hours later to send me on my way and to move the van onto its next location for a new client, who, unlike me, would have to pay for the privilege. After much hugging and thanks, I said farewell to the Robinsons and headed off to face a day of showers and occasional sunshine. My left leg was still pretty sore, but I was able to walk on it, albeit at a rather slower pace than I had been getting used prior to my latest injury. A series of uniformly tedious commercial forests, linked by very busy, fast roads, took me further up through the North Sperrins. I trudged through Cam, Springwell and Ballyhanna Forests and dodged the fast traffic on the Ringsend and Windy Hill Roads.

Windy Hill Road certainly lived up to its name, for it was all I could do to hold onto my flag and my cape as I pushed forward against the strong westerly wind. However, up until the 1970's this road was not called the Windy Hill Road, but the Murder Hole Road. This was due to the fact that a nineteenth century highwayman, called Cushy Glen, used to rob and dispose of his unfortunate victims in a 'murder hole' close to this road. So, when a police car pulled in and stopped just behind me, and I turned to see two large coppers emerging from the vehicle, my first thought was, Jaysus, surely they've apprehended Cushy by now? Mind you, I probably looked like a bit of a highwayman in my black cape. But then I recognised one of the policemen as none other than Chief Inspector Ian Magee, Head of Community Policing in the Causeway Coast and Glens. I had met Ian a couple of times in Portrush following my Ulster Way walk and he was a thoroughly decent chap. So, I put my hands down from the surrender position I had adopted and instead went to say hello to him and his colleague. Ian explained that he had been following my progress on social media, but he really hadn't expected to see me on this stretch of road today. But, when he had spotted me from the car, he had just had to pull in and wish me all the very best for the rest of my journey. He also confided in me that certain arrangements were being put in place for my arrival in Ballycastle, but he wouldn't be drawn on any of the detail. "I've been sworn to secrecy," he said, adding, "and I wouldn't want to spoil the surprise." His colleague took a couple of quick photos of Ian and I, before we headed off again on our separate ways. It was certainly an unexpected pleasure and I was intrigued to learn that arrangements were being made. I couldn't help but wonder what Ballycastle might have in store for my homecoming.

Once I emerged from the stony tracks of Ballyhanna Forest, I turned onto the Bishop's Road and followed this for the next eight kilometres towards Downhill. For the first couple of kilometres the views were restricted by the trees of Binevenagh Forest, but, once past these, I enjoyed great views over Benone, Lough Foyle and the Inishowen Peninsula and back to the cliffs of Binevenagh. As I proceeded, I was also able to keep an eye on the approaching rain fronts sweeping in from the North-West and had ample time to pull my cape on again each time before the rain arrived. As I neared the Gortmore viewing point, I caught sight of the Manannán Mac Lir statue standing on top of the hill behind the car parking area. Manannán Mac Lir is a sea god from Irish mythology, a bit like a Celtic version of Neptune, and grandfather of Síonnan, who gave her name to the River Shannon. The statue had been first erected a number of years ago and had become a popular tourist attraction. However, the original statue had been 'stolen' in 2015 and was missing from the site when I had undertaken my Ulster Way walk. Local people were quite aggrieved at the crime and the police even launched a 'missing person's appeal' at the time! It was later found but was so badly damaged that a new statue had been commissioned and this had since been erected on the same spot as the original. I really wanted to get a picture alongside this iconic statue and I hurried towards Gortmore viewing point, hoping to reach it before the next rain front blew in. As I climbed the steps up to the site of the statue, the wind started to pick up and by the time I got to the statue itself the wind was almost blowing a gale and the rain was starting. It was almost as if Manannán Mac Lir himself, with his arms outstretched before him, was commanding the weather and whipping up the wind and summoning in the rain from Lough Foyle. Luckily, there were a couple of tourists just about to run for cover when I arrived and I managed to persuade one of them to take a couple of quick snaps before we all retreated to the slightly more sheltered roadway again. He dashed for his hire car, while I simply continued walking along the road that now began a long, gentle descent towards Downhill. As I continued to limp along the road, between walls of rough stone and hedges adorned with red fuchsia blossom, I was rewarded with wonderful rainbows out to sea that split the dark skies with vibrant colour, as if in defiance of the rain. Straight ahead I could see Mussenden Temple perched on a headland overlooking the ocean and, further inland, the extensive ruins of Downhill House stretching over the hillside. Beyond this were hazy views of Portstewart Strand stretching into the distance and even hints of the towns of Portstewart and Portrush further along the coast.

The nicest part of the day's journey was undoubtedly the walk through Downhill Forest. I quickly forgot the monotonous commercial forests I had experienced earlier, as I fully immersed myself in the calm and beauty of this enchanting woodland filled with beech, sycamore and other leafy trees. The pathway through the forest followed alongside a fast flowing river for quite a time and the sound of the water spilling over the smooth rocks and stones only added to the peacefulness of this sheltered haven. The peacefulness was unfortunately shattered when I emerged from the woodland at the Bishops Gate entrance to the Downhill Demesne and joined a pedestrian footpath alongside the busy Coast Road. However, I enjoyed the views over the fields to Castlerock, the River Bann and the extensive sand dunes between the river and Portstewart Strand. At the pretty, thatched Hezlett Cottage, I turned left and headed towards the sea for the final kilometre stretch to the beach at Castlerock. I had been on the road for nine and a half hours and, by the time I stepped onto the sandy beach, my left leg was aching. But I hardly paid it any attention, as I savoured the significance of achieving this major milestone on my journey. I had reached the north coast of Ireland and had now technically walked the entire length of the island of Ireland – from the south coast all the way up to the north coast! Of course, I knew that I hadn't completed my journey just yet. The Ireland Way trail went on across the north coast to Ballycastle, which was the official end point. But I had now made it to the top of Ireland and my final destination was now very much within reach – only three more day's walking; if my leg held up! I shared my joy with two female tourists from America, who had coincidentally arrived at the beach at the same time as me and were curious about my challenge. I got one of them to take some photographs of me standing beside the Castlerock Beach sign, as evidence that I had made it, if nothing else. My friend, Carol Warke, then arrived to give me a lift to my place in Portrush for the night. But first, she brought me to The Rock Bar and Restaurant and bought me, not only a pint of Guinness, but also my dinner! The hospitality continued unabated.

****

Today's walk was going to be very special, as I would have the company of, not one, but three good friends for almost the entire journey. Gillian Beattie picked me up from my house in Portrush. This was actually the first time I had met Gillian, although we had been friends on social media for many months. She had first got in touch with me about her own challenge to raise funds for cancer research and Macmillan Cancer Support in memory of her husband, Davy, who she had lost to cancer the previous year. Her '354 hour walking challenge', acknowledging the fact that Davy had only survived for 354 hours following his diagnosis, was both brave and inspiring. I was delighted that Gillian was able to join me on part of my walk and, in doing so, would be able to contribute another few hours to her own very personal challenge. Gillian drove me back to Castlerock and here we met up with Gerard McAuley and Tom Clark, both of whom I knew through our shared passion for surfing. Tom had also brought his white pit-bull dog, Tia, along for the walk. After a few photos of our 'not so famous five' we set off under dark, grey skies for Coleraine, taking the quieter back roads into the town and then the busy main road out to Portstewart.

As the crow flies, Portstewart is actually only about four kilometres from Castlerock and a direct route would have involved walks along two of the most beautiful beaches on the North Coast for practically all of that distance. Unfortunately, however, we were required to walk a distance of sixteen kilometres on hard roads and pavements to reach Portstewart. The reason for this was due to the simple fact that the River Bann, the longest river in Northern Ireland, stood, or rather flowed, in our path. From Castlerock, we had to follow the West bank of the Bann inland into Coleraine, in order to find the first crossing point, and then follow the East bank out to Portstewart on the coast again. To take the beach route, we would have had to swim across the wide river at its barmouth (not easy with a rucksack) or get a lift across on some sort of water craft. As we trudged along the tarmac, I have to admit to being somewhat envious of Stephen Bell, aka Wildfoot, who had walked this route a few weeks before me and had crossed the barmouth with the help of a friend and a couple of stand-up paddleboards. I was slightly less envious of, but full of admiration for, the most notable achievement of Stephen's Ireland Way challenge though, which was his ability to complete the entire journey in his bare feet! I simply couldn't imagine attempting such a remarkable 'feet' of endurance – it was tough enough in boots.

Our wet gear was required on a number of occasions as several rain fronts blew in from the sea to give us a dousing. Poor Tia had to just put up with the rain, but, like most dogs, she didn't seem to mind too much. However, after crossing the footbridge over the River Bann in Coleraine, Tom left Tia home as he felt that she had gone far enough and was also getting cold. He lived nearby and so he was able to catch up with us again at the marina on the Bann, where Gillian, Gerard and I had stopped for a bite of lunch, which Gillian had very kindly prepared for us. We started our lunch sitting out in the open air, next to the jetties and the boats moored there, but we soon had to scarper for shelter in the porch of the nearby Coleraine Yacht Club, when another cloud burst suddenly descended upon us. Watching the wide, dark waters of the River Bann glide slowly past on their way to the Atlantic Ocean, I reflected on the fact that my Ireland Way journey had now brought me across both the longest river in Ireland, the Shannon, and now the longest in Northern Ireland, the Bann. The name of this northern river comes from the Irish *An Bhanna*, meaning 'the goddess', although the specifics of this naming seem to have been lost in the mists of time. It's not unusual for Irish river names to reflect the pagan worship of deities. I had found this out earlier in relation to the River Shannon taking its name from Síonnan, granddaughter of the Celtic God of the Sea, Manannán Mac Lir, whose statue I had passed only yesterday at Gortmore Viewing Point. I was reminded of how this island was not only tied together by geography and geology, but also by mythology and legend – a connection that would be reinforced again when I reached the very end of my journey. My reverie was broken as Tom arrived back to join us and, with lunch finished, the four of us then pushed on for Portstewart, following the footpaths alongside the very busy Coast Road.

My progress was rather slow, due to the pain in my left leg, but I was happy that I was still able to walk. That morning, when I had got out of bed and limped very painfully to the bathroom, I thought that I wasn't going to be able to walk any distance at all today. But, thankfully, the pain had gradually eased and I was now able to walk with care; although I had never relied on my walking poles more. They helped to take a bit of the strain of my leg, but it was frustratingly slow progress at times. I recalled my encounter with Peppe on my Camino in Spain two years earlier, when I had given him my walking poles as he had been struggling with a badly swollen and painful knee injury. He had been incredibly grateful to me and now I was incredibly grateful to the rest of the gang for slowing down to my pace, especially Tom who had long legs and was a naturally fast walker. Having company and being able to have proper conversations along the way was a real luxury and it certainly helped make the time pass a little quicker for me and also helped to take my mind off the almost constant ache in my leg.

Gerard had to leave us when we passed close to his home in Portstewart, but the rest of the gang picked up the cliff path near the entrance to Portstewart Strand and headed for the town centre. The skies had at last begun to clear a bit, although it had become very windy, particularly now that we were at the coast again. Along the way we met a lovely lady called Lucy, who was out for a walk with her children. I asked her to take a photo of Gillian, Tom and I and, not only did she very kindly oblige, but she also gave me a donation before we headed on our way again. We passed the impressive Dominican College and then crossed the town's busy promenade to pick up the coastal path into Portrush. This delightful path hugged the rugged coastline, weaving its way around grassy headlands and rocky coves for five kilometres or so. It then dropped down to meet the promenade skirting the long crescent of West Bay Strand, the first of Portrush's picturesque beaches. We arrived accompanied by glorious sunshine breaking through the clouds and strong onshore winds coming in off a choppy sea. Tom and I hugged Gillian and said farewell to her at this point, as she had to rush ahead to catch a train back to Castlerock, where she had left her car.

Tom and I continued on together for the final furlong, stopping at the Babushka Kitchen Café on the harbour breakwater wall to say hi to my friend, George Nelson, who provided us with complimentary coffees to go. From there we headed through the harbour area and followed a path up and round the stunning Ramore Head. Portrush is from the Irish *Port Rois*, meaning 'promontory port' and it takes its name from the fact that most of the original part of the town is located on a peninsula of volcanic rock that extends out to sea for over a kilometre beyond the surrounding coastline. Ramore Head is the rocky, elevated tip of that peninsula and on a clear day, as this day had now become, it offers superb views in all directions. Tom and I followed the path around the perimeter of the headland, stopping frequently to take in the fabulous panoramas on show that stretched from Portstewart and the Inishowen Peninsula in the West to the Skerries and the Giant's Causeway in the East. From this elevated vantage point, one could really appreciate the rugged beauty of this stunning coastline and I was reminded once again of why Jacqui and I had been so attracted to Portrush many years ago and had decided to buy a house here. A house that had witnessed so many joyful years, as we and our two children spent as much time here as possible, escaping the city life in Belfast and the pressures of work whenever we could. It had been a real sanctuary for Jacqui and I and I'm pretty sure we would have settled here in retirement if only things had worked out differently. 'If only' – probably the most frequently used and most utterly pointless words in the vocabulary of anyone who has lost a loved one. I still used the house on occasions for a change of scene or when the surf was good, but it would never be the same again – pretty much like everything else in my life really.

Tom and I completed the loop round Ramore Head and then headed into the town centre to stop with Andy Hill at Troggs Surf Shop for a photo and a very generous donation. We then walked a short distance up the street to Kiwis Brew Bar, where we were each served a pint of Guinness on the house! After grabbing something to eat in Kiwis, Tom put me to shame by setting off to walk the seven kilometres back to his home in Coleraine, while I waited on a taxi to take me the two kilometres to my place in Portrush. Mind you, I had already clocked up well over a thousand kilometres since setting off from Castletownbere and I was, of course, nursing a sore leg. It was hard to believe that I only had just over forty kilometres to go until I reached Ballycastle. I just had to hope that my left leg would hold out for a couple more days. My taxi driver was a gentleman called Joaquin and he refused any payment when he dropped me off at my house, having quizzed me about my challenge on the short five minute journey. Not for the first time it occurred to me that, if I had so desired, I could probably have kept my journey going on for as long as I wanted and continued to survive very well on the generosity of other people as I went. I thanked Joaquin and limped to my front door and opened it to enter an empty house full of memories.

****

When you embark on any long hike that involves many consecutive days of walking, it's inevitable that each morning, when you wake up, will have a certain feeling of 'Groundhog Day' to it. And so it was this morning, although, if anything, the feeling was even stronger on this occasion, for once again my left shin was throbbing. Initially, when I first stepped out of bed, my leg was very stiff and it was sheer agony to walk on it, but thankfully as I moved around the house, accomplishing my usual morning routine at a much slower pace than normal, my leg started to free up a little and the pain started to ease. By the time I had struggled into my walking boots, I felt ready to set off, but was genuinely concerned that my leg might not be able to endure much more punishment and might let me down at the eleventh hour. But, this was no time for such negative thoughts. I needed to be positive and believe that I could achieve my goal. So, as I closed the front door behind me, I set off, if not exactly with a spring in my step, then at least with a certain resolve and determination to complete my challenge. I had forty-two kilometres left to walk to Ballycastle and I planned to split it over the next two days.

I made my way on foot to the sands of East Strand, my official starting point for today, and, as I always did when I visited there, I paused for a few moments to whisper a few quiet words to Jacqui. Three years before I had visited this beach at dawn to scatter some of her ashes here, as she had requested. We had both loved walking on this beach and she knew I would continue to surf here. It was her way of saying that she wanted to stay close to me after she had gone. "I'm depending on you weather angels to look after me today," I whispered to her before setting off across the sandy beach that stretched for three kilometres round Curran Point and on towards Whiterocks. And the weather was certainly very pleasant, as I followed the wide strip of beach running between the pale-green, grass-covered sand dunes and the white-topped, windblown waves of the sea. Walking on this beach always engendered such a feeling of wide open space and freedom. It felt like a magical landscape where spirits could fly free and I have to admit that, just as Jacqui had wished, I always felt closer to her here than anywhere else. As I walked along these golden sands of time, happy memories of our walks together jostled for position with feelings of resentment that such occasions were gone, never to be repeated. There never seemed to be an outright winner in these tussles within the mind. They just kept sparring and bouncing off each other in an endless contest that would never be resolved. A horse thundered by, drawing me out of my pointless reverie. I watched as horse and rider moved together in perfect harmony, unlike my conflicting thoughts, the sand being churned up fiercely as they went, as if they had no time for the past. I would have quickened my step in response, if my leg would have allowed it. Instead, I continued to plod on at my own steady pace and tried to focus on what was ahead of me, rather than what was behind. And what I saw ahead of me were the white limestone cliffs and arches that gave Whiterocks its name. I also noticed a banner sticking up out of the sand and, just as I was wondering what it was for, it immediately became clear as a group of runners came streaming past me heading for the banner. It was the Portrush Parkrun and runners of all ages, shapes and sizes and sporting a striking variety of bright tops and shorts continued to jog past me, turn around the banner and head back the way they had come. It seemed like everyone was in a hurry this morning except me.

I left the beach and took the path over the white cliff tops, enjoying the gorgeous sea views as I went and moving ever closer to the dramatic cliff top ruins of Dunluce Castle. The stone walls and towers of the fortress seemed to almost emerge organically out of the very rocky headland on which they perched precariously. Beyond the castle, the views back along the coast to Whiterocks, Curran Point and the town of Portrush itself were magnificent under the cloudy but bright sky. I followed the Coast Road towards Bushmills, the home of the famous whiskey distillery, but when the road swung inland, I took the Ulster Way route down through some fields towards the sea again and into Portballintrae. The name of this coastal village is from the Irish *Port Bhaile an Trá*, meaning 'port of the beach settlement', and it overlooks its own sheltered and enclosed horseshoe bay as well as leading onto the much longer Runkerry or Bushfoot Strand on the other side of the Bush River. After taking the footbridge over the river, the route followed a wooden boardwalk behind the marram grass covered sand dunes towards the grandiose edifice of Runkerry House and the prominent headland of Runkerry Point.

I was now entering the magnificent realms of the Giant's Causeway, with the hexagonal stones and columns of the Grand Causeway itself, along with other impressive geological features, such as the Giant's Boot, the Organ and the Amphitheatre. I was very fortunate that a friend in The National Trust had alerted the Causeway Visitor Centre to my imminent arrival. So when I reported to the reception desk, I was welcomed by the manager, Bob Picken, who very kindly presented me with a complimentary pass. I picked up some lunch from the centre's café and sat at one of the picnic tables outside in the warm sunshine to enjoy my break. The Visitor Centre was absolutely hiving with tourists. I was amused to read a quote on the back of a tour coach parked outside, which was attributed to Octavia Hill, a co-founder of the National Trust - "*We all need space; unless we have it we cannot reach that sense of quiet in which whispers of better things come to us gently....*" I'm not sure that this was what she had in mind, though. The engines of tour buses rattled as they competed for parking space and tourists of many different nationalities noisily jostled for position as they waited to board their allotted coaches, while others poured out from coaches that had just arrived. However, I strangely welcomed and enjoyed all the activity and commotion going on around me as I relaxed over lunch and engaged in a spot of 'people watching'. I had had plenty of space over the weeks I had spent hiking the Ireland Way and, no doubt, I would experience some more before completing it. So for now, this brief exposure to the hustle and bustle of the 'madding crowd' was a novelty to be enjoyed.

After lunch, I joined some of the madding crowd to ride the small shuttle bus down to the famous hexagonal stones. Here I met Aaron, a tour guide for the National Trust, and he arranged for a photo to be taken of us standing on the stones of the Grand Causeway for their promotional sites – it's not every day that a famous hiker drops in on the Giant's Causeway! However, I tried not to feel like a charlatan, as I boarded the bus for the return journey back up to the Visitor Centre. Any feelings of guilt, however, quickly dissipated as I stepped down from the bus and immediately set off to continue my solitary walk along the cliff path, which provided spectacular elevated views over the coast. I had been so looking forward to this part of the walk and had been praying that the weather would be good, so I could enjoy it in all its glory. My weather angels did not let me down. It was a beautiful day and the views were stunning. Of course, it wasn't the first time that I had walked this stretch across these magnificent cliffs, but it never failed to instil a sense of wonder in me. As I passed the headland directly above the famous causeway, I approached the edge cautiously to look down and gazed in fascination at the finger of volcanic rock pointing towards Scotland and extending out into the perfectly deep blue sea surrounding it. Tiny dots of colour moved around and over the rock, like little mites searching out some shade from the burning sun above. However, closer examination revealed that these little colourful specks were actually brightly clothed tourists clambering over the hexagonal stones way below where I stood.

I moved on, traversing the cliff top path around the wide bay of Port Noffer, 'the bay of the giant', with 'aerial' views of the treacherously steep Shepherd's Path and the stone columns of the Organ. The path followed round the top of the Amphitheatre, encircling the smaller Port Reostan, to the Chimney Stacks overlooking Lacada Point, another finger of grey basalt rock jutting out into the ocean. This was where the Spanish Armada galleass, the Girona, met its fate in 1588. The wreck of the Girona still lies below the waters in the bay beyond Lacada Point, which has been known as Port na Spaniagh, 'Port of the Spaniards', ever since. The undulating path continued to weave around further grassy-topped headlands and rocky coves. Rathlin Island, Whitepark Bay and Fair Head soon came into view along the coast to the east. Without doubt, this section of the Ireland Way was, in my opinion, the most beautiful of them all. The Beara Peninsula and the south coast of County Cork had also been stunning, but it came at a price. It required long and tough climbs up into the Caha Mountains and, of course, I had often been moving inland and hence further away from the sea. Here, on the Causeway Coastal Path, I was generally walking along relatively easy terrain and the sea views were always right there with me. Added to this of course was the fact that it also involved traversing the famous Giant's Causeway, a World Heritage Site!

On and on, the route continued to delight and the sun continued to shine as I rounded Benbane Head and passed the pretty bay of Port Moon, with its little orange-roofed 'bothy', snuggled in its grassy nest at the foot of the cliffs. The sparse remains of Dunseverick Castle, which possibly date back to the fifth century, still stood defiantly atop its rocky peninsula. I made my way round the cove in which it rests, navigating my way through a flock of sheep as I went, and began my gradual descent towards sea level and onto Dunseverick Harbour. It was the epitome of peace and tranquillity, with just a few small fishing boats languishing in the calm waters of the harbour, and I stopped there briefly for a rest before pushing on to Gid Point. Once there, I enjoyed the magical experience of walking through a natural basalt archway in the headland and being suddenly confronted with the unbelievable splendour of Whitepark Bay opening up before me. A bit of a clamber around the rocks brought me into the tiny hamlet of Portbraddan.

My original plan for today had been to stop at this point, but I had been keeping an eye on the weather forecast and the forecasts for the following day were consistently dreadful. So, despite my injury, I decided to maximise the opportunity that today's good weather presented and walk as far as possible to shorten my journey tomorrow, which would, of course, be my final day and would hopefully see me arriving in Ballycastle. I contacted Sharon Tea, who was going to pick me up today, to let her know that I now planned to walk to the road entrance to the Carrick-a-rede Rope Bridge. So with my revised plan sorted, I set off once again and immediately began to make my way across the mass of slippery boulders at the base of a limestone cliff that provided access to the sands of Whitepark Bay. And it was here that my new plan was almost derailed before it had even begun. The tide was on its way in and quite a swell had begun to develop, sending consecutive waves crashing in over the rocks. I had to wait for a break in between the waves and then dash as best I could from one high rock to another and wait there for the next lull. The rising and retreating seawater only made the rocks more slippery and, what was already a tricky task, wasn't made any easier by my injured leg. I stumbled more than once and narrowly avoided getting soaked on a number of occasions. About half-way over the stretch of rocks, I realised that going back would just be as treacherous as going on. So, I played chicken with the waves some more and eventually made it safe and dry onto the beach. I looked back to see that I had only just managed to cross in time, as some of the sections I had passed were now totally cut off. But that was quickly forgotten when I turned round to take in the magnificent golden crescent of Whitepark Bay, stretching into the distance. The beautiful sands were fringed with an arc of white at the edge of the blue sea and backed by the soft green of the grass covered cliffs enclosing the bay. It was early evening and my elongated shadow stretched out ahead of me as I set off over the soft sands to walk the two kilometre length of this almost deserted beach.

By the time I had reached the far end, the path around the rocks to Ballintoy was, as expected, completely cut off by the rising tide. Fortunately, there was an alternative route. Unfortunately, it involved a very steep and strenuous climb over the headland between Whitepark Bay and Ballintoy. I managed to make it over, although my sore leg found the descent particularly hard going – it was noticeably sorer when my foot was angled down from the ankle. There were plenty of sheep and rabbits to distract me as I hobbled on towards the ever so picturesque Ballintoy Harbour. From the harbour, I had to walk up a fairly steep road for a time and now my leg really started to complain. It kept screaming at me, "Please stop. Please, I need to rest." I knew that I was punishing my leg by pushing on. I really should have been resting it. But stopping to rest was not an option I was prepared to consider seriously at this stage. So, I mentally screamed back at my leg, "Keep going, you bugger. We're almost there. You can rest all you want when this walk is over." Knowing that I would probably come to regret it, I struggled on stubbornly and turned off the road at the pretty, white-walled Ballintoy Church to follow a grassy path towards Carrick-a-rede. The views across the silvering surface of the ocean to Rathlin, Scotland, Fair Head and the Carrick-a-rede Rope Bridge were beautiful under the softening effect of the evening light and, as always, made my journey that much more bearable. I reached the car park for the rope bridge and then it was just one more final gruelling kilometre, up another fairly steep road, to my pre-arranged collection point, where Sharon Tea arrived in her car just as the rain was beginning to fall. It was as if my weather angels had stayed with me throughout the day and, now that they saw I was finished, they were content to let the rains come through. Sharon and I called at the nearby Fullerton Arms in Ballintoy village for an 'on the house' drink and a few photos with the manager, Colin Tweed, including one with me sitting on a replica of the iron throne from the popular drama series, Game of Thrones. Sharon then drove me back to my house in Portrush, where, before going to sleep, I reflected on what had been a very long, but fabulous day and continued to wonder what lay in store for me tomorrow.

Today's walk had ended up being a marathon hike lasting eleven hours. At thirty-four kilometres, it wouldn't normally have taken me so long, but both the pain in my leg and the stunning views had contributed, in their own ways, to slowing me down. Although my leg was now aching, I was nevertheless content that I had pushed things to the limit. The forecast for tomorrow was still looking abysmal, but I had now left myself with a short walk of only eight kilometres to Ballycastle and a late start might see me avoiding the worst of the weather. A small number of family and friends had been working behind the scenes to plan for my arrival into Jacqui's hometown. It was inevitably going to be an emotional day. There would be no avoiding that aspect of it, but I also hoped that it would be a day of celebration and joy. I wouldn't be disappointed.

****

I woke fully expecting my leg to be in excruciating pain after the punishment I had subjected it to the day before. It had disturbed me several times during the night and, as a result, I hadn't slept very well. I fully realised that I had brought it upon myself and perhaps I even deserved to be in agony. But something 'miraculous' had happened. I stepped out of bed to find that my left leg was feeling much better. Not totally without pain, but certainly a lot easier to move around on than it had been on the last few mornings. I knew I had taken a risk pushing it so far the day before, but it had paid off. I had shortened my final day's walk to Ballycastle to a mere eight kilometres and my leg had escaped any serious consequences. Just as forecast, the weather was pretty abysmal, but by the time I was ready to set off, the worst of the wind and rain had passed through. One might be tempted to say that someone up there was looking out for me!

My good friends, Catherine and Dawson Wray, picked me up in Portrush in the afternoon and drove me to the entrance to Carrick-a-rede Rope Bridge, just beyond the village of Ballintoy. I already had my wet gear on as I said farewell to Catherine and Dawson and set off up the main road into the rain. I stopped on the way to say hello to the donkey I had met here three years earlier – or, at least, I chose to believe that it was the same donkey – it was certainly as friendly and was obviously very pleased to have someone stop and pet it for a while on such a miserable day. I returned to the wet tarmac and, thankfully, only had a short distance to go before branching off onto a much quieter, but equally wet, back road lined with hedges of fuchsia doing their best to lend a little colour to a bleak, grey day. As I pushed on through various levels of rainfall and followed a mix of very quiet country roads and busy main roads towards Ballycastle, I caught occasional misty glimpses of landmarks such as Rathlin Island, Fair Head and Knocklayde Mountain along the way. It was ironic that my final companion on the last leg of my long journey would be my old adversary, Tar McAdam. We had certainly spent many hours in each other's company and we had developed a sort of 'love-hate' relationship over that time – mostly hate on my part, it has to be said. However, he was fairly kind to me on this final stretch. He was well and truly soaked and he had cooled down considerably from our early days together in County Cork. And, to be honest, when walking in the rain, it's undoubtedly much easier to be on the solid, flat surface of a road rather than tramping through wet grass land or marshy bog land. So, as I made my way towards Ballycastle, I found my attitude towards old Tar McAdam softening a little. He and I would never become best buddies, but on occasions such as today, I would be prepared to put up with him and be in his company for a few miles. Strangely, given the dreadful weather conditions, I actually ran into a few hikers going the other way - on today of all days! First I met a young Danish couple, Peter and Melgi, who were hiking along the Causeway Coast and planning to stop for the day in Ballintoy. I was able to cheer them up by telling them that they were almost there and would soon be able to get out of their dripping wet gear. And later, I bumped into a young Australian guy called Marcus, who had just cycled round Scotland and was now making his way round Ireland. Only mad hikers and donkeys go out in the pouring rain.

I would certainly have loved a better day for my arrival in Ballycastle, but while the weather was awful, the date of my arrival was very fortunate indeed. I had, of course, originally planned to reach Ballycastle on 1st August to coincide with mine and Jacqui's wedding anniversary, but a herd of Tipperary bullocks had put paid to that. So, personally, today had never been my preferred date. But, as it turned out, the date of my arrival could not have been better. For this was the day that the town of Ballycastle really cranked up the celebrations to herald the start of its famous Ould Lammas Fair. This is a traditional fair held in Ballycastle every year on the last Monday and Tuesday of August. It is associated with the Lammas harvest festival and has been running for nearly four hundred years, dating back to the seventeenth century. It is without doubt the biggest occasion on Ballycastle's annual calendar of events and it draws in thousands of visitors every year. Tomorrow and the next day would see the town jam-packed with fairgoers to such an extent that it would be difficult to move. But today was mainly for the locals to celebrate the advent of the fair and, whilst it would certainly be busy, it would not come anywhere close to the mayhem of the two subsequent fair days. Many locals actual avoid going into the town on fair days because it is so manic and takes an age to get anywhere due to the multitudes that descend on the market stalls and fairground rides. But for me to arrive on the eve of this most significant event in the town where Jacqui was born certainly added a whole new dimension to my homecoming. To be honest, if I had arrived as originally planned on our wedding anniversary, although highly significant personally, it would probably have gone largely unnoticed, except among close friends and family. That might have been fine by me on a personal level, but, in terms of raising awareness of my challenge and raising money for cancer research, it would have made little impact. Today's arrival date gave me a wonderful opportunity to reach out to so many more people. However, as I continued to plod through the rain, drawing ever closer to the mist blurred profile of Fair Head, I had little knowledge of the extent to which some people had gone to mark my arrival into Jacqui's hometown.

As I walked on, still limping slightly, I played the song that Andy Hall had recorded for me and sung along to the lyrics.

It's a long way from Tipperary,
It's a long way for you.
It's a long way from Tipperary,
For the sweetest girl I knew.

Off to Ballycastle,
See you at the fair.
It's a long, long way from Tipperary,
But my love lies there.

I arrived at the outskirts of Ballycastle at just after 3pm and made my way to Ramoan Parish Church, or St James, where Jacqui's remains lay. Just her earthly remains, I reminded myself. Her spirit lives on in everyone who knew her and loved her. We all carried a little piece of her in our hearts, just as she had asked us to. "Well, my dear," I began, as I got down on my hunkers beside her grave, "I decided to do that wee summer walk after all." I was remembering our 'discussion' back in January, after I had returned from my treacherous hike on a snow covered Knocklayde. "Sorry I didn't make it here for our anniversary," I continued, "but I had a wee problem with some crazy cattle along the way. 'Feckin' bullocks!' you might say – if we weren't minding our language in these church grounds, that is. Anyway, I've walked, hobbled, stumbled, fallen and limped my way north and I'm here now. And just in time for the fair. Do you remember how the song went?

At the Ould Lammas Fair in Ballycastle long ago
I met a pretty colleen who set me heart a-glow

My heart still glows when I think of you; even though it's broken. And I think of you pretty much all the time. Thanks for looking after the weather.....mostly," I added with a smile, as I felt the raindrops continue to patter softly on the hood of my jacket. I read again the epitaph on the black marble surrounding the plot, '*You can shed tears that she is gone or you can smile because she has lived*', and I smiled again. It was a line from a beautiful poem we had chosen together to be read at her funeral service. If there is anything good to be said about dying from cancer, or any other serious illness I suppose, as opposed to a sudden death as a result of say an accident, it is that it gives you time to prepare. Prepare for the immediate arrangements that is – not for the aftermath; nothing can prepare you for that. Jacqui had always been a great organiser and, even under the dreadful circumstances she was facing as her time on this Earth drew to a close, she continued to organise - she simply didn't think it fair to leave it all up to someone else. So, yes, together we planned her funeral, or 'celebration of her life' as we described it, and we chose the words for her service including the poem from which her epitaph was taken. I had read it many times over the years since Jacqui had passed away and it was only now, over three years later, that I could honestly say that the weight of my response to the words had shifted more towards the smiles. With the odd exception, the tears had largely dried up and, although I still missed her terribly, I now found that I did smile a lot more as I continued to remember the many happy times that we had had together over the thirty-five years we had been in each other's lives. It had taken a long time, and I had often despaired that it would never happen, but the balance between the tears and the smiles did eventually shift and I gradually found myself smiling much more – and not feeling guilty about it! "Thank you for everything," I said to her, and then I added, "Oh, by the way, I really think I've walked far enough now. I've clocked up over three thousand kilometres over the last three years. But more than the kilometres travelled, what is even more significant is the huge distance I have travelled in my own mind – in learning to live without you. It hasn't been easy, but I think that I've finally got there. Anyway, it's maybe time to hang up the boots now - what do you think?" I didn't get a response, so I took that as a tacit agreement. "Okay, I'd better go now. There are some very special people waiting on me outside and I believe they have a few things organised for me. I wish you were here to see it. I'll tell you all about it later. Bye for now." With that I got to my feet again, nodded to her parents, Jack and Annie, who rested with her, and turned to leave the graveyard.

On the pavement outside, I joined Jacqui's sister, Christine Mitchell, her cousin, Joan Bailie, and Joan's husband, Jeremy, who were waiting patiently in their 'We are beating cancer' tee shirts to welcome me. We were soon joined by my daughter, Hannah, friend (and poet), Ashley Todd, and my neighbour, Barbara Lewers. There were hugs galore, before we set off on foot towards the town centre, armed with collection cans and buckets. We stopped off at the Spar store on route to meet my nephew, Derek Mitchell, and Assistant Manager, Sean Hamill. Derek had undertaken a sponsored beard shave earlier in the year and had raised an incredible £450 for Cancer Research UK and he presented me with a thick envelope containing the money on my arrival. It was a very proud moment, as we all huddled together in a group to get a photo to mark the occasion. Our small, but formidable gang then descended on the Diamond in the heart of the town, where I was forced, against my will of course, into the Diamond Bar. My daily finishing ritual was, by this stage, the stuff of legend and in the bar the owner, Charlie McVeigh, had a pint of Guinness with my name on it waiting for me. There was an incredible buzz in the bar and more donations followed as word spread among the customers about my arrival. I was amazed to see a picture of Jacqui and I on a poster displayed in the bar. Christine told me that it was a 'lottery square' poster to raise funds for Cancer Research UK and that they were on display in a number of venues in the town. It was just one of the many ideas that a small 'planning committee', comprised of Christine and friends Joan Quigg and Aidan Toner, had come up with for my homecoming.

After enjoying my Guinness and the craic in the Diamond Bar, we headed down to the sea front and over to the 'Children of Lir' sculpture for the requisite 'end of route' photo. The rain had finally stopped, although the sky was still leaden and a thick covering of grey cloud stretched out over the equally grey sea. Hannah took several shots of me standing under the flying swans of the metallic sculpture, with the iconic profile of Fair Head brooding darkly in the background. As I stood posing for photographs, with the swans 'flying' overhead, it was perhaps inevitable that the tragic story of the Children of Lir would come to mind once again. The age old legend of how the children, turned into swans and banished by their jealous stepmother, spent three hundred years on the cold and desolate Sea of Moyle behind where I was standing. And how, after their total of nine hundred years of exile was finally over, the swans came ashore on the Beara Peninsula and were immediately changed back into their human form and then died, freed from their exile at last. It was the saddest of tales, but it was also remarkable to realise that the Ireland Way, either by accident or design, connected these two locations at opposite ends of the island of Ireland that played a key part in the legend. It was also remarkable to realise that my epic challenge was over. I had done it. I had walked all the way from Castletownbere on the south coast of Ireland to Ballycastle on the north coast - from one castle to another; and with plenty in between. In the process, I had covered in excess of eleven hundred kilometres – that's close to seven hundred miles 'in old money' - and it had taken me a total of forty-two days walking; plus one day resting (in Millstreet) and twenty-five days recovering from injury.

Unfortunately, the nearby Visitor Information Centre was closed by the time we got to it, so I would have to wait to pick up my Ireland Way completion certificate and the final stamp in my passport. But it didn't matter. My support team had a more important engagement lined up for me. After a brief rest at Christine's home, she, Hannah and I were chauffeured to the Marine Hotel by Ashley, where I was received as the 'special guest of honour' at the Mayor's dinner to mark the Lammas Fair weekend. Prior to dinner being served, Mayor Chivers formally welcomed me to Ballycastle and presented me with a bottle of ten year old Bushmills Malt Whiskey. In return, I presented her with a signed copy of my 'Camino' book and said that I hoped that she would enjoy it as much as I would undoubtedly enjoy the whiskey. The dinner was excellent and there must have been close to one hundred guests. Unfortunately, we had to skip the dessert course and leave a little early for yet another planned event. Christine,

Hannah and I hurried to where Ashley had parked her car and we piled into it once again for the drive round to Pans Rocks at the end of Ballycastle's long strand. I had told Aidan Toner a few days before during a phone call that I was planning to burn my walking boots at Pans Rocks at the end of my walk. I had felt that this would be a fittingly symbolic gesture that would truly mark the end of my long distance walks in Jacqui's memory. Aidan, an old friend from school days, had embraced this idea, ran with it and added bells to it! It now transpired that my boot burning ritual would act as a signal to start of the town's firework display that would officially launch this year's Ould Lammas Fair. The display was scheduled to begin at precisely 9pm and my boot burning ceremony obviously had to take place immediately prior to this. It was a fantastic idea and, although I had originally envisaged my ritual as being a fairly private and personal affair, I was now happy to embrace this exciting plan and allow my simple boot burning ritual to be the trigger for a much bigger conflagration in the sky. The only problem was, it was now 8:40pm, leaving us very little time to get to Pans Rocks. On any other day this might not have been such a problem, but the streets were now jammed with traffic as the crowds flooded in to watch the upcoming firework display. And to compound the problem, when we reached the sea front in Ashley's car we found that the police had closed off the road we needed to take if we were to stand any chance of reaching Pans Rocks in time. When we encountered the police barrier, I really thought that it was the end of things – the carefully planned signal to begin the fireworks would be no more than a damp squib. But I hadn't allowed for either Ashley's determination or her powers of persuasion. She drove up alongside a young police man manning the barrier, wound down her window and appealed to him, "Please, can you let us through?" followed with the immortal words, "this man needs to get to Pans Rocks urgently to burn his boots!" I think the young policeman was so stunned by the absurdity of the request that he quickly moved the barrier aside and waved us through. Either that or he judged Ashley to be totally mad and thought it better to wave her off the road and trap her inside the cordon. But no – we were allowed to pass on through and Ashley then drove like a woman possessed to the car park at Pans Rocks a couple of kilometres away.

As soon as the car came to a halt, I immediately jumped out and, totally ignoring my injured leg, managed to run across the short section of pebble beach to the wooden footbridge giving access to the rocks. I could see two figures out on the rocks, standing beside a tall structure and waving at me to hurry up. When I arrived at the footbridge, the tide was coming in and seawater was washing up around the end of the bridge, but I succeeded in clambering onto the steps without getting my boots soaked and then dashed across the bridge towards the jagged, black rocks. The light was fading by this stage and it made crossing the uneven rocks that bit more challenging, but I stumbled on over the pits and cracks to finally be welcomed by Aidan Toner and his wife Karen. I could now see that the structure was in fact a rather makeshift, but nonetheless impressive beacon, which Aidan had rigged up earlier that day. It was a tall wooden post, held upright by three wooden legs, taped to the bottom of the post in tripod fashion, with a wire basket attached near the top, like a basketball net, and stuffed full of combustible material. Aidan was desperately trying to light the beacon, but there was a stiff breeze that was making it very difficult. However, he was as determined as Ashley to make this plan work and, after many frantic attempts, punctuated with much agitated cursing, he managed to get a strip of cloth to light with a liberal, some might say reckless, application of lighter fluid. He threw the lit piece of cloth into the wire basket, but before any of the material in the basket could catch light, a gust of wind caught the burning piece of cloth and whisked it away onto the rocks where it continued to burn. Aidan quickly retrieved it and, at much risk to himself, placed it into the basket once again. This time a little of the material in the basket caught light and, once again, Aidan reached for the container of lighter fluid to assist the process. I had nightmarish visions of 'The Wicker Man' as I watched Aidan splash lighter fluid over the basket to encourage the flames. Thankfully, Aidan escaped unharmed and the material in the basket was soon sending flames and glowing sparks into the darkening sky. By this stage, Christine, Ashley and Hannah had joined us and we all cheered, as much in relief as in celebration of Aidan's success as a firestarter. I then removed my faithful boots that had carried me for almost seven hundred miles over the length of Ireland and pulled on another pair that Hannah had brought for me. Then taking each of the old boots in turn, I added some lighter fluid to each, lit it using Aidan's lighter and hoisted it into the burning basket, using a large branch that Christine had somehow had the foresight to lift off the beach and bring with her. I did feel a touch of regret at seeing my trusty boots going up in smoke, but they had served me well. They were quite worn and the left boot was letting in water, so they had come to the end of their life anyway; and they deserved a grand send-off rather than being tossed unceremoniously into a wheelie bin somewhere. With both boots deposited in the burning basket, the beacon was well and truly lit and it presented a fabulous sight out on the dark rocks, surrounded by the inky seawater under a darkening night sky. It was fire; it was primal; it was symbolic; it was magical!

It was just after 9pm and, almost on cue, the town's fireworks display started, lighting up the night sky over Ballycastle and we all cheered again. As we made our way back to Ashley's car, I looked back towards Pans Rocks to see the flames of the beacon still burning brightly, while the cacophony of sound and light played out in the sky over the town as one firework exploded after another in luminous showers of colour. When we got to the car, it was clear that we were not going to be able to drive back into town for a while, as the roads had now become congested with traffic due to the number of people that had made their way out to watch the firework display from this excellent vantage point. But, I had one more engagement to make it to, which meant that I couldn't hang around waiting for the fireworks to finish and for the traffic to clear. Ashley stayed with the car, while the rest of us walked back through the darkness to the town, taking off-road shortcuts through the golf club, over the River Margy footbridge and past the 'Glass Island' and the tennis courts, using the torches on our phones to light the way. We made it back to the Marine Hotel, where we joined the Mayor's group once again and then we all walked up the Quay Road towards the Diamond. As we approached, the raucous sound of live music began to fill the air and we were soon weaving our way through the crowds that had gathered to watch local band '30 Mile Limit' perform their Lammas Fair set. We made our way to the side of the stage and, when the band reached the end of the song they had been playing, the Mayor and I climbed the steps up onto the platform and took our position centre stage. Mayor Chivers was handed a microphone and after welcoming everyone to this year's celebrations, she introduced me and then handed me the microphone. I had taken my spare boots off before climbing onto the stage and made a joke about having burned my boots on Pans Rocks earlier and now having nothing to wear on my feet except my socks – holding up one foot for everyone to see. I then became more serious and explained why I had walked seven hundred miles in memory of my Ballycastle girl and why I believed that it was so important to raise funds for further research into tackling cancer. I finished by encouraging the audience to part with their money, as a small but determined team of volunteers passed among them with their collection buckets. My words appeared to have struck a chord with many and they were met with raucous applause from the crowd. The Mayor and I were about to leave the stage, when one of the band members invited us to stay and join them in singing a special song. The band then launched into a slightly modified performance of '*I'm Gonna Be (500 Miles)*' by the Proclaimers and the mayor and I sang along. It was another unbelievable moment in a day filled with unbelievable moments! After what would probably be our first and only ever live performance singing together, the mayor and I parted company and I pulled on my spare boots again. I then gathered up my loyal team of volunteers, who had, by this stage, extracted all the money they could from the audience – some of whom, Aidan joked, had only donated on the promise that the Mayor and I would stop singing! We continued collecting as we all headed back down to the Marine Hotel to enjoy a few well-earned drinks to celebrate a hugely successful day, while Aidan and Ashley, who had re-joined our party in the Diamond, entertained us with a non-stop barrage of jokes!

Pure adrenaline had kept me going until I reached my bed sometime after 1am. I was out for the count before my head even hit the pillow. The following morning, I learned that we had collected over £1000 for Cancer Research UK on that one day alone, bringing my total to almost £40,000. It had been an incredible day and an incredible finale to an incredible journey. But, as always at high points such as this, my emotions were inevitably mixed – a never ending struggle between the joy of the occasion and the sadness of having to experience it without the person I most wanted to experience it with. As I struggled to find the words to express the range of feelings and emotions that I experienced during my 'homecoming', Ashley sent me a beautifully perceptive poem and I had to look no further.

A Journey

He knelt by her grave, his walk over,
As he spoke quiet words to his love.
She lay silently sleeping,
Yet still watched him from above.

His journey was long and so tiresome,
Each step brought him closer to home,
And there, she was patiently waiting
To share again the love they had known.

His words were soft as the teardrops
That now from his eyes freely spilled,
The relief and release of returning
Flowed out in a flood of free will.

His spirit regained all that sustained it
His strength steadied and held him again,
His humility rose into the limelight,
As humble words touched hearts, in the rain.

The flames that burned his old footsteps,
Were a beacon of hope in the dark,
His love burns more brightly than ever,
Overcoming the grief in his heart.

Chapter Fifteen: Swan Song
(Ballycastle to A Coruña)

I returned to Ballycastle's Visitor Information Centre a few days later and collected the final stamp in my passport and picked up my Ireland Way completion certificate. After a few photos were taken to mark the occasion, I hobbled over to the car park opposite the Centre and took a seat at a picnic table bathed in warm sunshine. My left leg was still a little sore, but it was gradually improving with rest and a little complimentary physiotherapy from my Portrush friend Andy McClelland - I had managed to build up a considerable network of physiotherapists as a consequence of my Ireland Way! The picnic table I was sitting at was near the 'herring sculpture' next to the Harbour and, on seeing the sculpture of the swimming fish, a memory suddenly swam into my mind. Of how Jacqui had often told me that, as a child she had been terrified of an old character who used to walk the streets of Ballycastle with his fish cart, shouting, "Herrin', herrin'". To her, he had seemed like the Child Catcher from the movie 'Chitty, Chitty, Bang, Bang' and she would hide whenever she heard him coming, convinced she was going to be snatched away from her family home! I smiled at the memory. And not far behind me, less than a stone's throw away, was the place on North Street where Jacqui had been born and had grown up. I had visited her and stayed in 16 North Street many times when we had started going out together. However, the two storey house that had stood there for decades was, like Jacqui, now gone – only a level plot behind a fence now marking where they both had once been. I examined the Ireland Way certificate in an attempt to distract my mind from the maudlin direction my thoughts were heading in. The certificate included a wonderful artist's impression of four swans, the Children of Lir, flying over the Sea of Moyle off the coast of Northern Ireland and at the bottom of the certificate were the following words in Irish:

> *Go n-éiri an bother leat*
> *Go raibh an ghaoth go brách ag do chúl*
> *Go lonraí an ghrian go te ar d'aghaidh*
> *Go dtite an bháisteach go mín ar do pháirceanna.*

It was a traditional Irish blessing and I had last encountered the words in English when I was on the Camino del Norte in Spain, two years before. There, in an *albergue* run by the British Confraternity of St James in the village of Miraz, a woman named Paula from Belfast had recited the blessing to me and my friend Sara, just prior to our departure on the next stage of our Camino:

> *May the road rise to meet you,*
> *May the wind always be at your back.*
> *May the sun shine warm upon your face*
> *And rains fall soft upon your fields.*

It was another lovely little link between my walks in Ireland and my walk in Spain. And it wasn't to be the last!

It was a beautiful early September's day and, from where I was sitting, I had a good view over the harbour and the boats in the marina and beyond to Fair Head and Rathlin Island and then across the Sea of Moyle to the east coast of Scotland. As I was drinking in the view, I felt a familiar presence by my side. I looked around and nodded to Donal Cam and he simply nodded in response. Then, after a few moments, he said, "Well, you made it. You walked all the way from Castletownbere to Ballycastle. That's considerably further that I marched over four hundred years ago."

"And it took me considerably longer," I added with a wry smile, "but, yes, I made it. All the way to Ballycastle. And just as O'Neill had left before you arrived at Slieve Gallion, my Jacqui left long before I ever got here. But, of course, I knew that before I ever set off. Your march had a real purpose behind it. My walk was merely symbolic."

"Symbolic it may have been, but it has touched the hearts of a lot of people along the way. And Jacqui is very proud of what you have achieved."

"Ha, everybody says that, but how do they know?" I asked, not really expecting an answer. It was, after all, just something people said to make me feel better. For nobody could possibly know what Jacqui thought about my achievements; if indeed she thought anything at all.

"Well, I can't speak for others," he said, "but I know it for a fact because she told me so."

I looked at him again, with an eyebrow raised in question, not quite sure if I had heard him correctly. "Sorry, what did you just say?"

"I said that I know for a fact that Jacqui is very proud of you because she told me so," he repeated.

"You've spoken with her?" I couldn't believe what I was hearing. "When was this? You've actually met her? How is she? Can you talk to her now? Is she........." My questions were spilling from me almost as quickly as my heart was now racing.

"Slow down there, young sir," Donal Cam said calmly, "before you give yourself a heart attack and join her before your time. Of course I have spoken with her - and a lovely lady she is too. But it was before you and I first met; in fact, just before you set off on your journey. She asked me to look out for you and keep you company along the way."

"But, why did she ask you?" I asked, somewhat puzzled. "Why did she not accompany me herself, like I felt she had on my previous two journeys?"

"Well," he replied, "Jacqui has been very fortunate to have completed her own journey – her journey through the spirit world to her final resting place. She stayed in touch with you until she was sure that you could manage on your own – until she felt that it was time to completely let go – time for you to set her free. I was really just a little extra security as it were, in case you showed any signs of regressing. And I'm pleased to say that you coped really well with all the mental and physical challenges thrown at you. There were a few wobbles along the way, but throughout it all you remained strong and resolute. You should be proud of yourself."

"Hold on," I said, "how come you haven't reached your final resting place? Jacqui died less than four years ago – it's been four hundred years since you died!"

"It's a question of atonement," Donal Cam said with a heavy heart, "and let's just say that some of us have more to atone for than others."

"But four hundred years!" I exclaimed. "That's a hell of a long time!"

"Not if it's hell you're trying to avoid," he replied with a laugh. Then gesturing to the picture of the swans on my certificate, he added, "The Children of Lir were exiled for nine hundred years and they had done nothing wrong, so I suppose I can't really complain too much. As you know, I was responsible for many deaths during the rebellion, some of which you witnessed, and they can't be easily ignored or excused. I attempted to atone for my sins while exiled in Spain, but it wasn't enough and, if truth be told, I was still angry at having lost my lands on Beara and at never being able to return to Ireland. Even when I was in Spain, I wrote to King James in England promising obedience if my estate was restored. Not surprisingly, he refused."

"What exactly happened when you went to Spain?" I asked, adding, "I remember you saying that you were reunited with your wife there."

"Yes, my wife Ellen had arrived in Spain earlier with our two young sons, Donal and Dermot," he began.

"Ha, one named for each of us," I laughed.

Donal Cam dealt with this interruption by simply rolling his eyes and continuing, "My uncle Dermot - whom my second son was actually named after, by the way - and his wife and children and other close kinsmen also joined us. We were very warmly welcomed by King Philip of Spain and we were treated very generously by the Spanish. I was given a pension of three hundred gold pieces a month by the king and my uncle received fifty a month. The Irish were held in high esteem in Spain and we enjoyed rights and privileges far above other foreigners in the country. In fact, for all intents and purposes we were generally treated as Spaniards. I was actually the first Irishman to be knighted by the Spanish King. As I told you when we first met, I became a Knight of the Order of Santiago."

"You did indeed," I replied, remembering our first encounter in the dead of night in Ballingeary. I knew from my Camino de Santiago pilgrimage in 2018 that the Order of Santiago, also known as 'The Order of St. James of the Sword', was established in Spain in the twelfth century. I also knew that it owed its name to the Patron Saint of Spain, Santiago or St James, and that one of the Order's initial objectives was to protect pilgrims making their way to the holy site of Santiago de Compostela in Galicia. "And I made it to St James as planned," I said. "The St James here in Ballycastle, that is, where my late wife now rests." Then, pulling up my tee-shirt sleeve and showing Donal Cam the Camino tattoo I had had tattooed on my right shoulder following my Camino pilgrimage, I added, "It seems that we are both connected to Santiago in our own ways. And, it certainly seems that my pilgrimages in Spain and Ireland have been more connected than I previously thought. It's almost as if our meeting was destined to be!"

"You might say that," he said smiling. "That's why Jacqui asked me to watch out for you on your latest pilgrimage. Not only did she know that I knew the part of the route that you were unfamiliar with, but she also knew that I was a protector of pilgrims. Nice tattoo, by the way."

"Well, I'll be damned," was all I could say for a moment, as I continued to struggle to take in the revelation that it was Jacqui who had sent this Irish Chieftain and Knight of Santiago to watch over me. Then something suddenly occurred to me and I said, "Hang on! You didn't protect me from those bloody bullocks very well, did you?"

"But, sure, didn't it all work out for the best?" he replied with a chuckle. "Look at all the friends you made because of it and look at the brilliant reception you had when you reached your destination at the start of the Ould Lammas Fair, on a date much later than you had originally planned."

"That's very true," I admitted, but my suspicions were aroused further. "It did all work out very neatly indeed – perhaps too neatly! Some might be tempted to say at this point that God works in mysterious ways. I'm not so sure about that, but I now suspect that a certain knight, aided and abetted by a certain angel, might have had a hand in it." But Donal Cam just sat impassively and clearly wouldn't be drawn. I took his silence as tacit agreement. "Anyway," I continued, "I suppose it was good to have a Knight of Santiago watching over me all that time, even if he did let a herd of bullocks attack me! And I certainly learned a lot about your incredible march that I wouldn't have otherwise."

"It was an honour, young sir," Donal Cam said with a deferential bow of his head, then adding, with a wink, "but, to be honest, it wasn't totally without self-interest. I'm hoping that my good deed might go a little way to helping with my atonement."

"I hope it does," I said with sincerity. "Four hundred years is a long time to be doing penance!" After a moment, I then added, "So, if you don't mind me asking, when and how exactly did you die?"

"Well, that unfortunate event occurred on 16th July 1618 outside the *Iglesia de Santiago* in A Coruña in North-West Spain," he replied, his right hand automatically drifting up to caress his neck, as it had done before whenever the subject of his death came up. Then, with a broad smile crossing his face, he added, "I can show you if you like."

"Oh God!" I said, "I'm not so sure I ......"

But before I could finish my sentence, the warm and bright September sunshine of Ballycastle harbour was swapped for the cool, shaded interior of a church, which I presumed to be the *Iglesia de Santiago* in A Coruña that Donal Cam had just referred to. The high vaulted ceiling of the stone church created a magnificent space and the modest stain glass windows allowed sufficient light to stream in from the daylight outside to illuminate the interior. I could see that there were many statues and carvings around the building representing St James in his various guises, as pilgrim, knight and saint. The church was quite obviously dedicated to the saint and named in his honour; *Iglesia de Santiago* being Spanish for 'Church of St James'. There was no service under way, although it appeared to me that mass was not long ended. There were a few individuals still scattered around the church, kneeling or sitting in the pews. Donal Cam was by my side as usual and, when he caught my eye, he nodded towards a figure near the front of the church. The figure was kneeling, with his head bowed and he seemed to be lost in deep prayer as he fed his black rosary beads between his fingers. He was dressed in clothing very similar, perhaps identical, to that worn by Donal Cam beside me. "You?" I whispered the question. Donal Cam nodded and added, also in a whisper, "I had become even more devout in Spain, perhaps attending mass two or three times a day. There wasn't much else to do," he added with a smile, "being in exile was rather tedious and, as I said earlier, I had much to atone for."

Just then there was a disturbance at the back of the church as the door was flung open and a man hurried up the aisle towards O'Sullivan Beare. Ignoring the sanctity of the church, the man called to O'Sullivan Beare loudly, "Count you must come quickly."

"Count?" I enquired of Donal Cam. He may have mentioned this before, but if he had, it had escaped my memory.

"Yes," he replied, "King Philip had awarded me the title of First Count of Berehaven the previous year, much to the indignation of King James and my cousin Owen. However, they were soon to have the last laugh."

O'Sullivan Beare had sat up and spun round in his pew to look at his anxious messenger. "What is it," he demanded, "that merits disturbing me from my devotions?"

"It's your nephew Philip," cried the other man. "Come quickly. Please. He's in great danger."

O'Sullivan Beare leapt to his feet at the mention of Philip's name and rushed down the aisle towards the door of the church, with his messenger hurrying to keep up with him. Donal Cam and I quickly followed them out, being momentarily blinded by the bright

Spanish sunlight as we stepped through the doorway onto the stone steps outside. We remained at the top of the steps where we had a good view over the small plaza below, which was hemmed in between the surrounding tall buildings. Here a small crowd had gathered around two men who were facing each other with swords drawn. The air was palpable with tension. O'Sullivan Beare pushed his way through the crowd and shouted, "John, please, lower your sword man. Philip, what is this all about? Whatever it is, I'm sure it can be settled peacefully."

"This scoundrel has insulted you and insulted our family," said the younger of the two swordsmen. This was obviously Philip and he was clearly in a rage.

"Is this true John?" O'Sullivan Beare demanded of the older man. Neither man had lowered their sword. They were clearly still ready to settle their argument with a duel.

"All I did was tell the truth," snarled the older man.

"And what truth is that," enquired O'Sullivan Beare in a tone carefully measured so as to not inflame the situation further.

"The truth that you ran your people into the ground back in Ireland," hissed John, "and then cleared off to live a life of luxury here in Spain. Lording it up like nobility. Count of Berehaven," he spat, "what the blazes does that even mean, when you're hiding out here in Spain?"

"John, please," appealed O'Sullivan Beare, obviously keen to defuse the quarrel, "it distresses me to hear you talk like this. But your argument is not with Philip. Put down your sword and let's talk about this like civilised gentlemen."

But John was too fired up by this stage to be so easily talked down. Philip had obviously challenged him to a duel and he was not ready to lose face. "Like civilised gentlemen," he laughed scornfully. "Get out of my way you dandy, so I can teach this young guttersnipe a lesson."

Philip, who had only just been reigning in his anger since O'Sullivan Beare's intervention, was further enraged by this latest insult and he suddenly lunged forward with his sword towards his opponent. O'Sullivan Beare, being a fighting man of some experience, had clearly anticipated Philip's move and he stepped in to block Philips sword arm, forcing the blade of his sword wide in the process. However, John had already moved to counter Philip's attack and he quickly thrust his sword towards Philip, coming at him high and aiming for his neck. John's sword found flesh. But it wasn't Philip's. It was O'Sullivan Beare's throat that was pierced. A loud gasp erupted from the crowd as crimson blood suddenly stained his white ruff, like a dreadful flower suddenly coming into bloom. Seeing what he had done, John quickly turned, pushed his way through the crowd and ran off. Philip dropped his sword and caught O'Sullivan Beare around the waist as his gravely wounded uncle began to slump. O'Sullivan Beare's hands, still tangled with his rosary beads, were pawing desperately at his own neck, hopelessly trying to staunch the flow of blood. But the wound was too serious and he quickly started to lose consciousness and his legs buckled beneath him. No longer able to support the weight of his body, Philip gently lowered O'Sullivan Beare to the paved ground of the plaza and he himself fell to his knees beside him. "I'm sorry uncle," he cried, as the crowd moved back in horror, seeming to instinctively know that this man could not be saved. As the circle of the crowd widened, so too did the pool of dark blood spilling out from sprawled figure lying at its centre.

And with that, I was back in Ballycastle next to the harbour. I looked round at Donal Cam beside me. I must have looked as shocked as I felt because he said, "Sorry, maybe I should have warned you."

"You don't say!" I replied in exasperation. "Good God! I obviously knew you were going to die, but I never expected it to be in such a bloody manner. And not in Spain, where I thought you were safe."

"Well," he said, "some say that if you live by the sword, you will die by the sword. But, yes, I never expected it to happen there either, years after my fighting days were behind me. However, some people had long memories and were prepared to wait for their moment of revenge. Although, I believe the title of First Count of Berehaven bestowed upon me by the King of Spain the year before, may have hastened my departure."

"Who, was that man called John?" I asked. "You appeared to know him well."

"I did indeed," Donal Cam replied. "His name was John Bath and he was a member of my own household. He was an Anglo-Irishman from Dublin, who had worked tirelessly to promote the standing of Irish Catholics to the King James. He was the last man I would have suspected, but unknown to me at the time, he was also a spy acting on behalf of the English Crown and he had been ordered to kill me. He had created that argument with my nephew out in the plaza knowing that I would be summoned from inside the church. It provided him with the opportunity to stab me, while making it look like an accident. And he executed it very well; I have to give him that. And I also have to admit that his words cut almost as deep as his sword. There was, after all, some truth in what he said. Anyway, after carrying out my murder, he escaped and became a politician."

"Ha, some things never change," I said, rather sarcastically, before asking, "it must be really weird to watch your own murder?"

"It is," he replied, "and each time I think what I might have done differently to have avoided my early demise. I was only fifty-seven you know?"

"Good God," I exclaimed, "the coincidences just keep coming. That's the very age I am now!"

"Kind of spooky, for sure," he said, adding a spooky laugh for good effect. Then he added, somewhat wistfully, "I'm sure I had a good few years left in me yet. My Uncle Dermot lived until he was over a hundred! But, there's no point in 'what ifs'. It was what it was and it is what it is."

"Tell me about it," I said, "if there's one thing I've learned the hard way over the last few years, it's that you can't wish your life away, wishing things were different."

"That's easy for you to say," he laughed, "I haven't got a life to wish away, even if I wanted to."

"Sorry," I said, laughing also, "but you know what I mean." We were both silent for a while and then I asked the question I had been longing to ask since Donal Cam had mentioned that he had met Jacqui. "Where exactly is Jacqui now?"

"Son," he began, "the truth is I really don't know. Yes, I'm dead. Have been for a long time, as you know. But my spirit journey isn't finished yet. I'm in this sort of limbo, or purgatory, or perdition; call it what you will. I'm stuck here for now, but hopefully not forever. What I do know is this. There is something much, much better beyond where I am now. Somewhere where I will no longer be tortured by my past; where I'm not forced to wander this earth as a ghost, neither properly in one world nor the next; somewhere where I will finally find that blissful peace I have so craved for centuries. And that, my friend, is where your Jacqui is now."

"Hmm, that sounds okay to me," I said, "I just want to know that she's happy."

"Of that, you can be sure," said Donal Cam, "and hopefully I will be able to join her soon – and my own wife, Ellen, of course."

"Well, if you see Jacqui before me," I said, "tell her that I love her and look forward to being with her again."

"I will," he replied, "but, she already knows that. When I last saw her, she told me to tell you that she will be waiting, however long it takes. But she also said to remind you that there were no shortcuts and to stay away from cliffs."

"Ha ha, I can't promise that," I said with a smile, "but, I'll try to stay away from the edge."

"Good man," he said. And then after a short pause, he announced abruptly, "So, that's it. My work here is done. Your journey is finished and I'm no longer required here. It's been a real pleasure meeting you and telling you my story. And please don't take this the wrong way, but I hope to never see you again – not here on Earth anyway! I've really had enough of exile – first in Spain and now in this purgatory. Maybe Jacqui will put in a good word for me."

"I'm sure she will," I said, "particularly after the way you have looked after me. Before you go though, could I ask just one more thing of you?"

"And what might that be?" he enquired with a frown.

"When I write my book about this journey and our adventures together, would you provide a Foreword?"

"Ha, I'm not sure that too many people will believe that you met with a four hundred year old ghost as you travelled through Ireland," he responded with a laugh, "but I would be very happy to do that. I'll communicate my thoughts to you when you're ready. I suppose I could be your 'ghost-writer'," he added, laughing again.

"Oh, how I'm going to miss your little jokes," I said, with a dose of good natured sarcasm. "Anyway, thanks for agreeing to that. And you never know; it might just be the last little act of kindness required to get you out of purgatory?"

"That would be very nice indeed," he said with a smile.

"Good luck," I said.

"And to you, young sir," he replied, "and goodbye."

And with that he began his last disappearing act and moments later I was sitting by myself, with only the sound of the seagulls crying overhead to break the silence. I looked out across the Sea of Moyle, towards Fair Head and the coast of Scotland, where the Children of Lir had spent three hundred years of their nine hundred years of exile, and wondered about my own feelings of exile. For that's what my life over the last few years had felt like. As if I was exiled here on Earth, while Jacqui was somewhere else; somewhere unreachable. Not exiled from my home or my country obviously, but exiled from the life I had known before Jacqui's untimely death; the life I felt that I should still be living. But as Donal Cam had said, "*it is what it is*", and as I had said in return, "*you can't wish your life away, wishing things were different.*" I just had to accept my circumstances as they were. Just as Jacqui had had to bravely accept her circumstances, when she was faced with her imminent death. And of course my exile wouldn't be for ever. I was convinced, now more than ever, that I would join with Jacqui again at some stage in the future. I had no idea how long that would be, but if the Children of Lir could manage nine hundred years and Donal Cam four hundred or more, then I was prepared to wait for however long it took. And at least, in the meantime, I was exiled among friends – I wasn't banished to a sea of loneliness nor was I living among strangers in a foreign land. And I was meeting new friends all the time. Once again I gave thanks for the many generous and hospitable people that I had met along my Ireland Way, who had become my friends and had helped me reach my destination.

And as I thought again about my destination – this special place on the north coast of Ireland that I had walked over one thousand kilometres to reach – I took the folded (and, by now, slightly frayed) sheets of paper from my pocket that had been with me since the start of my journey. I flattened the sheets out on the picnic table and read once again the words that Jacqui had penned just before her death.

Final words

I was born on Friday 13th January 1961, third daughter to Jack and Annie Greer and baby sister to Heather and Christine. Five years later, I became a big sister to Jonathan. We grew up on North Street in Ballycastle with the ever changing sea on our doorstep, and the unmistakeable Fair Head in front and Knocklayde Mountain behind us.

I had a very happy childhood. My mum was always there with her pinny on to look after us - which was no easy task without all the modern amenities we take for granted today! Dinner was on the table at six o'clock, and always shepherd's pie on a Saturday.

I remember sitting on my father's knee when he came home from work and asking him to tell me a story. He was good at that. He might sing me a nonsense song, like "Suzanne was a funny wee man", with oinking and raspberry noises thrown in for good measure!

My biggest sister, Heather, was always organised and in charge – but not in a bossy way - I always felt secure when she was around. Her boyfriend, and later husband, Terry, has been part of my life since I was about seven years old. I shared a room with my sister Christine, and I remember her always reading to me in bed. I eventually got the room to myself when she married Nigel. Having two sisters meant I got to be bridesmaid twice!

Heather and Terry later moved to live in London. Christine and Nigel lived locally and had three children, Emma, Derek and Andrew, and I was just the right age to be able to babysit for them as they were growing up. I have loved being part of their lives.

Our brother Jonathan was active and wakeful as a baby, but I think my older sisters were too quick to lift him from his cot if he made any sign of waking! That's what Mum said anyway! He was a quiet child, and I fear I was probably a bossy big sister! I have to say I'm proud of the adult he has become. He and his lovely wife, Heather, are great parents to Ewan, Arran, Hollie and Skye. I love them all dearly.

At the age of three, I was invited to play with Carolyn, who lived on Strandview Road, just round the corner, and thus began a close friendship which lasted throughout most of our school days and still exists today. We became part of each other's families and, living in Ballycastle, spent a large part of our Summers swimming at the Glass Island or Boat Slip, playing tennis, having picnics across the Strand, or just amusing ourselves making up games to play in the garden. When we discovered gymnastics, we probably spent as much time walking upside down on our hands, as upright on our feet!

I loved school. I cannot remember not being able to read, and I often had my head in a book. We didn't have TV in our house until I was about eleven, so apart from the radio, reading was a great pastime for me. There were a few tears over maths homeworks, and I never really got to grips with numbers until I became a teacher myself. I remember getting the bus to Ramoan Primary School. The Reverend Goulden once brought a donkey into the school. I also recall Mrs Campbell, my infant teacher, shifting us all outside, the desks, chairs and big blackboard easel, whenever the weather was sunny. I loved the school dinners - the stew, and cake and custard!

I loved singing and when I was in P6, our Principal, Stanley McIlwaine, decided to produce The Snow Queen and I was cast in the principal role as the Snow Queen herself. The show was put on at the Quay Road Hall in the middle of town to a packed house! That was the first of many school productions I participated in, and when I went to University, I was an active member of the drama society there, although I was always nervous before a performance.

When I was at Ballycastle High School, I had the opportunity to try different sports. I loved gymnastics, played hockey through all my time there, and was Captain of the First Eleven at one stage. I enjoyed trampolining, and did a coaching award when I was 16. I was also lucky enough to be awarded a bursary to attend Rhownair Outward Bound Centre in Wales. I spent three weeks there during the Summer, and had a fantastic time, canoeing, hill walking, bouldering, rock climbing, abseiling and trekking through the mountains, learning map reading and camping out. While I was at the High School, there was a cross community initiative, where young people from our school and the 'Cross and Passion' school across the road were invited to get together to organise a Youth for Community week in Ballycastle. My friend Noelle and I were two of the people selected from the High School to participate. The 'initiative' was facilitated by the Catholic Curate, Raymond Fulton. The 'Youth for Community' week was a great success. I have very fond memories of that time, and remained friends with many of those involved.

I left Ballycastle High School in June 1979 and started a four year English Honours Degree at Queen's University Belfast in October that year. I thoroughly enjoyed the independence of University life, and the social life too! It was at one of the Elms Halls parties that I first met my wonderful husband to be, Dermot, in the Spring of 1980. I couldn't believe it when he actually rang me when he said he would – remember there were no mobiles then! – and we were soon going out together regularly. Of course, being at Queen's and living in Belfast, there was no shortage of events to go to, or we would just meet up with friends in the Union on a Friday night. Dermot and I both graduated from Queen's in the Summer of 1983.

I subsequently applied for Stranmillis College and was accepted onto the one year PGCE course, starting in Autumn 1984. I have to thank my big sister Christine for undertaking all the form filling required to enable me to get a grant. Whilst at Stran, I met a great group of like-minded people, and there are a few of us "Stran girls" – Sandra, Diane, Rosemary and Heather - who have kept in touch and enjoy catching up with each other a couple of times a year. Sandra and I became running partners all those years ago, and she recently persuaded me to accompany her on a 10K run in Enniscrone, while holidaying with my brother in law, Michael. Our run together gave me a great sense of enjoyment – and we didn't mind at all that we finished almost last! I have thoroughly enjoyed their friendship over the years.

Having completed the PGCE, I was appointed to Rathcoole Primary School on 1st October 1985, to teach a P3 class. I stayed there for four years before moving to Greenisland PS when jobs were lost at Rathcoole. I taught both P1 and P3 in both schools and remained at Greenisland for the next twenty-five years. My friends and colleagues at Greenisland, and indeed many of the parents whom I have got to know through my work, were very encouraging and supportive during my treatment, and their thoughtfulness or gestures of kindness often gave me a lift when I needed it most.

On 1st August 1987, Dermot and I were married in the Church of the Good Shepherd, on the Ormeau Road in Belfast. We had a wonderful wedding day celebrating with family and friends. My beautiful niece Emma was my bridesmaid. I felt like a princess in my wedding dress, with my hair specially done by my long-time friend, Roisin. What was already a strong partnership, became a happy marriage, and I was warmly welcomed into the Breen family circle. I have very much appreciated and enjoyed the warmth and friendship I have received from the wider family, Dermot's brothers and sisters, and especially from his amazing dad Artie, and step mum, Rosaleen.

Dermot and I were delighted to become parents to Matthew on 28th February 1991, and couldn't have been happier when we welcomed Hannah into the world, two years and four months later, on 2nd July 1993. Dermot, Matt and Hannah have been everything to me, and I know that we have created many happy memories together. Over the years, we have had family holidays to the North Coast and Donegal, to be close to both our families. We also ventured to Spain and France for sunshine holidays, which were always wonderful and a chance to experience new things.

As the children grew up, I loved taking them to gymnastics, to swimming lessons, football coaching, music lessons, and horse riding. I ferried them, and their friends, to and from birthday parties, and loved seeing friendships blossom, and their confidence grow as they experienced new achievements both in and out of school. We were all blessed throughout those years, to have the friendship, loyalty and unwavering support of Maura Mullen, who was our child-minder from just before Matthew was one. She was, and is, a wonderful caring person who enabled us to make the most of our family life. She was a positive influence on all our lives.

I loved being a mum, and enjoyed all the stages of Matt and Hannah growing up. There were a few hiccups and heartaches during the teenage years, but I am so proud of the values and principles they now hold; their loyalty to their friends and each other, and I love the adults they have become. Their hearts are in the right place and I wish them a future filled with happiness and fulfilment.

I want to pay tribute to Dermot, my steadfast partner in life. We have been together since we were nineteen, and have shared so much love and laughter as well as the responsibilities and decisions which come along with being parents. We have always had confidence in each other, and been very happy and content in our own company. We are lucky to have a similar outlook on life, although Dermot has been the one who has made the great decisions about enjoying life to the full. A number of years ago we made the decision to invest in our little house in Portrush, and we have spent so many happy family times there. In 2012, we discovered a little piece of paradise when we visited Maiori on Italy's beautiful Amalfi Coast for our 25th Wedding Anniversary. We enjoyed the food, hospitality, sea and sunshine so much that we went back again the following year! Our life together really has been wonderful. I have no regrets.

But I am heartbroken that I will not share in so much that has yet to come, especially in Matthew, Hannah and Dermot's lives, but I hope that they will be strong for each other, and go on to be happy in whatever way they can.

I have been blessed throughout my life with a loving family, many loyal friends, wonderful opportunities and happiness and, up until last year, very good health. I have been incredibly touched by the kindness and support shown to me and Dermot by so many people over recent months. There are just too many of you to name, but you know who you are and I want you to know that your thoughts, prayers, acts of kindness and support have been appreciated more than words can say. Thank you so much to you all.

I hope that each of you will always carry a little piece of me in your hearts.

With much love,

Jacqui

January 2015

Acknowledgements

I consulted a lot of material while carrying out my research for this book. Listed below are my main sources of information. Thank you to all concerned. Without access to this wonderful material, my book certainly wouldn't have been as well informed. Any errors are, of course, my own. Thank you also to all the wonderful people who helped me and looked after me on my journey. Without their help, there might still have been a story to tell, but it certainly wouldn't have been such a special one. Thank you to the small number of volunteers who read an early draft of my manuscript and provided me with valuable feedback and corrections. Thank you to Ashley Todd for the wonderful poem at the end of Chapter Fourteen. And lastly, thank you to you for purchasing this book. By doing so, you have contributed to Cancer Research UK (CRUK), the cancer charity so dear to mine and Jacqui's hearts. Thank you very much.

Dermot Breen

Books:

Philip O'Sullivan-Beare, Ireland Under Elizabeth, first published in Dublin, 1903 (Reprint by General Books, Memphis, 2010)

Patrick Weston Joyce, A Concise History of Ireland, 1910

Peter Somerville-Large, From Bantry Bay to Leitrim, Arrow Books Limited, London, 1974

Morgan Llywelyn, The Last Prince of Ireland, Tom Doherty Associates, New York, 2001

Dermot Somers, Endurance: Historic Journeys in Ireland, The O'Brien Press Ltd., Dublin, 2005

Richard Crawford & Richard Jordan, Donal O'Sullivan, Prince of Beare: The Long March, Irish River Press, 2012

Caroline Allen, A Guide to Hiking the Ireland Way, Ireland Way Guides, 2017

Online articles:

Beara Breifne Way committee, Beara-Breifne Way, History

Jerry O'Sullivan, Ballingeary & Inchigeela Historical Society, The Retreat of O'Sullivan Beara

John Jeremiah Cronin, The Battle of Aughrim, 1603: a talk given to the South East Galway Archaeological and Historical Society

Susanne Iles, The Ring of Beara Blog, Children of Lir Mythical Site, Allihies, County Cork, Ireland, 2009

Hikelines, Glengarriff to Adrigole, 2017

Irish Railway Record Society, The Stolen Railway today: The Parsonstown and Portumna Bridge Railway (1868-1878)

Websites:

The Ireland Way: https://www.theirelandway.ie/trail.html

The Beara-Breifne Way: https://www.bearabreifneway.ie/

The Ulster Way: http://www.walkni.com/ulsterway/

Note: If you didn't in fact buy this book, but borrowed it or acquired it by other means, fair or foul, you might be feeling a little guilty at this point. But don't worry, this can be easily resolved by making a donation to CRUK. Just go to:

http://www.cancerresearchuk.org/support-us/donate

or send a cheque to:

Cancer Research UK
PO Box 1561
Oxford
OX4 9GZ

Other books in the Pilgrim Trilogy

Book One: The Edge
Walking the Ulster Way with my Angels & Demons

'The Edge: Walking The Ulster Way With My Angels & Demons' by Dermot Breen, is a unique and very personal account of one man's journey around one of the longest and most stunning way-marked trails in Britain and Ireland.

When Dermot lost Jacqui, his wife and soul mate of 35 years to ovarian cancer in 2015, he was totally devastated. However, in the wake of her death, and seeking some purpose to his own life, he resolved to undertake a 1,000km pilgrimage round the Ulster Way in her memory and to raise funds for cancer research. What followed was a physically and emotionally challenging journey, as Dermot struggled to overcome episodes of injury, exhaustion, anguish and grief; often made possible only through the incredible kindness and support shown by friends and strangers alike.

This is an inspirational and searingly honest account of his 'unlikely pilgrimage'. Told in his own unique style, mixing traditional narrative with flights of imagination, and tales past and present, join him as he treks through isolated wilderness and stunning landscapes alike, with his dark demons and guiding angels never far from his side.

What Amazon customers have said about The Edge:

"A very evocative read which captures the spirit of the Ulster Way."

"Full of raw, honest emotion it made me laugh, cry, hold my breath and at times left me speechless."

"Sad and yet wonderfully uplifting at the same time. You will not be disappointed."

"I loved this book. It's honest and heart breaking. I loved the detail of the local legends and place-names."

"Beautiful book. Both heart-warming and heart-rending in equal measures. I would thoroughly recommend it! Wonderfully written!"

"An excellent book. Dermot is open and honest and this makes for difficult reading at times, but a rewarding experience. Highly recommended."

"Dermot's story provides an inspirational gift to readers."

"I cried, I laughed, I put the book down for a breath and I walked around with it. I can't wait until the next book ... this man is a wonderful writer."

"Honest, heart-breaking and uplifting. This book packs an emotional punch.

"A gripping read comprising simple language and complex feelings."

"Inspirational yet written with a true sense of humility. Almost thinking of dusting down the old walking boots myself!"

"An in-depth insight into the beautiful countryside of the Ulster Way. This is a fantastic read and I would definitely recommend reading it."

"Dermot's honesty provides readers with a true sense of the depths of his grief and how difficult it must be to go through the loss of a soul-mate. Dermot's travel logs include plenty of humour and light-hearted moments!"

"I would strongly recommend this book to anyone, be it someone who has lost a loved one, or simply someone who is interested in travel, walking or Ireland!"

"Emotional, compelling reading about love and loss, heartbreak and hope, and the power of walking it all out. A must read."

"An excellent book, hard to put down. Moving."

"A superb and bittersweet journey."

Book Two: The Man with the Camino Tattoo
Searching for sanctuary on the Camino de Santiago

The Camino de Santiago, or The Way of Saint James, is a network of pilgrim routes leading to the Cathedral of Santiago de Compostela in north-western Spain, where the remains of the saint are believed to be buried. Over the centuries, many hundreds of thousands have followed its various routes as a form of religious or spiritual devotion. The path to Santiago is also known as the Way of the Sword. It's reputed to be the path where you fight your demons and find your strength.

In 2016, Dermot decided to undertake a gruelling 1,000 kilometre pilgrimage along the challenging Camino del Norte in memory of his wife Jacqui, who had been cruelly taken from him fifteen months earlier by ovarian cancer. As he carries his rucksack and great sense of loss with him along the centuries old route, he dearly hopes to achieve some sort of peace - perhaps even find a place of sanctuary. And as the land he passes through gradually reveals many of its wondrous myths and legends associated with St James, he begins to believe that miraculous events are perhaps not only confined to the past. Through the tremendous camaraderie he experiences on his Camino, and particularly through his encounters with the enigmatic Jane, he gains a much better understanding of himself and his loss, which ultimately results in a surprising and life enhancing revelation. Told with great honesty and passion, this is a story that reaches into the very heart of the reader and demonstrates that, even when life can seem utterly hopeless, the human spirit is a powerful force that can rescue even the most vulnerable of souls.

What Amazon customers have said about The Man with the Camino Tattoo:

"A truly inspiring and thought provoking read"

"I was looking forward to this book and it did not disappoint."

"A highly recommended read. Once started, this is a book I simply couldn't put down! Dermot Breen's ability to weave the history of the area into his own experience of the walk is indeed remarkable."

"A beautifully written and honest account of the emotional roller coaster of life. Brilliant read - so personable without being sentimental. Such vivid descriptions of people and places make the whole book come alive. "

"A great read. Loved this book."

"It's noticeably more reflective, even upbeat in tone compared to his previous work on the Ulster Way."

"The descriptions of his daily walks and the accounts of the characters he encounters along the way made me laugh out loud at times."

"Great book and works on many levels. Even those who like to do their long distance walking from imagination and comfort of an armchair will get drawn into the narrative and enjoy this account, not least its conclusion!"

"Loved the narrative and the quirky sense of humour Dermot has brought to this second book."

Printed in Great Britain
by Amazon

53106137R00184